Latin Music Trivia Book

From the Bolero to Salsa

Thousands of Fascinating
Facts, Fallacies, Tidbits & Tales

By
Joe Hernández

ALSO, BY JOE HERNÁNDEZ

Conjurer's Wisdom Vol. 1
Conjurer's Wisdom Vol. 2
Phonetastic
Magic Babylon

The Latin Music Trivia Book

From the Bolero to Salsa

Thousands of Fascinating
Facts, Fallacies, Tidbits & Tales

Written by
Joe Hernández

Layout and Design by
Joe Hernández

Edited by
Isabel Hernández

Book Cover by
Joe Hernández

Published by
Joe Dez Publications

Copyright © 2024 by Joe Hernández

All rights reserved. No part of this publication may be used, reproduced, stored in a retrieval system, or transmitted in any form or by any means (including electronic, mechanical, photocopying, recording, or otherwise) without the written permission from the author or publisher.

First Edition
Printed and bound in the United States of America
Published by JOE DEZ PUBLICATIONS

To my brother Vitico (Tony) and my sister Delia

Acknowledgments

Authoring this book has been a captivating journey. It's not just another Latin music history book. It's a deep dive into the 'trivia' of the main characters that shaped its history, with a special focus on Afro-Cuban or salsa, but also touching on other genres. The idea for this book was sparked after I completed a trivia book on magic last year. Initially, I had envisioned a 200-page book, but the rich and complex history of Latin music, filled with captivating characters, led me to delve deeper into the subject. This book is a comprehensive exploration of the players of Latin music's origins, evolution, and impact, with a particular focus on Afro-Cuban rhythms and salsa. While I know I have only scratched the surface, I plan to continue exploring this vast subject in future volumes, or someone else will take up the mantle.

It has been a profound honor and a privilege to not just study the works of these legends, but to also forge personal connections with them. Graciela, Cachao, Johnny Albino, Joe Cuba, Raul Azpiazú, Marco Rizo, Lou Pérez, and many others have not only enriched my understanding of Latin music but have also become dear friends, their stories and music woven into the fabric of my life.

The pinnacle of my journey was the extraordinary privilege of meeting Dr. Cristóbal Díaz Ayala and stepping into his world at his museum in Santurce, Puerto Rico, during the 90s. His warm and genuine hospitality, as he selflessly shared his vast collection with me, left an indelible mark on my soul. I am profoundly grateful for this unforgettable and cherished experience, a moment that will forever be etched in my memory.

I want to express my deepest gratitude to Pat Lombardi, my son's friend, for his meticulous proofreading of the first draft and insightful suggestions. I also extend my profound thanks to John Resto, my old friend, for his thought-provoking input and enlightening conversations while covering the material. I am genuinely indebted to Chico Alvarez, the producer and former host of 'The New World Gallery' on WBAI in New York City from 1986 to 2017, for his thorough reading of my manuscript and invaluable feedback on specific details. Additionally, I want to thank Bobby Sanabria, a Berklee College of Music graduate, multi-talented musician, and Grammy Award nominee for Best Latin Jazz Album, who hosts WBGO's 'The Latin Jazz Cruise.' Bobby's unwavering support and the critical historical details he provided were not just instrumental but also heartwarming in shaping this book.

Lastly, I want to thank my wife, Isabel, for her tireless support and understanding, which allowed me to dedicate a significant amount of time to this project, even though it meant spending less time with her.

Introduction

> *It is a very sad thing that nowadays there is so little useless information.*
>
> ---Oscar Wilde

The **Latin Music Trivia Book** is a delightful collection of Latin music trivia, a continuation of the author's work for a Latin music magazine that is no longer in print. This book is a joy to read, offering hours of information about your beloved Latin music artists, from the romantic bolero to the lively salsa. It's the perfect companion for your favorite reading spot, even if it happens to be the bathroom.

This book is not an academic or historical account of Latin music history but rather an informal read and the first of its kind. It is a fascinating compendium of facts, fallacies, tidbits, and tales about the artists and events that have shaped and entertained the world with the most dynamic and pulsating rhythms that have ever afflicted humanity - Latin music.

Feel free to open this book to any page and delve into the rich history of Latin music. You will discover bizarre stories, inventive minds, odd facts, and exciting and amusing "bits and pieces" of information. Reading this book might spark your interest in learning more about the history of Latin music.

It's worth noting that most of the information included in this book comes from various sources. The author sifted through hundreds of magazines, newspapers, books, and other sources related to Latin music, such as the back covers of LPs. The author utilized various sources of information, some of which were extrapolated from lesser-known sources, and some were obtained through oral history or gossip. Furthermore, the author has over fifty hours of recorded personal conversations with many artists he had over the years. The author also watched hundreds of hours of television interviews.

Indeed, some of the information we hear or read in the news may be fake or inaccurate. This phenomenon has existed for a while, as phony news existed long before the printing press was invented. Therefore, it is crucial to be cautious when consuming news and not unquestioningly believe everything we hear or read.

Moreover, sometimes, the musician can be the source of misinformation about their events or happenings. They can tell one story one day and then change it the next day. Some famous musicians, such as Rafael Hernández, Pedro Flores, Tito Puente, Daniel Santos, Joe Cuba, Cheo Feliciano, and many others, are known for providing different accounts of the same events. Therefore, we should take their stories with a grain of salt and realize we may not get the whole picture.

The author has attempted to verify everything in it with at least one other source. However, the author does not vouch for the integrity of these sources or vice versa. The book contains subjective, objective, rational, irrational, hysterical, serious, and sardonic stories. As you read the content and try to determine the validity of any story, it is worth remembering the wise words of Leonardo da Vinci: *"I take no more notice of the wind that comes out of the mouths of critics than of the wind expelled from their backsides."*

This book is intended to be an entertaining read rather than a comprehensive guide to Latin music. The trivia is not presented in chronological order, so you can start reading from any page. Each trivia stands independently; you don't need to read previous information to understand it.

Some musicians, singers, and composers are featured more prominently in the book due to their significant contributions to Latin music over the years. These include Tito Puente, Celia Cruz, Daniel Santos, Ismael Rivera, and Eddie Palmieri.

The author has kept repetition to a minimum, but there may be some overlap to present specific trivia as accurately as possible and provide a coherent reading experience. The author takes full responsibility for any omissions or errors in the book and apologizes for them.

Surprisingly, some of the best musicologists often repeat information from erroneous sources. Like parrots repeating what they hear, many musicologists write about stories taken from other sources without verifying their accuracy. Some events that they discuss may not make sense on their faces.

The author has attempted to minimize subjective opinions, but that is not always possible. On topics such as the controversy over the origin of the term "Salsa" or the correct documentation of dates, the author presents different sides of the argument so the reader may make an informed judgment.

The reader should approach each trivia to be amused, entertained, and learn something new about their favorite musician, composer, singer, or event. The author believes that reading "history" as trivia makes learning and retaining information more accessible.

Overall, the author had fun researching this book, even though he sometimes got frustrated with the contradictory information, especially when it came from the same source as the artist himself. But the author hopes that this book will bring back pleasant memories for you, particularly when you read about the music of your parents and grandparents.

Joe Hernández
New Jersey, 2024

The Latin Music Trivia Book

From the Bolero to Salsa

Thousands of Fascinating
Facts, Fallacies, Tidbits & Tales

The Latin Music Trivia Book

From the Bolero to Salsa

Bolero is a musical genre born in Santiago de Cuba at the end of the 19th century. It is the Romantic language of Latin America and the most Romantic of its popular languages. This musical genre has cultural elements from Spain and Africa, including influences from France.

The Cuban musician, singer, and composer José "Pepe" Sánchez, born on March 19, 1856, in Santiago, is known as the father of the *trova* music style and the creator of the Cuban bolero. He was initially a tailor, then co-owner of a copper mine, and a representative in his hometown of a cloth manufacturer in Kingston, Jamaica. Pepe had no musical training but an abundance of talent. He composed many numbers in his head but never wrote them down; these are lost forever. However, a few survived because some of his friends and students wrote them down. His first bolero, "Tristezas," is still remembered and played today. He taught some great *trovadores* from Cuba, like Sindo Garay, Rosendo Ruiz, Manuel Corona, and Alberto Villalon. Pepe died on January 3, 1918.

Son Montuno, a musical genre, has been called *"Salsa"* for fifty years. The first one to use the word salsa in a Son was the Cuban musician Ignacio Piñeiro when he used the word salsa in a song he wrote called "Échale Salsita" (1933). However, the word salsa in his tune was used by Piñeiro to describe a food condiment and not as a musical term for the *son*. In the late 1930s, the great vocalist Bény Moré often shouted, "Salsa!" in the middle of his performances. In 1962, Willie Torres wrote the song "Salsa y Bembé," already referring to salsa to describe the son montuno as something new. Also in 1962, Pupi Legarreta released "Salsa Nova," and then, in 1963, the final recording of Charlie Palmieri's *Charanga Duboney Orchestra* released a tune titled "Salsa Na' Ma." In 1966, Federico and his Combo released an album titled *Llego la Salsa* (Salsa Arrived) in Venezuela. In 1968, Richie Ray and Bobby Cruz released *Los Durisimos Salsa Y Control.*

Let's not forget that the great Cal Tjader released a top-selling LP under the Verve label, *Soul Sauce,* in 1964 as he was already starting to use the word "Salsa" (sauce) to describe his music. Four years later, on November 16, 1968, Morris Levy, president of Tico Records, hired the *Machito Orchestra* to back up La Lupe at a performance where she was crowned the Queen of Salsa.

Early on, many artists, inadvertently and without realizing it, were already at the forefront of the "salsa" renaming that was to come.

Salsa is a pseudonym for a Latin music genre that has existed for almost one hundred years. As a marketing term, it evolved over ten to fifteen years, from the 1960s through the mid-1970s, as it crossed the oceans from Cuba to New York to Puerto Rico, Venezuela, Peru, Columbia, and back to New York. Many musicians, disc jockeys, and promoters had a hand in the term's evolution to describe an existing genre and as a marketing strategy to promote the Son Montuno as a new genre, which it was not. However, like the guaracha, guaguancó and the son montuno, salsa has developed into its own unique style due to more modern arrangements from musicians like Rene Hernández, Ray Santos, Bebo Valdés, and Chico O'Farrill, etc.

Curiously, the word Salsa is not mentioned in the movie *Our Latin Thing*, which symbolizes the beginning of the "Salsa movement." Throughout the movie, they keep referring to the music as Latin music. Even in the original Fania All-Star LP sleeve, it reads "The Best in Latin Music." During the movie's introduction, you can hear Izzy Sanabria yelling, *"Qué viva la música Latina,"* and not *"Qué viva la salsa."* In the 1972 souvenir book *Our Latin Thing*, "Salsa" is mentioned only once in parenthesis to describe a new sound breed. However, the phrase "Latin music" is mentioned fifteen times.

The movie, which premiered on July 19, 1972, in New York City, received favorable reviews from the New York Times and the Daily News, and yet, the word "Salsa" is not mentioned anywhere in the reviews. This lack of use for the term "Salsa" demonstrates that it was used only occasionally to describe Latin music. The label salsa wasn't used frequently or rigorously until the release of Larry Harlow's 1974 album SALSA with the great hit "La Cartera," originally composed by the father of the son montuno, Arsenio Rodríguez. It wasn't until approximately 1976 that the term "Salsa" began appearing more consistently on album covers to describe the music as "hot and saucy."

However, the genre of the Son Montuno began to be called Salsa when the first radio program dedicated exclusively to this musical "genre," *La Hora del Sabor, La Salsa y él Bembe*, appeared in Caracas, Venezuela, in 1964. The announcer, Fidias Danilo Escalona, used this word to refer to the "new experiences" reflecting the lives of those who listened to the Son Montuno in New York, mainly the Puerto Rican community.

The term was a way to use an all-inclusive "catchphrase" to describe the music of the *Son*, guaracha, danzón, mambo, guaguancó, cha cha chá, rumba, etc., Phidias, who was among the first to use the term daily on his radio program, although more to describe the "flavor" of the music. Also known as El Bigotón, he was from Caracas. He was born in La Pastora, where every day he was in the homes of the Venezuelan listening audience through the radio station Radio Difurosa Venezuela, with his program *La Hora de la Salsa,* which garnered a large audience in the decade of the sixties.

La Hora de la Salsa is part of the collective memory of neighborhoods and popular areas of Caracas; it represented for the Venezuelans of that time, a free lecture on "Salsa, Sabor, and Bembe," entertaining, illustrated, and dictated by their beloved radio personality Phidias. The music he played in his daily one-hour program represented the sounds created in Cuba and enriched in Puerto Rico and New York.

Phidias Danilo Escalona knew how to select and air the music that was then "happening" and, in the process, used the term salsa to describe the music in an original, authentic, and fresh way. A term that was then used as a marketing strategy to describe all the different and complex sounds of the *son* and its integration and evolution within the "Barrios" of young New York Puerto Ricans who were seeking to express their own unique identities through music that they heard through their parents. This music was part of their upbringing and culture, yet they still needed to make their statement and stamp it with their mark to make it part of their identity.

The Latin Music Trivia Book

The term Salsa has always created controversy in discussions about its origin. The Cuban purists of the "Son Cubano" refuse to see it as a new rhythm; that is why they dismiss the name Salsa and tend to consider the genre as it is. On the other hand, Puerto Ricans highlight the differences with *son* and their influences within the genre. Venezuelans and Colombians prefer to call it Afro-Caribbean music in particular because of Salsa's undeniable African influence, making it familiar to those from the Caribbean.

Salsa is a Cuban-based dance music cultivated in New York City by Latinos who listened to and performed it. Most of these individuals were from the Puerto Rican community, making them the most prominent proponents of this musical form outside of post-revolutionary Cuba. Salsa was created by adding something extra to Cuban music elements, creating something new and unique. Its commercializatFania the level of records by New York recording houses, such as Alegre, Tico, and Fania, gave it cohesion and a name as a musical movement.

Dominican musician Johnny Pacheco and Brooklyn-born Italian American impresario Jerry Masucci were instrumental in the success of Salsa. They exploited the possibilities of Salsa from a large-scale advertising point of view, as most commercial enterprises do. Their marketing approach involved using the term "Salsa" to re-brand Cuban-based dance music as it was played in New York City. This marketing strategy led to a successful campaign with New York City-based radio disc jockeys. Masucci used this as a springboard to expand the audience for the music by producing large-scale concerts, two critically acclaimed theater-released documentaries, and eventually tours to South America,

Europe, and even Africa, the rhythmic birthplace of the music. This made Masucci and his partner, Johnny Pacheco, wealthy men.

However, in the process, there seems to have been an intentional "cover-up" to ignore the Cuban roots of the Salsa movement. On the records, under the pretext that there is no copyright exchange with Cuba, the names of well-known authors, such as Matamoros, Piñeiro, Rodríguez, etc., were covered with the well-known phrase "Derechos Reservados" (Rights Reserved), or the abbreviation of "DR." In one of its films, Fania gives the false impression that Salsa had come directly from Africa to settle in New York.

The debate surrounding Salsa's origins is driven by a desire to understand the rich tapestry of influences that shape this musical style. Some argue that Salsa is a fusion of many different musical genres, while others believe that it is simply a variation of the *son* rhythm. The *son* rhythm, with its five core elements- the introduction, the verse, the montuno, the mambo, and the finale- is a testament to the depth and diversity of Salsa's musical heritage.

It is crucial to recognize that the U.S. embargo against Cuba has had a profound impact, contributing to a lack of recognition for Salsa's Cuban roots in mainstream American and Latin American music culture. This political barrier has hindered the full appreciation of Salsa's origins and its cultural significance.

The debate will continue without being resolved, especially among the purists. The term salsa evolved over the years with so many variables and input from so many different segments of the music community, representing a host of countries with diverse perspectives that, by definition, can never be traced to one source. In short, no one person or entity created the term. Like the word "love," we all know what it means, but no one knows who produced it first.

The fact remains that the term *Salsa* within a dozen years, became the new term to describe the old and became so popular that even those who were against the term came to accept it. Some, like Celia Cruz, saw the writing on the wall and became comfortable with its use early on to describe what she sang. She always stated that she would continue with her Cuban music until the end. To Celia, you can call it *Salsa*, or you can call it whatever you want. Her accent will always be Cuban no matter where she is, whether in Mexico, Venezuela, Spain, or Argentina.

In 1951, Celia Cruz sang "El Yerbero Moderno" with *La Sonora Matancera,* which was considered a *son.* However, when the same tune was recorded in 1974 by Johnny Pacheco, it became a *Salsa* tune. In the fifties, the compositions played by bandleaders such as Machito, Tito Puente, Tito Rodríguez, and many others were known by specific names such as guarachas, mambos, and son montunos, among others. But by the sixties, the same tunes were called *Salsa*, a general term that included all of them.

Salsa, a musical form that originated in Cuba, found its unique voice in the U.S.A., particularly in the bustling streets of New York City, as a fusion of son montuno, mambo, and guaracha, reflecting the diverse cultural influences of its surroundings.

Joe Hernández

However, many of the top musicians in Latin music, at one time or another, objected to the term *Salsa*. Some were:

"For me, salsa is the ketchup you put on French fries or the salt and pepper on salads..."

--- Tito Puente

"First and foremost, the term salsa is a new invention which allows people who do not know it very well to identify a musical style. It's simply a marketing ploy.

--- Ray Barretto

"I don't like the word salsa because it's too vague, too generic. Young people today don't know about the son, the guaguancó, the danzón, the guaracha, or a mambo or rumba. To them, it is all salsa."

--- Cheo Feliciano

"In fact, what they call salsa is nothing new. When Cuban music was at its height, the youngsters didn't want to know. Now they call it salsa, and they think it's theirs. It's nothing more than a publicity stunt."

--- Mario Bauza

"The naming of salsa is a colossal error. I didn't know any genre that's called Salsa."

--- José Curbelo

"Salsa is envious because you could hear Cuban music in Puerto Rico, and they were the best interpreters of

Cuban music, so why does salsa have to appear? Salsa is not a new rhythm. Salsa is the flavor given to food." (author's translation from an interview given in Spanish).

--- Graciela

"I'm talking about "la música" que se llama salsa. Unfortunately, this is a misnomer, which is to present the most incredible rhythmical patterns that ever crystallized the evolutionism that came out of Cuba and influenced the world."

--- Eddie Palmieri

"Salsa is what you put in food. It's not really music."

--- Machito

"It is bullshit..."

--- Miguelito Valdés

"In 1967, I performed on a Venezuelan radio program that always played Sonora Matancera recordings. The program was hosted by a gentleman named Fidias Danilo Escalona, may he rest in peace. The show was called La Hora de la Salsa (The Saucy Hour), and that's where I think salsa was born. I say that salsa is just a marketing term applied to what originally was Cuban music."

--- Celia Cruz

There are other musicians that define Salsa in more positive terms:

"Salsa is Cuban music the way it's played in New York City by Puerto Ricans."

---Ray Santos

"You ask me what salsa is? I always say it's Cuban music played with a freakin' Nuyorican attitude."

---Bobby Sanabria

Interestingly, both Cubans and Puerto Ricans, experts in this music, agree that *salsa* is nothing more than Afro-Cuban music.

The Fascinating Story of "Pedro Navaja" (Mack the Knife).

"Pedro Navaja," from the album *Siembra*, may have been the first time Latinos heard the song in Spanish. Those who do not speak English may not realize that the song is a translation of "Mack the Knife," done in 1978 by the Panamanian singer Rubén Blades. However, the song's premise has a long history, and the character that inspired it goes back to March 4, 1702, in England, with the name Jack Shepherd.

Jack Shepherd was one of the most famous criminals of the 18th century, not only because of his crimes but also as an escape artist because each time he got arrested, he would manage to escape.

Jack grew up extremely poor, and for a couple of years, he worked as a carpenter until he met a prostitute. She became his lover and taught him how to be a criminal. Jack started a career as a criminal and, within a brief period, became incredibly famous for his evil deeds.

His ability to escape made him a living legend. His exceptional skills as an escape artist prevented the authorities from detaining him. Then, at 22, he was caught for the fifth time. The authorities, desperate, frustrated, and demoralized from his escapes that made fun of their security system, decided to put an end to his escapades and sentence him to death by hanging.

Little did they realize that he would also "escape" his death because the public loved him and idolized him so much that they would make sure he would remain immortal. On the very day of his sentence to death, his autobiography came out, where he described in detail his life as a criminal and his escape from jail. This book inspired many other works, books, and stories for theatres about his life, so much so that authorities, fearing that his story would inspire other criminals, prohibited for 40 years any play or book with the name Jack or Shepherd in it.

However, the story doesn't end there. It's just the beginning. So, what does "Pedro Navaja" have to do with "Mack the Knife" and this story? It's the same person; four years after Jack Shepherd's death, John Gay reincarnated him in the play *The Beggars Opera,* where he continued to be the same thief. Still, to avoid legal problems, the author changed the character's name to

Captain Mackheath. But Mackheath continues with his life as a criminal, falling in love with a prostitute, going to jail, and escaping.

Years later, he made another appearance, but this time as a pirate, in the book *Polly*, also written by John Gay. This story remained for over 200 years until 1928, when he reappeared in Germany in the *Three Penny Opera*, written by Bertolt Brecht, and music by Kurt Weill. This time he appears a lot crueler and more sinister under the name Von Mackie Messer (In English, it translates to Mack the Knife and in Spanish, Mack el Navaja), whose crimes included rape and murder, transforming him into a modern antihero which in the song tells of a knife-wielding criminal of the London underworld. He remained the central character of this opera until the arrival of the Nazi party in 1933. By then, the opera had appeared in over 18 languages, with over ten thousand interpretations in European theatres.

The play starts and finishes with a street singer who sings, describing Mackie as a shark with sharp teeth and a knife in hand that no one can see. In 1956, the song became a massive hit in the United States when it was translated and sung by Louis Armstrong. The song has become a standard for many artists after being recorded by Louis Armstrong. In 1959, Bobby Darin recorded it, and it became the most popular version, becoming a number-one hit in the US and UK and earning him two Grammys. In 1961, Ella Fitzgerald also received a Grammy for her performance of the song.

Rubén Blades, with the same arrangements, resurrected Jack Shepard, Captain Mackheath, Von Mackie Messer, and "Mack the Knife" by adapting the story to a barrio in New York City. This adaptation was not just a change of setting, but a transformation infused with the vibrant rhythms of Son, the lively beats of guaracha, and the infectious melodies of mambo, all under the name "Pedro Navaja." The legend of Mack the Knife, a literary and musical character that has endured for over three hundred years, was given a new musical life by Blades. As Rubén Blades sings, *"la vida te da sorpresa, sorpresa te da la vida"* (life gives you surprises, surprise give you life).

Rafael Hernández composed many songs in his lifetime, but the rumba "El Cumbanchero" was the most lucrative. Interestingly, Rafael didn't think much of the song; he wrote it in just ten minutes to soothe his baby to sleep. When the song debuted, it was a complete failure. However, it eventually became incredibly popular and generated significant royalties for Rafael. When Rafael was invited to the White House in 1961 to honor Luis Muñoz Marín, Governor of Puerto Rico, under the Kennedy Administration, the President greeted him by saying, *"How are you, Mr. Cumbanchero?"*

Despite being condemned and looked down upon in many parts of the world, Tango was still immensely popular. Its popularity was so great that a New York physician claimed to have discovered a new disease called "Tango foot," which caused pain below the ankles. However, even the fear of contracting this "dreaded" affliction could not deter Tango enthusiasts from indulging in their favorite dance. Despite being labeled "immoral," Tango continued to captivate and attract people from all walks of life.

Joe Hernández

—⚏—

During the early days of recording, the speed of the first discs varied between 72.73 and 81.82 RPM. These variations in speed caused variations in tone and key (clave), which was particularly noticeable in human voice recordings. However, over time, the speed stabilized around the average of 78 RPM, which became the standard speed for vinyl records.

—⚏—

A myriad of factors have shaped Latin music's growth and evolution. One intriguing aspect that warrants exploration by musicologists is what influence organized crime had on the Latin music industry, a phenomenon that echoes its influence on jazz.

—⚏—

Ray Barretto and Joe Hernández

Raymundo "Ray" Barretto Pagán, a.k.a. Ray Barretto, was born in New York City on April 29, 1929. His parents had moved to New York (Brooklyn) from Puerto Rico in the early 1920s, looking for a better life. His father abandoned the family when Barretto was four years old, and his mother, who loved music, especially jazz, moved the family to the Bronx. In 1946, at 17, Ray joined the U.S. Army. While stationed in Germany, he learned how to play the conga. Upon his return in 1949, Ray visited clubs and participated in jam sessions, where he perfected his conga playing. He developed a unique playing style and soon was noticed and sought by other jazz band leaders. In 1962, Ray formed *Charanga Moderna* and recorded his first hit, "El Watusi," for Tico Records. The rest, as the cliché says, is history.

During the 1940s and 1950s, New York City was not only a destination for Puerto Ricans seeking a better life, but also for a specific community of the Puerto Rican population - musicians. In fact, of the 61,000 Puerto Ricans living in the city by 1940, more than 5,000 were musicians, making up over 8.5% of the Puerto Rican population. When you add the Cuban, Panamanian, Dominican, Mexican, and other Caribbean populations of musicians to the mix, it's clear that this concentration of musicians played a vital role in the development and growth of *nuestra música* Latina in New York City.

The vibrant cultural fusion in Spanish Harlem, a melting pot of young Latinos, primarily Puerto Ricans and African Americans, gave rise to a generation that would shape the Salsa movement and pioneer 'Latin Boogaloo.' This neighborhood, a hotbed of creativity, also saw the emergence of numerous Rhythm and Blues vocal groups. The proximity of these communities naturally led to a rich musical growth and evolution, with influences from Jazz and Latin music permeating the air. Notably, groups like Frankie Lymon and the Teenagers, a blend of Puerto Ricans (Herman Santiago and Joe Negroni) and African Americans (Frankie Lymon, Jimmy Merchant, and Sherman Garnes), were products of this unique environment.

The phenomenally successful song "Quimbara" was composed by a young Puerto Rican named Junior Cepeda. He sent a demo tape to Johnny Pacheco at the Fania New York City office but never received a response. Junior then takes it upon himself to visit the Fania headquarters and meet with Pacheco. Pacheco loved the song and agreed to record it in their "Celia & Johnny " album with Celia Cruz.

Sadly, Junior, who was only twenty-two, never had a chance to hear Celia Cruz's interpretation because he died two days before the album was released on July 29, 1976. His live-in girlfriend killed him. Celia had also recorded "Dime si Llegue a Tiempo," another Junior composition.

Between 1954 and 1955, American musical groups nationwide released 30 songs with mambo titles. Similarly, between 1953 and 1962, there were 25 songs with cha-cha titles and another 12 songs during the same period with elements of both mambo and cha-cha. Howard Kane, a member of the New York-based group *Jay and the Americans*, spoke about how Cuban rhythmic patterns and the Doo Wop sound influenced their music. The popularization and blending of Latin music with other styles in the 1950s and 1960s contributed to the development of new genres such as Latin Boogaloo, R&B, and Rock 'n Roll and the evolution of the Son-Montuno into Salsa.

The Puerto Rican salsa romantic singer Jose Antonio Torresola Ruiz, a.k.a. Frankie Ruiz (1958-1998), did a three-year stint in federal prison for being involved in an altercation with a flight attendant. He also served two jail sentences for possession of crack cocaine between the years 1988 and 1992.

As a young boy, Pedro Aguilar, also known as Cuban Pete, went to live with his uncle in New York. Unfortunately, the living arrangements did not work out, and he was sent to an orphanage. Later, he was placed in a foster home. To help manage his anger issues, he took up boxing. However, despite his efforts, he remained an abusive husband to Millie Donay, his wife and dancing partner.

Felipe Rodríguez was the first Puerto Rican to sing the national anthem, "La Borinqueña," at a sporting event that was televised in the United States coast to coast when fellow Puerto Rican José "Chegui" Torres won the World Light Heavyweight boxing title against Willie Pastrano at the Madison Square Garden in New York City in 1965. Chegui knocked Pastrano down for the only time in his career with a powerful left hook to the liver. The ringside doctor asked the daze looking

Pastrano if he knew where he was, to which Pastrano answered, *"You're damn right. I know where I am! I'm in Madison Square Garden getting the sh*t kicked out of me!"*

Olga Guillot

According to some music historians, Olga Guillot was the first Latin female artist to perform at New York's Carnegie Hall on October 13, 1964. However, Celia Cruz claimed she was the first Hispanic woman to perform there on June 18, 1962. But neither of them was the first. In 1947, the Argentinian singer and actress Libertad Lamarque had already appeared in a sold-out performance. However, the first Latina to perform at the renowned concert hall was Rosalía "Chalía" Herrera in 1915, 108 years earlier than Guillot and 47 years earlier than Lamarque.

Willie Colón's musical journey took a significant turn at the age of fourteen when he formed his first band as a trumpeter. However, it was the powerful trombone playing of Barry Rogers, heard with Puerto Rican timbalero Joe Cotto's band, that sparked a transformative inspiration in him. This led to a pivotal decision-he switched to the trombone. Under the Fania label, his first recorded album was *El Malo*, marking the beginning of a new era in his musical career.

Celia Cruz had her cousin Nenita and her daughter, Silvia, a nurse, come from Havana to care for her during her illness. They took diligent care of Celia for three months, day and night, and did all the domestic chores and anything else that Celia needed. Two months later, Celia passed away. For all the arduous work and care they gave Celia during her last days, Celia's husband Pedro gave them a meager $500 to split between them. Despite their hardships in Cuba, Pedro removed the names of all the members of Celia's family from the will. The family is still fuming over Pedro Knights's legendary stinginess and disregard.

Before the Palladium ballroom became popular, members of the Jewish community would often attend Latin dance halls and socialize with people from other ethnic groups. During the 1940s and 1950s, various New York newspapers, including the New York Post, published announcements advertising Latin dance events to attract the Jewish community.

The grandfather of bandleader and TV star Desi Arnaz, Don Desiderio Arnaz, was President Teddy Roosevelt's doctor, and he participated in the charge up San Juan

Hill with the Rough Riders during the Spanish-American War in 1898. Desi's ancestors were influential citizens in Cuba before it became Fidel Castro's country and influential in California. Ventura County in Southern California is named after Desi's great-great-grandmother, Doña Ventura! His mother, Dolores de Acha, was the daughter of one of the founders of the Bacardi Rum Company.

There were multiple factors for the growth of Latin music in the United States, especially in New York that music historians have overlooked; among them was the different system for obtaining recordings. All the record companies adopted, like Victor and Columbia, an approach that took local figures from other countries (Cuba) to record in the United States. Occasionally, the artist or musician whom a record company hired managed to take advantage of that trip and make recordings with another record company, generally smaller, by changing their names. These trips also left some musicians who settled permanently in the United States and were creating, together with musicians who previously emigrated or were born in the new country, a third raw material of music originators: local talent. That was the case, for example, of the Cuban Antonio Machín and many Puerto Rican artists. The results were recorded music printed for the Latin colony of New York, other cities, and other Latin American countries.

In the field of Latin ethnic music, the big record labels immediately noticed a very favorable characteristic for them: in other markets, the ethnic record areas were drastically marked for different languages; that is, what interested the Serbians was not enjoyable in the least to

Ukrainian, because they are logically different languages. And even in the case of using the same language, the music of interest to the Irish, for example, was different from the taste of the English or the Scots.

That didn't happen in the Latin market. There was music that, although produced in a specific country, attracted the interest of other Latin American countries. This interest occurred, for example, with the Cuban son, the Argentine tango, and the Mexican corrido. Guty Cardenas, the Mexican singer and composer who made numerous recordings for Columbia, included duets with Cuban singers such as Tomasita Nueñz, Conchita Utrera, and Adolfo Utrera, as well as a Puerto Rican, Fausto Delgado, and a Colombian, Jorge Anez.

Izzy Sanabria's artistic contributions were instrumental in the development of the Fania brand. His creativity as an artist was evident in the unique look of Fania's record sleeves and advertising flyers, which played a significant role in establishing the label's identity and contributing to its success. Izzy's journey began with design projects for Allegre Records, owned by Al Santiago. However, the mystery of his first album cover remains. It's believed it was for the Panart label, but to confirm this, the author talked with Izzy, who needed help remembering.

The famous Cuban composer Ernesto Lecuona, at seventeen, debuted in 1913 at New York's famed Aeolian Hall.

In the North American recording industry, another crucial moment arose in 1925, as part of the first stage of its history, when Victor and Columbia put the first electronically recorded records on sale. And Brunswick brought the first electric phonographs to the market.

Oscar D'León was the first salsa artist to fill the Plaza Mayor in Madrid.

Tito Puente was a world-renowned musician who gained widespread recognition after his appearance as a solo artist with Gloria Estefan during the closing ceremony of the Summer Olympics in Atlanta, Georgia, in 1996. The performance was watched by an estimated billion viewers, making it the most-watched event in the Olympics history. Today, the timbales he played during the performance have become a symbol of his musical talents and are displayed at the National Museum of American History in Washington, D.C. In recognition of his contributions to music, Tito Puente was awarded the National Medal of Arts in 1977 and was inducted into the International Latin Music Hall of Fame in 1999.

Héctor Lavoe was born Héctor Juan Pérez Martínez on September 30, 1946, in Ponce, Puerto Rico. He was one of eight siblings whose father, Luis, supported them by singing and playing guitar with tríos and big bands.

In the early 19th century, recording technology was limited. It was found that human voices were the most suitable sound for reproduction. This led to the first record companies mainly recording opera and its great singers, such as Caruso. Although instruments were eventually added, they did not record as well as the human voice. It was impossible to record a symphony orchestra with 100 musicians using a single microphone. Therefore, the first orchestral recordings were made with a few musicians, with piano and violin solos among the first instrumental recordings.

Ida Carlini

In the mid-1950s, Tito Puente's girlfriend, Ida Carlini, filed a lawsuit against Tito for child support of their son, Richard Anthony Puente. Initially, Tito denied being the father of the child, and the court ordered a blood test to confirm the paternity. The test results returned positive, proving that Tito was the father. This author possesses a copy of the blood-typing test and the results that Ida Carlini had given him.

In 1963, Eydie Gormé recorded "Blame It on the Bossa Nova," which became a Top 10 hit in the US and worldwide. According to legend, she purposely sang poorly on the song because she disliked it so much that she hoped Columbia Records wouldn't release it. However, it was the final solo Top 40 hit of her career. It's worth noting that Johnny Pacheco played percussion on the track.

La Lupe was born in Santiago de Cuba in 1938 as Guadalupe Victoria Raymond Yoli. She recorded approximately 29 albums and appeared in American talk shows, such as *Merv Griffin Show, The Dick Cavett Show,* and the *Tonight Show*. She died of a heart attack in New York City on February 29, 1992. She was *"La Reina de la Música Latina."*

In America, in the late 1920s and early 1930s, every Latin beat was erroneously called Rumba. However, Rumba is the term given to the secular Afro-Cuban party music that came out of the community halls of African slaves in Cuba. The music is for dancing and for telling stories. The genre is singable and danceable, born from the Afro-Spanish side, with a unique trace of the first element.

It originated in the urban setting where the humble black population abounded (quarters, plots) and in the semi-rural setting around the sugar mills. It is performed by percussing drums (tumba, caller, and quinto) or simply wood (cod box, candle box), accompanied by claves and, sometimes, spoons. There are three distinct types of Rumbas: Guaguancó, Columbia, and Yambu.

The famous Cuban trumpet player Alfredo "Chocolate" Armenteros was Bény Moré's maternal cousin.

Despite his enormous popularity, Bény Moré was unofficially banned from the Tropicana club in Havana due to his drinking problem and his reputation for being unreliable. While other cabarets put up with his antics due to his star stature on the island, the Tropicana had strict standards under the ownership of the corrupt Martin Max. Eventually, after many attempts, Bény convinces the owner that he will behave, and he is given a two-week engagement during the Christmas and New Year holidays.

El Bárbaro del Ritmo came through with enormous success as he packed the club every night, especially on New Year's Eve. Shortly after midnight, the club was rocked by an explosion, and pandemonium ensued as every patron made their way out. Someone had planted a bomb. Bény and his orchestra escaped unscathed.

Joe Hernández

—⁂—

Starting in 1935, María Teresa Vera formed another excellent duet with Lorenzo Hierrezuelo, and they sang for 27 years. They constituted one of the duos that experienced incredible popularity, forming an indispensable part of the radio programs of Radio Álvarez, Radio Cadena Suaritos, and the CMQ Circuit. Later, they were also on television.

—⁂—

Toña La Negra

Toña La Negra was the only Mexican vocalist to sing with the *Sonora Matancera*.

—⁂—

In the mid-1940s, Libertad Lamarque feared working in the United States, so much so that she turned down an offer from Hollywood for a seven-year contract, partly because she could not speak English and was afraid of being taken advantage of. Nevertheless, despite her fear, in 1947, she accepted an engagement at Carnegie Hall and sold out.

The song "Toro Mata" is a Peruvian composition that Celia Cruz heard when performing in this Andean country by another performer, coincidentally with the same name of Celia in the mid-1960s. Celia brought the song to Johnny Pacheco and recorded it.

Celia Cruz

Celia Cruz graduated from Teachers College (Cuba) in 1949 at 23. However, she never pursued a career as a teacher. A teacher whom Celia admired and respected, Miss Marta Rainieri, told her in response to Celia's asking how to pursue the path of becoming a teacher not to waste her time because she had a God-given gift that would afford her a much better living and could make people happy. Deep inside, Celia knew she was right, and she was thrilled to hear her advice. At that moment,

Celia made up her mind and decided that she would follow her fate and pursue a singing career.

―⁂―

Like the danzón, the *son* originated from the Oriente province of Cuba, but unlike the Contradanza, which began as music for the upper classes, *son* was music that came out of black slums. Another difference was that the Contradanza began as instrumentals, whereas the *son* had vocals.

This vocal genre constitutes one of the primary forms of Cuban music. It presents, in its structure, elements from African (Bantú) and Spanish music but already fused into the Cuban, converging in the rhythmic turns, choruses, percussive modes, intonations, and sonorities of the plucked strings that denounce its two sources.

Soneros (singers) would sing a pre-arranged part of the song followed by a montuno section (originally called the "estribillo) where the singer would improvise over the chorus's response.

―⁂―

In the 1960s, Joe Cuba had two million-selling hits, El "Pito" and "Bang Bang." The success of Joe Cuba became a springboard for other young New Yorkers, such as Larry Harlow, Willie Colón, Joe Bataan, Rafi Pagán, and Harvey Averne, to start their bands.

―⁂―

Thomas Edison recorded 205 cylinders in Havana in 1905.

In 2001, *La Lupe: My Life, My Destiny,* directed by Carmen Rivera and starring Nuyorican actress Sully Diaz, was produced by Miriam Colón's Puerto Rican Traveling Theater in NYC.

Miguel Faílde

The danzón is derived from the French *contradanse.* When the Haitian Slave Revolution occurred at the end of the 18th century, many enslaved people and colonists escaped to the Eastern Province of Cuba, known as Oriente. The Danza, Danzón, and Habanera developed out of the contradanza. The dance genre derived from Creole dance, and the name of the dance from a collective figure dance, formed in part by couples provided with arches and bouquets, widespread in the second half of the 19th century. Miguel Faílde composed the first danzón, "Las Alturas de Simpson," which premiered on January 1, 1879, at the Liceo de Matanzas (but written in June 1877).

One of Ismael Rivera's last performances was in Paris as the opening act for Bob Marley in 1978.

Arsenio Rodríguez

The classic salsa hit "Fuego En El 23" ("Fire at the 23"), initially called "Hay Fuego En El 23" ("There's A Fire at the 23"), is a song by Cuban songwriter and tres player Arsenio Rodríguez, a.k.a. "El ciego maravilloso" ("The blind marvel"). The inspiration for the song was from a fire in Arsenio's apartment in the wee hours of one morning in 1955 at 23 West 65th Street and not, as in subsequent remakes of the song, on 110th Street. Arsenio had moved to mid-town from the Bronx into a better neighborhood because his livelihood had improved.

The original tune was recorded in 1956 in Cuba and released in 1957 under the Puchito label in the LP *Arsenio Rodríguez y su Conjunto*. In the recording, you can hear Arsenio's lead singer and close friend, the Puerto Rican singer Luis "Wito" Kortright (Luis "Guito" Courtwrite), in typical Spanglish, sing, *"En el twenty-three West de la sixty-fifth, Wito agarro Arsenio y del fuego lo saco."*

In the Puchito release, Arsenio gives composing rights to his wife, Lucía Martínez. In the first version, played by *la Sonora Ponceña* in 1969, the lyrics changed to 110th Street; however, out of respect, Arsenio's wife is still credited for the composition. However, when the Ponceña recorded the tune for a second time in 1985 in their Jubilee Album, they correctly credited Arsenio.

The fire started in the middle of the night and quickly spread, causing chaos and panic among the residents. The protagonist and the neighbors try to extinguish the fire before the firefighters arrive to avoid getting burned and losing everything they own. The song describes folks screaming to get Arsenio out of the building, but little did they know that Wito had escorted Arsenio safely out a lot sooner and taken him across the street from the fire.

Daniel Santos was married twelve times and reported to have fathered twelve children.

Musician Willie Colón, born William Anthony Colón Róman on April 28, 1950, grew up in the South Bronx,

New York, and without his knowledge, his father was serving time in prison.

Puerto Rican bassist Bobby Valentin was named "Mr. Soul" by Ray Barretto.

Salsa/Mambo dancing is the most popular partner dance in the world, enjoyed by an estimated 200 million people. This is more than the combined popularity of Bachata, Swing, and Tango.

María Teresa Vera

María Teresa Vera was born in Guanaguay, the former province of Pinar del Río, on February 6, 1895. Of black ancestry and enslaved people, she spent her childhood in Havana. She sang from an early age and learned to play guitar with Manuel Corona and Patricio Ballagas. Her first public performance was on March 18, 1911, at the Teatro Politeama Grande, singing the creole "Mercedes" by Manuel Corona. She then continued singing in the theaters of Havana.

Rafael Hernández, who would become Puerto Rico's most popular and prolific composer of the twentieth century, wanted to avoid becoming a musician. He wanted to become a cigar maker or anything else other than a musician. He fought with his grandmother, who raised him and pushed him to become a musician. The belief that all who played cornet died of tuberculosis existed in his hometown of Aguadilla. The cornet was the first instrument young Rafael learned to play. To get away from playing the instrument, he would prick his gums with a pin to extract blood, then spit the blood and tell his grandmother that he had tuberculosis because of her insistence. The grandmother stood firm with his musical studies, although she allowed Rafael to switch from cornet to violin and the trombone.

Maxwell Hyman, a Jewish businessman, owned the popular mid-town Latin dance venue known as the Palladium. He made his fortune in the fur business and was a survivor of the holocaust, having spent time in a concentration camp.

Willie Colón tried out for his high school band and didn't make the cut, so he dropped out and went professional with his *Latin Jazz All-Stars* at 14.

At one time, the Cuban singer Roberto Ledesma played timbales with flutist José Fajardo's Charanga.

La Lupe's actual name was Yolanda Guadalupe Victoria Raymond, also known as La Yiyiyi. She graduated from the University of Havana as a teacher.

Bény Moré

Bény Moré was the stage name of Bartolome Maximiliano Moré Gutierrez. He was born at 7 a.m. on August 24, 1919, in Santa Isabel de las Lajas, Cuba, a former province of Las Villas (currently belonging to Cienfuegos), in the crowded neighborhood of Pueblo Nuevo. He was known as *El Barbaro del Ritmo* and *El Sonero Mayor*. He started his career with the *Trío Matamoros*. He was the eldest of 18 children.

Bény's great-great-great grandfather was the king of a tribe in the Kingdom of Kongo (present-day northern Angola). He was captured by slave traders and sold to a Cuban plantation owner named Ramón Gundo Paredes, who owned private homes, and Silvestre Gutierrez, a blacksmith sold him to another Cuban landowner named Conde Moré. His parents were Virginia Moré, a descendant of blacks from the Congo, dedicated to domestic work in profession. Bény would take his mother's last name for lack of paternal recognition. Shortly after the firstborn's birth, the family moved to the neighborhood of La Guinea, where Bartolome spent his childhood. There, he received a decisive influence on his future career as a musician, thanks to a black brotherhood called *Casino de Los Congos* or *San Antonio*, founded around 1850 by freed Congo blacks from central and western Africa.

Bény died at 9:15 p.m. on February 19, 1963, at 43, in Havana. He suffered from alcoholism and died of cirrhosis of the liver. Tens of thousands of people attended his funeral.

If you listen to Tito Puente's 1957 LP Night Beat, you can hear Doc Severinsen, the band leader of the Johnny Carson Tonight Show, playing all the whip-snapping solos. Doc was a long-underrated New York studio sharpshooter at the time.

Puerto Rican salsa vocalist José Cheo Feliciano fell into tough times due to substance abuse. He went into rehabilitation in Puerto Rico with a program called

CREA. While in the program, he recorded with a group called *Impacto Crea*, composed of other musicians also undergoing treatment.

In planning his comeback, Jerry Masucci, owner of the Fania label, got together with the composer Tite Curet Alonso to have a few songs written for the album, which was called *CHEO*. The orchestra was top notch with Larry Harlow on piano, Orestes Vilato on timbales, Bobby Valentin on bass, Ismael Quintana playing the maracas, claves, and singing chorus with Santitos Colón and Justo Betancourt, Johnny Rodríguez on bongó and Cencerro (hand bell), Charlie Rodríguez on Tres, Louie Ramírez on vibraphone and the great Johnny Pacheco as the musical director, chorus and on conga.

The LP was released under Vaya Records (a subsidiary of Fania Records) in 1972 and was a remarkable success. Tite composed eight of the ten songs with such hits as "Anacaona," "Pienso en Ti," "Pa' Que Afinquen," and "Franqueza Cruel." However, the first release was in 1971 on the Discos Meiser label based in Bogota, Colombia, whereas Masucci was developing a distributorship for South America.

―∞―

Did you know that Charlie Palmieri revolutionized Salsa music by replacing the traditional piano with an organ? His innovative approach to Latin music brought a new sound and energy that captivated audiences worldwide. It's incredible how one small change can make such a significant impact!

―∞―

Willie Colón was a teenager when Irv Greenbaum engineered his demo. Willie didn't have the money to pay for the night's recording, so Irv's boss kept the tape and Willie's jacket, which he had carelessly left behind. The following day, Willie showed up with his mom, and she paid for everything and got his coat back.

Tito Puente and The Latin All Stars

Frank Peri, a former ballroom dancer, founded Roper Records in New York City in the early 1960s. The Roper label specialized in Latin instrumental records, many of which were played by Tito Puente. Even today, some of these tunes are used in Ballroom Competitions worldwide. Tito Puente's rendition of "Hava Nagila" is also immensely popular among thousands of Jewish gatherings around the world, as well as the dance school classic "Hokey Pokey." However, many people are unaware that Tito Puente is performing under the name of the Roper Dance Orchestra.

At the turn of the 19th century, the phonograph played a vital role for someone who did not speak another language (other than English). The phonograph facilitated an emotional return to the homeland in a country with strange values and customs and where people spoke an unfamiliar language. Records of family songs reinforced traditional values and the sense of dignity of every immigrant. For their part, record companies were astute enough to recognize the need for records in foreign languages at the beginning of the 1900s, when they began seriously to develop and diversify their catalogs and offers.

By 1908, Columbia, Victor and other small companies printed popular double-sided records for 75 cents, the equivalent of $25.00 in today's market. Amid World War I (1914), selling records and phonographs to people not born in the United States was a huge business. The record companies looked at every market and analyzed its potential. Even small ethnic groups were considered. For example, the Albanian-American community was small and record sales were low. Still, every person who wanted a record could be persuaded to buy a phonograph and other kinds of records. In the case of Albania, Columbia and Victor maintained a series of Albanian records for a time, and the records they pressed of each selection fluctuated between 300 and 325.

The Panart label was responsible for recording the initial sessions of what became known as The Cuban Jam Sessions, with their first LP-8000. These types of recordings, which would later be given a very Cuban name, "Descargas," by the Gema label, marked a significant moment in the cultural history of Cuban music. However, Panart recorded the first of these sessions, laying the foundation for a new era in Cuban music.

Celia Cruz

Celia Cruz was once engaged to a young bass player named Alfredo León, son of Bienvenido León, who was a member of the *Septeto Nacional*.

One day, Tito Rodríguez called Pete Bonet and asked if he would sing with his orchestra at Casa Borinquen in Brooklyn. Pete became flabbergasted and honored, and he accepted. During the evening, after singing a few tunes, Tito asked Pete to sing a song and suggested "Marisol," a number that was composed by Pete. Pete was ready to sing, but Tito would not leave the stage. Finally, Tito told him to get started, but Pete was confused and told Tito, "But you are still on the stage."

Joe Hernández

Tito told Pete, "I'm going to sing coro (chorus) for you." Pete was dumbfounded and elated at the same time to have the great Tito Rodríguez give him the stage to sing and have him sing coro. That was a big moment in Pete's life.

In the 1920s and 1930s, the government of Cuba attempted, unsuccessfully, to eradicate all aspects of black culture on the island. President Alfredo Zayas (1921-1925) outlawed the Rumba. Dictator Gerardo Machado y Morales (1928-1933) prohibited *carnival comparsas* and made playing the *son* publicly illegal. He also banned the bongós for being too "African." Machado's minister, Rogelio Zayas Bazan, attempted to close all dance schools. Desi Arnaz's father, Desiderio Alberto Arnaz y Alberni II, following the example set by Machado and as the youngest mayor of the Providence of Santiago (1923-1932), prohibited the playing of congas and bongós. Desi's uncle was the Chief of Police, guaranteeing enforcement of the law. Ironically, Desi became famous by playing the instrument his father forbade.

Miguel Berdicia Matamoros chose not to use his father's last name because the father had abandoned the family when Miguel was a lad. He decided instead to use his mother's maiden name, "Matamoros."

Gladys Serrano was a beautiful dancer who was always enthralled by Ismael Rivera's voice, even though she had never met him. She was in Puerto Rico looking for Daniel Santos, her former husband, and the father of their two-year-old son, after being separated from him for two years.

While in Puerto Rico, she hears the voice of Ismael Rivera, and she quickly walks towards him when she notices he is with her cousin. The cousin introduced them, and they quickly began to talk to each other. At this time, Ismael was divorced from Virginia Fuentes, with whom he had three children. Gladys began to tell Ismael her plight and how she was looking for Daniel Santos. To her surprise, Ismael said Santos was his friend and often heard him talk about his little boy. Ismael told her he would contact him.

The next day, he showed up with Santos, and they bumped into the Puerto Rican composer Pedro Flores. Don Flores invited them to his home for lunch. They had a wonderful time together. Don Pedro then played romantic music and took Santos to the yard to show him his roosters and chickens. From that moment on, something special began with Ismael and Gladys. Eventually, they married, and Ismael raised Daniel Santo's son as if he were his own. Of course, rumors and stories were plentiful (lots of gossip).

The composer Bobby Capó then wrote "Que Te Pasa a Ti," thinking of the relationship between Ismael and Gladys. Capó then told Rivera he wanted him to sing this song for Gladys. So around 3 a.m., Ismael goes to Capó's home. By 5 a.m., they call Gladys, with Capó on piano, and Ismael sings the song.

The song was eventually recorded in the LP Traigo de Todo, which also included the tune "El Nazareno." The

LP was released in 1974, and all the compositions were arranged by the pianist Javier Vasquez. The LP was a big hit.

Ismael and Gladys had one son, Carlitos Rivera. He would eventually sing chorus with his father. Unfortunately, he died young. With regards to Ronnie Santos, the son of Daniel Santos, whom Ismael raised and encouraged him to pursue his music and appears singing the chorus in the album by Ismael Rivera, Soy Feliz, he took his life at an early age. Gladys died in 1992, the same year that Daniel Santos passed away.

Marion Sunshine

In the winter of 1929, Miss Marion Sunshine, a vaudevillian actress, was on her honeymoon with her husband, Antobal Azpiazú, in Havana, where she became interested in Cuban music. During her stay, she met her brother-in-law, Don Azpiazú, for the first time and encouraged him to embark on a musical invasion of the United States. She suggested he add the tune "El

Manisero" to his repertoire. Thanks to her connections with George Godfrey and Charles Freeman, who were then the Keith Circuit overlords, she secured Don Azpiazú's April 1930 engagement at the New York Palace Theatre. Miss Sunshine produced and staged the event, which later turned out to have made history.

Printing musical compositions in Havana started in 1803. In 1812, Esteban Bolanos printed the first musical newspaper in Cuba, *El Filarmónico Mensual.* Then, in 1814, Don Antonio Coleho established the first known musical academy to teach singing, violin, and piano. Finally, in 1816, the Santa Cecilia Music Academy was founded.

Johnny Pacheco & Joe Hernández

In 1964, Gennaro Massucci, an Italian American, and his client, Johnny Pacheco, a Dominican, founded the Fania

Recording Company with a capital of five thousand dollars. While Massucci was a high school dropout, he earned his diploma while serving in the U.S. Navy in Guantánamo. Later, he studied business administration in Mexico and obtained his law degree from New York Law School while working as a New York City police officer. Unfortunately, Masucci passed away on December 21 while undergoing exploratory surgery for stomach pains in Buenos Aires, Argentina. He died on the operating table.

The first live recording and release of *the Fania All-Stars Volumes 1 and 2* was at the Red Garter in 1968—the success led to recording the *Fania All-Stars: Live at The Cheetah, Volumes 1 and 2*.

According to the Cuban pianist Alfredo Rodríguez, the steps for the cha-cha-chá existed before Enrique Jorrín's creation. Rodríguez recalls seeing dancers performing the steps at home parties his mother gave back in the mid-1940s.

The Mafia oversaw the Palladium in New York City. At one point, despite the enormous success it experienced at the hands of promoter Federico Pagani, they told him to curtail the number of blacks frequenting the dancehall, even though they were thrilled with the business he was generating. Pagani responded by telling them that blacks also bring in the greens. To the Mafia, money talks, so they give Pagani a pass and let him continue doing what he was doing.

The notion that Millie Puente was Tito Puente's niece makes no sense since Tito's siblings died young. Cousin? Perhaps. No one seems to know for sure.

Augusto Cohen (Left)

In the spring of 1935, there was a significant shift in the music scene when Augusto Coen, a prominent figure in Alberto Socarras's band, decided to start his band. He teamed up with Davilita and set up their new band at the Golden Casino Ballroom, which was buzzing with anticipation. As a promotional masterstroke, Fernando Luis, Campoamor's talent director, proposed a musical battle dance between Socarras and Augusto. The parties agreed on a percentage of the ticket receipts, setting the stage for a thrilling showdown.

The event was billed as the "War between Cuba and Puerto Rico." The week of the event, at the Park Palace theatre, after the featured movie ended, across the screen, it repeatedly read *"FLASH!"* followed by *"WAR!"*... *between Cuba and Puerto...between Alberto Socarras of Cuba and Augusto Coen of Puerto Rico*. The event was sold out with no room to move, as Socarras played on one end of the ballroom and Augusto at the other.

Part of the attraction was the dislike that existed at the time between the two groups (as well as between Socarras and Coen), fueled by the resentment that Puerto Ricans were citizens, thereby free to travel in and out of the country. At the same time, Cubans' stay in the United States was limited to 29 days. With more Puerto Ricans at the event and fearing that Socarras would be declared the loser, Cubans threatened to wreck the place. In the end, no one was declared the winner. The irony was that Socarras's band consisted mainly of Puerto Ricans and Dominicans, while Coen's band consisted mainly of Cubans and Panamanians.

—⚏—

La Lupe, a musical force to be reckoned with, captivated audiences with her raw and intense performances. After witnessing one of her live shows, Pablo Picasso hailed her as a musical genius. Her stage presence was electrifying, as she would kick off her shoes, tear her clothes, and bite her hands and arms. Amidst this chaos, she would laugh, cry, and scream, '¡*Ahi na ma!*', leaving the audience in awe.

It has been said that La Lupe was not a woman on the edge of a nervous breakdown, but a nervous breakdown dressed as a woman.

Besides being the Queen of Salsa, Celia Cruz was also the *Queen of Wigs*, having a collection of over one hundred and fifty of them.

In the mid-1940s, CBS had a weekly radio show, *Saludos Amigos*. The show aired some of the most popular Latin orchestras and was heard overseas by our American Armed Forces.

Selena's 1994 mega-hit and signature song, "Bidi Bidi Bom Bom," is considered one of the best compositions recorded by Selena that led to her commercial access. It peaked at number one on the United States *Billboard Hot Latin Songs* and remained there for four weeks. This song was Selena's second consecutive number-one single. It was the most-played Latin song in 1996 and won the *Tejano Music Award Song of the Year*. Selena and Pete Astudillo wrote the song, and the title means the sound of a female's heart when she sees her man pass by, "bidi bidi bom bom!"

Armando Peraza, the Cuban percussionist born in 1924 and passed away in 2014, left an indelible mark on the world of music. His early life was marked by adversity, growing up as an orphan and facing homelessness by the age of seven. Yet, he managed to play semi-professional baseball and co-wrote a song, 'Cepeda Forever,' in honor of his friend, baseball player Orlando Cepeda. His musical journey was equally remarkable, with notable stints in Cal Tjader's band for six years, The Judy Garland Show's orchestra on television from 1963 to 1964, and a legendary collaboration with Carlos Santana for almost two decades.

After being honorably discharged from the Navy during WWII, Tito Puente attended the renowned Juilliard School of Music in New York City as a "special" student, as he never completed high school. Despite some misconceptions, Puente did not receive a degree from Juilliard.

According to Jerry Masucci, in an interview on television, the cost of renting Yankee Stadium for the August 24, 1973, Fania Latin-Soul-Rock concert was $280,000 (equivalent in purchasing power for 2024 of 1.94 million dollars). There was an additional $50K ($350K adjusted for inflation in 2024) deposit to ensure no damage to the field by the fans would occur.

Tejano music incorporates rhythmic elements of Colombian cumbia, melodic elements of Cuban bolero, and influences from pop, rock, blues, and European polka. It began to gain mainstream recognition and popularity in modern times thanks to the late and legendary Selena.

Mongo Santamaría first worked as a mechanic and a mailman (from 1940 to 1948, he worked during the day as a mailman) before becoming one of the world's top conga players.

Canario Group

Supposedly, Manuel "Canario" Jiménez was the first to record Rafael Hernández's famous "Lamento Borincano" on July 14, 1930. Accompanied by his two guitarists and his maracas and clave players, they were each paid twelve dollars for the recording. However, some historians disagree with the above version and claim that the Canario group went to record it with the voice of its singer, Ramón Quiros, who became hoarse, so they called Davilita (Pedro Ortiz Davila) to replace him. This song was Davilita's first recording ever made and the first that was made of Rafael's immortal tune.

—⚙—

The Panart "Descargas" would significantly influence the development of Latin music. Two new rhythms were born on Panart albums: Enrique Jorrín's "El Cha Cha Cha" with the *Orquesta America* and Pachanga with Eduardo Davidson.

—⚙—

There was a time when the authorities in many municipalities in Cuba prohibited slave descendants from playing drums, except on Sunday. Instead, the participants would use various packing boxes, with the ones used for codfish as a favorite. The different boxes had different pitches. From approximately 1909 to 1933, many of Cuba's presidents issued edicts to prohibit the expression of African culture or any manifestations of their culture, such as secular rumbas, comparsas, and the bongó drum.

—⚙—

The tune "Oye Cómo Va" was written by Tito Puente around 1956. However, it was first recorded in 1962 and included in his album *El Rey: Bravo*. Carlos Santana popularized it with his release of the album *Abraxas* in 1970. It was then released as a single in 1971, reaching number 13 on the *Billboard Hot 100*, 11 on the *Billboard Easy Listening survey,* and 32 on the *R7B chart*. Gregg Rolie sang the song.

—⚙—

From its early history, the blacks in Cuba have been the creative force behind Cuban music. For example, according to the 1827 census, the data shows that among the 16,250 whites dedicated to trades, there were only 44 musicians, while there were 49 musicians among the 6,754 free blacks dedicated to trades; that is a ratio of one musician for every 369 in the white population vs. one musician in 137 in the black population, almost triple.

The Cheetah

Although the release of the first Fania All-Star album was a success, the live event at the almost unknown club, *Red Garter*, which was at the border between the South Bronx and Harlem River Drive, was a fiasco. To avoid repeating the same mistake, promoter Ralph Mercado was brought in by Masucci to promote the next concert at the *Cheetah Ballroom* on August 26, 1971. The concert was a resounding success, with more than four thousand fans attending.

Joe Hernández

Many have written that the tune "Oye Cómo Va" came to Tito Puente from Arcaño's orchestra when, in 1957, they recorded "Resa del Meletón" for the Gema label under the title "Chanchullo." In 1963, Puente then added his magic touch from its introduction to produce what would become a worldwide hit. Whether or not Tito was "inspired" by the Arcaño piece is not as relevant as realizing that a careful listen shows Arcaño's tune of "Chanchullo" is nowhere the same as "Oye Cómo Va." Cachao was a friend of this author. He never mentioned that he thought there was any similarity or, as some would conclude, that Tito "copied" Cachao's work. "Oye Cómo Va" was meant to be one of those tunes to fill up space in an album, never the mass hit it became. It featured Johnny Pacheco on the flute.

Battle of Leyte

Tito Puente was drafted in 1942 and served in World War II for three years. He was a war hero, having participated in nine battles on the escort carrier USS Santee (CVE-

29), and was honorably discharged. For his service in the Battle of Leyte, he received a Presidential Unit Citation, serving under the overall command of General Douglas MacArthur.

Bauza composed a tune titled "Lona" on September 10, 1934, in honor of his first wife, whom he affectionately called "Leona" (Lion) in Spanish when she was upset. To prevent her from noticing, he altered the spelling on the record, but it didn't work out as planned. When she heard it, she exclaimed, *"Quien carajo es Lona?"* (Who the **** is Lona?)

The records at El Cerro, Cuba's municipal district, indicate that Celia Cruz was born on October 21, 1925. However, the reliability of the dates is questionable since her parents only registered Celia's birth fourteen years later, on January 1, 1939.

Jerry Masucci was a fan of Latin music, a taste he developed while stationed in the military base in Guantánamo, Cuba.

On April 29, 2000, the Fania All Stars performed before thousands of salsa fans in the historic Hiram Bithorn Stadium of Puerto Rico. This author presented the International Latin Music Hall of Fame induction award to Cheo Feliciano on stage. Cheo then introduced Celia

Cruz, and she received an unwelcome reception as the fans booed throughout her performance for her political intolerance against the island's beloved Andy Montañez.

Celia left the stage crying and blamed Andy Montañez by arguing that he had planned everything. This concert was her only public humiliation in her glorious career. However, in the summer of 1997, the promoters were forced to cancel Celia's appearance at the World Salsa Festival in San Juan under the threat of a boycott for the same controversy. This entire *brouhaha* resulted from Montañez, who, in April of 1997, warmly embraced and welcomed Silvio Rodríguez, the famous Cuban Revolutionary singer of the *nueva trova,* to Puerto Rico.

Jerry Masucci and Johnny Pacheco decided on the name "Fania" from a son montuno by the Cuban composer Reinaldo López Bolaños, titled "Fanía Funché," and recorded by *Estrellas de Chocolate* in 1958. This song, combined with a visit by Masucci and Larry Harlow to a cafe shop in Havana called "Fania" (without the accent mark), sealed the name.

Chino Pozo, who falsely claimed to be Chano Pozo's cousin, left the jazz world in the mid-1960s to work for the singer Paul Anka. However, it is important to note that according to Cuban researcher Helio Orovio, who worked at the Institute of Ethnology and Folklore of the Cuban Academy of Sciences, Chino and Chano were cousins.

Rita Harlow, Larry Harlow's former wife, made a significant contribution to Latin music history by forming an all-female salsa band named *Latin Fever*. This groundbreaking group recorded its only album in 1978 on the Fania Label, a production that was masterfully overseen by Larry Harlow himself.

Cándido Camaro

The Cuban conguero Cándido has performed and recorded with 97 of the top 100 billing names in the Encyclopedia of American Jazz and Pop Music.

Eduardo Brito was the Dominica Republic's first famous popular singer known worldwide. He was born Eleuterio Aragónez in Puerto Plata on February 21, 1906. In 1929, while in New York to record and perform at the Waldorf Astoria, the RKO, and Lowe's State Theatres, he worked alongside Eduardo Cansino, the father of the famous movie actress Rita Hayworth. In 1941, during the Second

World War, he returned to the Dominican Republic from Spain and shortly after suffered a psychological breakdown and was committed to a mental hospital. He died at the early age of 39 on January 5, 1946.

In the late 1940s and early 1950s, Tito Rodríguez was spotted at the Palladium Ballroom breakdancing, spinning on one hand while dressed in his tuxedo, well before breakdancing became widely popular in the 1980s. In the 1955 short film *Mambo Madness*, you can witness a young Tito showcasing his floor gyrations.

Copacabana

The famous entertainment night spot, the Copacabana, opened on November 10, 1940, at 10 East 60th Street in New York City. Like many nightclubs, the person on the lease was just the "front" man for the one being in charge. It was no different at the Copa; whereas Monte Proser was the name on the lease, the powerful mob boss

Frank Costello ran the joint. All entertainers, including Tito Puente, knew who was really in charge.

Music and dancing have a long history in Cuba. Documentation shows that in 1798, there were at least fifty public dances in Havana, and the dancers preferred the black orchestras, even back then.

Tropicana

Night Club

The famous open air night club in a typical Cuban atmosphere.

Presenting this great show:

JOSEPHINE BAKER
First World's Vedette

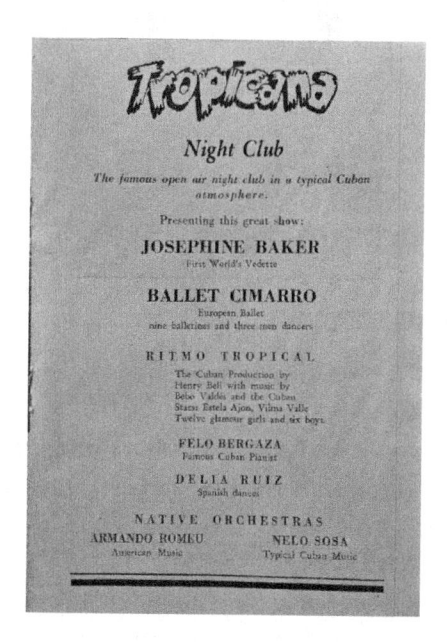

BALLET CIMARRO
European Ballet
nine balletinas and three men dancers

RITMO TROPICAL
The Cuban Production by
Henry Bell with music by
Bebo Valdés and the Cuban
Stairs Estela Ajon, Vilma Valle
Twelve glamour girls and six boys.

FELO BERGAZA
Famous Cuban Pianist

DELIA RUIZ
Spanish dancer

NATIVE ORCHESTRAS
ARMANDO ROMEU   NELO SOSA
American Music   Typical Cuban Music

Promo Jan 6, 1951

Prohibition, when The United States took over most of the Cuban economy. As North American tourism grew, discrimination also grew. Bands that were once integrated were now frowned upon. In 1950, the Hotel Naciónal refused to allow Josephine Baker to enter their property during her visit to the island because of her skin color. Eleven years later, in 1966, Fidel Castro invited her to perform in Havana as the guest of honor and headliner of the Cuban Revolution's 7th anniversary celebrations.

Ernesto Lecuona

Ernesto Lecuona wrote over 600 (some sources state over 1,000) songs during his career; among them are "Malaguena," "Siboney," "María La O," "Siboney," "Always in My Heart," "Andalucía," "Para Vigo Me Voy" and "La Comparsa."

In the early 1960s, Tito Puente did many recordings under the Roper Record label while under contract with RCA. To disguise his participation, most of the LPs did not have his name, and the orchestra he led was called The Latin All-Stars. In the early 1960s, Tito Puente did many recordings under the Roper Record label while under contract with RCA. To disguise his participation, most of the LPs did not have his name, and the orchestra he led was called *The Latin All-Stars.*

Johnny Pacheco suggested to singer Héctor Pérez that he change his name to Héctor Lavoe. This name change would allow Lavoe to build a personal brand.

During the filming of *The Mambo Kings,* Celia Cruz told a group of the cast that Pérez Prado was the inventor of the mambo. This comment by Celia made Tito Puente livid when he learned of it. He explained to others who the actual inventors of the mambo were, followed by a few expletives. Whether Tito told Celia or if she ever heard about his outburst, no one knows.

Barry Rogers was a renowned jazz, pop, and salsa trombonist, born Barron W. Rogers on May 22, 1935, in New York City. He belonged to Jewish ancestry and was raised in Harlem and the Bronx. Besides being an exceptional Trombone player, he was passionate about playing the Cuban *tres*. He learned to play the instrument after his wife bought one for him in the Bronx as a birthday gift. Barry's love for the Cuban *tres* can be heard in a few Latin recordings, such as in the Cesta All-Stars, Eddie Palmieri's "Si Las Nenas Me Dejan, Que," in "Tierra Bendita" with Típica Novel, and on Johnny Pacheco and Pete "El Conde" Rodríguez's swinging tune, "Sonero."

Joe Hernández

In the 1930s and '40s, Ernesto Lecuona wrote eleven music scores for MGM, Warner Brothers, and 20th Century Fox films. He was nominated for an Academy Award in 1942 for the song "Always in My Heart." He once wrote four songs in a single night that would become hits: "Blue Night," "Siboney," "Say Si Si," and "Dame Tus Dos Rosas" (Two Hearts That Pass in the Night).

Celia Cruz

Celia Cruz made her big-screen debut in 1955 in the Cuban film *Gallega en La Habana* (*A Spanish Woman in Havana*) with the great Argentine comic actress and leading box office draw Nini Marshall. Celia's husband, Pedro, also makes an appearance in the film. Celia also appeared in the 1957 film *Affair in Havana* with John Cassavetes and Raymond Burr of Perry Mason fame.

The Yankee Stadium concert by the Fania All Stars in the summer of 1973 was repeated at the Coliseo Roberto Clemente in San Juan, Puerto Rico. When the album The *Fania All Stars: Live at Yankee Stadium* was released, the public felt deceived because Fania combined the two concerts to give the impression of one event.

"El Manicero" (The Peanut Vendor) was a Cuban son-pregon composed by Moisés Simons in 1922, earning him over $100,000 in royalties by 1943 (the equivalent of $1.8 million in 2024). The tune was first recorded by Rita Montaner in 1928 under the Columbia label. "The Peanut Vendor" has been recorded more than 180 times, including by such notables as Stan Kenton, Louis Armstrong, Anita O'Day, Dean Martin, and the Beatles. Cuban Don Azpiazú and his *Havana Casino Orquestra* first popularized it in the States on April 26, 1930, at New York's Palace Theatre. It was also the first authentic Cuban song to be a best seller in the United States and to sell over a million records in 78 RPM form.

"Bésame Mucho" (Kiss Me a Lot) was a bolero song composed in 1941 by beloved Mexican singer and songwriter Consuelo Velázquez. She was only 15 years old when she wrote it in bolero style. The young Consuelo was inspired, despite never having been kissed, as it was considered sinful, by the piano piece "Quejas, O La Maja y el Ruiseñor" composed by the Spanish Catalán of classical music, Pantaleón Enrique Joaquín Granados Campina.

The song has been interpreted by the likes of Elvis Presley, Frank Sinatra, Nat King Cole, Plácido Domingo, Andrea Bocelli, Diana Krall, Cesaria Evora, Luis Miguel, Dean Martin, Dalida, Chris Isaak, and The Beatles. Among its most famous versions were sung by *Trío Los Panchos*. It is one of the most popular songs of the 20th century and one of the most important and most recorded songs in Latin music of all time.

Ray Barretto's album *Ritmo en el Corazón*, featuring Celia Cruz and Adalberto Santiago, won him his first and only Grammy in 1990.

Cuban musicians, particularly trumpet players, would often feel intimidated by Pérez Prado due to the challenging nature of his arrangements, which required playing many high notes. He was commonly regarded as the Beethoven of the mambo, and only the most exceptional trumpet players could collaborate with him.

Orestes Vilato was born on May 12, 1944, in Camaguey, Cuba. Vilato is a renowned Cuban percussionist who moved to New York with his family in 1956. At the age of 12, he began playing with the Charanga Orchestra of Belisario López. In 1962, he played with José Antonio Fajardo before joining Johnny Pacheco. Vilato has had the privilege of working with other legends, such as Ray Barretto, Cachao, and the Fania All-Stars. He has also collaborated with Carlos Santana.

Eydie Gormé

Eydie Gormé, born Edith Gormezano, was an American singer of Jewish descent. Her journey from a translator and interpreter at the United Nations to a renowned singer is a testament to her talent and determination. Born on August 16, 1928, she grew up in the Bronx, New York, on East 168th Street. After graduating from Taft High School, she embarked on a career at the United Nations. However, her true passion lay in music, and she became famous for her Latin music songs, with her signature tune being "Sabor a Mi," a heartfelt melody she recorded with *Trío Los Panchos*. Her untimely passing on August 10, 2013, in Las Vegas, Nevada, marked the end of an era in the music industry.

The first time that Celia Cruz cried "Azucar" on a record was when she recorded the album *Nuestros Exitos de Celia Cruz* with the number "Te Solte La Rienda" in 1971.

Tito Puente's arrangement of "Picadillo" was retitled "The Arthur Murray Rhumba" by Gabriel Oller, the owner of SMC records.

Palladium Ballroom

Louis Levine, Sylvia Cole, and Hyman Siegel filed the Certificate of Incorporation of the Palladium Ballroom, Inc. with attorney Louis J. Lefkowitz on January 19, 1946. Later, Louis J. Lefkowitz served as the Attorney General of New York State for 22 years. The Palladium Ballroom was granted its liquor license on April 17, 1947. On September 19, 1950, the Palladium Ballroom was officially renamed Morton Ballroom Inc. However, it kept operating to the public as the Palladium Ballroom.

In 1925, María Teresa formed a group called *Sexteto Occident* to play the popular *son* genre of music. The group recorded for the Columbia label and worked for Brunswick and Odeón. María Teresa frequently changed the name of the sextet for commercial reasons. However, she stopped performing between 1933 and 1935 due to her religious beliefs in the Yoruba religion. She eventually sold the group to Ignacio Piñeiro, who renamed it *Sexteto Nacional de Ignacio Piñeiro,* later known as *Sexteto Nacional.* With the addition of a trumpet, the band became the *Septeto Nacional.*

Vitín Avilés was a Puerto Rican singer born as Victor Manuel Aviles Rojas in Mayagüez on September 30, 1924. He started his career as a barber, a skill he learned from his father. Vitín participated as a singer in amateur radio shows and later became the lead singer for the *Orquesta Hatuey* in 1943. Throughout his career, he sang with several orchestras, such as the *Miguelito Miranda Orchestra, Orquesta Anacaona, Pupi Campo's Band, Lecuona Cuban Boys, Enric Madriguera, Xavier Cugat, Tito Puente, La Playa Sextet, Carlos Varela* and *Charlie Palmieri.* He was also a soloist, and his voice was often compared to Tito Rodríguez's. Vitín was featured on many of Tito's recordings, singing the chorus. He passed away on January 1, 2004, at St. Vincent's Hospital in New York City.

In 1972, Eddie Palmieri received an advance from Jerry Masucci to record an album with the Fania label. The recording never occurred. As things turned out, Palmieri never needed to record with Fania or the Fania All-Stars to achieve fame.

Tite Curet Alonso learned to speak Portuguese because his oldest sister married a Brazilian. He was fond of saying that the Portuguese language was just Spanish, badly spoken.

Edyie Goemé, fluent in Spanish, had a mega-hit throughout Latin America in 1964 with a song titled "Amor," accompanied by Trío Los Panchos.

Author and Raúl Azpiazú

Raúl Azpiazú was the son of Don Azpiazú, the famous pianist, composer, and band leader who pioneered Latin music and the rumba craze in New York City with the infamous tune "El Manicero." Raúl was born on September 23, 1924, in Havana, Cuba. He was a singer, conguero, and saxophone player who performed at the Roseland Ballroom for many years with the Lecuona Cuban Boys, Lester Lanin, Peter Duchin Orchestra, and

Ramón Argueso. Raúl had the honor of playing at four Presidential Inaugural Balls.

In 1957, the renowned singer Celia Cruz visited New York City for the first time. She was invited to receive a gold record award for her hit song "Burundanga" at the Saint Nicholas Arena in the Bronx. The event was enormous, with other famous performers like *Machito and His Orchestra* and Graciela performing. However, things worsened when the police intervened due to some fighting that broke out, which may have been caused by overcrowding. As a result, everyone had to leave the venue abruptly, and Celia was escorted out of the nightclub without knowing what had caused the chaos.

In 1963, Julio Iglesias attended law school in Madrid and was a goalkeeper for one of Real Madrid's youth soccer teams. However, On September 22 of the same year, he was in a severe car accident that not only put an end to his career in soccer but left him paralyzed for two years. While hospitalized, he learned how to play the guitar.

To keep the Fania label growing and meeting the increasing demand for new songs, Johnny Pacheco and Jerry Masucci used to travel to San Juan, Puerto Rico, to purchase new songs. They visited a famous street called Calle Sierra in Santurce, a hub for songwriters selling their latest works. They would stay there for a few days

Joe Hernández

and return with ten hits, such as Ray Barretto's "Mirame de Frente," purchased from a Cuban composer named Hugo Gonzalez.

Pete Bonet tells the story of a fellow coming weekly to The Corso and asking him to hire him to perform. Pete would reject him weekly, telling the person that no one knew who he was and that he only hired well-known bands. The fellow was persistent and continued to drop by each week, asking for work. Finally, Pete gave him a break to play one evening. The fellow and his band were so fantastic that Pete hired them for six months. That fellow was Willie Rosario.

Don Azpiazú and His Orchestra

In the late 1920s and early '30s, Don Azpiazú incorporated some form of Afro-Cuban percussion with drums. Note the instrument at the feet of the third musician on the right in the above photo.

Enrique Jorrín, the chachacha inventor, initially called his new rhythm "mambo-rumba."

Tommy Morton, the actual "owner" of the Palladium, was assaulted in the ticket booth by four men while the place was jumping upstairs. Morton, then 45, was hit on the head with a gun. The New York Times edition of April 11, 1947, headlines, "Bandits Routed in Dance Holdup." This incident took place one week before the approval of its liquor license. Under normal circumstances, this would usually delay a liquor license approval, but somehow it did not. The following week, the liquor license was approved.

Musician Willie Rodríguez was the pianist on two Grammy-winning Albums; the first is *Machito and His Salsa Band,* recorded in 1982 in Utrecht, Holland on the Timeless Label. The other was in the Celia Cruz album *La Negra Tiene Tumbao* 2002 on the SONY Label. Rodríguez earned a BSA in Psychology, a master's in education, and, in 2002, a Doctorate in Music Education degree from Columbia University, Teachers College.

Between 1946 and 1956, Bény Moré participated as a singer in 11 films during his stay in Mexico.

Celia Cruz's father, Simón Cruz, was a stoker for the Cuban railroad, one of the first to take on this role. His modest salary was stretched thin, barely providing for his immediate family and certainly not for the nine other 'relatives' who shared their home. The household was a bustling one, with Celia's cousin Serafín Díaz and his two children, Aunt Nena (Agustina Alfonso) and her four children, and Celia's mother Catalina, who had an adopted child, all under one roof.

Johnny Albino with author Joe Hernández

The Puerto Rican bolero singer Johnny Albino (1917-2011) played with *Trío Los Panchos* from 1958 through 1968. He was also a member and lead voice of the *Trío San Juan,* which, like *Los Panchos*, became an internationally acclaimed group. His career spanned over 300 albums and CDs. He was a World War II veteran. Before starting a music career, he worked as a radio repairman. Johnny would never forget to call and sing "Feliz cumpleaños" to this author's wife on her birthday.

The first charanga orchestra in the United States was the *Orquesta Gilberto Valdés*, which was formed in New York in 1952. The group lasted less than one year.

Olga Guillot (1923-2010) was known as the "Queen of Bolero." She made her public debut when she was only nine, and as a teenager, she performed with her sister, Ana Luisa, as the *Duo Hermanitas Guillot.*

Trío Borinquen and Rafael Hernández (2nd from the right)

Rafael Hernández founded the *Trío Borinquen* in 1926 and the *Cuarteto Victoria* six years later in New York City.

Singer Edyie Goemé attempted five times to try out for *Arthur Godfrey's Talent Scouts* and, incredibly, was rejected each time. She would joke, *"The last time they saw me coming up the stairs, they locked the doors."*

—⁀∞⁀—

While with the *Panamerican Orchestra,* Rafael Cortijo was motivated and inspired by Bobby Capó and Miguelito Valdés and formed his own group on January 28, 1954.

—⁀∞⁀—

Birdland

Jazz musician Cal Tjader was introduced to mambo music by bassist Al McKibbon while they were on a break from performing at Birdland. McKibbon took Tjader to the Palladium, a nearby ballroom, where they entered through the service entrance on 53rd Street. It was there that Tjader heard Machito and Tito Puente for the very first time and was blown away by the sound. The rhythms were unlike anything he had ever heard before, and he became hooked on the style of music from that point on.

Arsenio Rodríguez's grandfather was born in the Congo and taken to Cuba as an enslaved person, where he lived until the age of 103 (possibly 104). Arsenio himself was a member of the Palo religion.

The Puerto Rican singer Ruth Fernández was elected to the Senate of Puerto Rico, representing the district of Ponce as a member of the Popular Democratic party. She was in office for eight years between 1973 through 1981.

Fernando López, who appears as the author of the music of many boleros with lyrics by the Argentine Roberto Lambertucci, is actually the Cuban Fernando Mulán López.

The Casino de la Playa in Cuba achieved remarkable success in the late 1930s and early 1940s, thanks to the contributions of Anselmo Sacasas and Miguelito Valdés.

Joe Hernández

Israel "Cachao" López

Bass player Israel "Cachao" López is credited with creating the dance-hall mambo when he played with flutist Arcaño y Sus Maravillas in the mid-1930s. However, Cachao's brother Orestes López, who created the danzón-mambo, admitted that without Arcano's flute riffs, they would not have been able to develop the mambo.

—⚋—

Miguelito Valdés's mother was Mexican of Maya Indian ancestry, born in Yucatán. His father, Emilio Izquierdo, was a white Spaniard and Spanish Army Colonel. Miguelito was one of seven siblings, five brothers and one sister, all raised in the neighborhood known as "Cayo Hueso," Cuba.

—⚋—

In the 1940s, for a record to go gold, it had to sell five thousand copies.

—⚋—

Apollo Theatre

The Apollo Theater was initially known as *White & Seamon's New (Burlesque) Theater*, which opened in 1913 as a burlesque venue for only white patrons.

—ഝ—

The Puerto Rican pianist Noro Morales was known for recording without a contract, only a handshake.

—ഝ—

Mario Bauza's composition "Tanga" is considered the birth of Afro-Cuban jazz. He wrote it while Machito was away, having reported to Camp Upton for basic training on April 23, 1943. The song eventually became the opening and closing theme for the *Machito Orchestra*.

—ഝ—

By 1815, the Catholic church denounced the waltz in Mexico as it considered it a corrupt importation from France, a degenerative country in the view of the church.

Joe Hernández

None other than the great Dizzy Gillespie, in the documentary that was filmed in the summer of 1991 by Boston's TV station WGBH *Notes from The Mambo Inn: The Story of Mario Bauza,* admits that Mario Bauza was not only his mentor but the first to play Afro-Cuban jazz.

When Willie Colón sought a vocalist early in his career, Johnny Pacheco suggested Héctor Pérez (Lavoe).

Machito's father was Rogelio Grillo, the owner of a business that supplied food to sugar mills. He was a good singer in his own right. By 1926, his dad had taken a job as a cigar maker in Pogolotti, and the young Machito went to live with the folks of vocalist Graciela Pérez.

Edyie Gormé was the cousin of singer-songwriter Neil Sedaka.

Tito Puente's body was buried at Saint Anthony's Church Cemetery in Nanuet, Rockland County, New York. Other famous memorials at this cemetery are World Bantamweight Champion Joe Lynch (1898-1965), Mario Paul Perillo (owner of Perillo Tours, 1926-2003), and Sculptor Louis Richard (1869-1940), who sculpted the lions that are outside of the main entrance to the New York City Public Library.

One night, at the renowned jazz club *Blue Note*, Mongo Santamaría was performing with his band. As the band members arrived, Mongo introduced a girl to the singer, Pete Bonet. He informed Pete that the girl would be singing with the band from that night onward and asked that he teach her all the songs. This girl marked La Lupe's debut.

Pérez Prado's version of the mambo, initially considered too American for the Cubans and too commercial for the hipsters at the Palladium in New York City, found its home in Mexico. On March 30, 1949, Pérez recorded 'Que Rico El Mambo' in Mexico, becoming the first hit recorded mambo that sparked a global craze. The mambo, a massive sensation in Mexico and the rest of Latin America, soon spread its infectious rhythm worldwide. Within a few years, Pérez recorded dozens of mambos, and some claim that by 1952, he had sold over six million records. Regardless of the actual sales, his success was truly phenomenal.

Rafael Hernández was a well-trained musician and a prolific composer, a graduate of the musical conservatory in Mexico. He was known to compose several songs in one day, with some authorities claiming he had written more than two thousand songs before his death at 72.

Felipe Rodríguez

Luis Felipe Rodríguez was born on May 8, 1926, in Caguas, Puerto Rico. Known as "La Voz," it has been estimated that he recorded over five thousand songs. His hit song "La Ultima Copa" (The Last Drink) was one of the most extraordinary musical successes in Puerto Rico; it sold over five million copies. He died on May 26, 1999, in San Juan, Puerto Rico.

What Was the True Birth of Lamento Borincano?

Rafael Hernández recorded his famous song "Lamento Borincano" on July 14, 1930, for the RCA Victor label in New York. He wrote this signature song the year before while sitting in a restaurant in Spanish Harlem, drinking rum with some friends on a gloomy rainy day. His friends felt nostalgic and melancholy as they reminisced about their tropical paradise. Rafael sat on an old, run-down piano in the restaurant's corner. As he visualized Borinquen's beauty and heartache, he was transported to that beautiful land of beaches and swaying palm trees. The melody for "Lamento Borincano" began to flow from his fingers as if by magic.

His sister, Victoria, claimed he wrote the song on the sidewalk outside her music store, Almacenes Hernández, one summer day in 1929. Victoria had to give a student a lesson, so she asked Rafael to leave the room. Rafael obliged and left the room with a guitar and a tin can of black coffee. He sat on the sidewalk near the curb with his feet in the gutter, and with paper and pencil in hand, he began to sing and write the lyrics for what would become his most popular and famous composition.

However, for the record, Rafael Hernández, in an interview, said that the version describing the scene in a restaurant, as written above, was the way "Lamento Borincano" came about. So, which is the true story? Perhaps neither; we will never know. Authors are known to create fictitious stories or forget or believe something that never happened. No one in the restaurant ever came forward to confirm what happened or act as a witness. Either one of the above stories sounds plausible. Does it matter? In either scenario, the result was pure genius. What makes it even more interesting is that despite the setting and conditions of the island, the song was born in New York.

Ray Barretto was inducted into the International Latin Music Hall of Fame in 1999.

Joe Hernández

Alfredito Valdés was the father of Alfredito Valdés Jr., and the brother of singer Vicentico Valdés.

Don Azpiazú's Havana Casino had an orchestra that showcased several musicians who later became big Latin music stars. At their debut performance of "El Manicero" in the Palace Theatre of New York City in 1930, the orchestra members included Julio Cueva on trumpet, an eighteen-year-old Mario Bauza on saxophone, and Antonio Machín as the singer.

Carlos Eleta dedicated the bolero "Perdónala Señor" to the 'Chinese' composer Hassan, his friend, when he was "jilted" by a girl he wanted and who left with "another."

In the middle of a big scene of The Mambo Kings, as the film is rolling, Tito Puente abruptly stops the music and yells at all the dancers, "Estan fuera de clave..." In short, they were out of sync with the rhythmic mantra/building block of Afro-Cuban music known as the clave. The director needed to figure out what Tito was referring to.

In Cuba during the first half of the nineteenth century, blacks were most of the professional musicians.

Despite having a record contract with the Verne label, Machito recorded as the backup orchestra to Chano Pozo, Olga Guillot, and Rene Hernández under Gabriel Oller's Coda label.

The Clave, a rhythmic pattern that underpins the soul of salsa music, has a fascinating historical journey. Its roots can be traced back to the vibrant cultures of West and Central Africa, and it continues to thrive in Cuban-based dance music. The small wooden sticks used in Cuban music, known as 'Clavijas' in Spanish, have an intriguing origin. They are believed to be descended from the wooden pegs used to secure ropes on ships. It's a curious fact that these sticks were never used as a musical instrument by the slaves, adding a unique twist to their story.

The Cuban Contradanza was heard in the U.S. via sheet music as early as the 1850s.

Willie Colón's tough guy image received a spectacular boost with the 1970 infamous cover of the album *Wanted By FBI/ The Big Break-La Gran Fuga,* designed by Izzy Sanabria, whose cover had a photo of Willie Colón, fronting him as a gangster, accompanied by fingerprints all inserted in an FBI "most wanted" file, similar to the one employed by the agency of the United States Federal Bureau of Investigation. The advertising and cover design caused such a stir that the FBI demanded that

Fania Records remove the label "Wanted by the FBI" from the cover.

Cándido Camero
(Photo courtesy of Bobby Sanabria)

Cándido Camero, a true pioneer in percussion, is often revered as the father of the modern multi-percussion setup. His groundbreaking invention, the first foot-operated cowbell, not only transformed his own playing style but also revolutionized the entire percussion world. This innovative creation allowed him to play the congas while keeping a steady rhythm with his foot. Cándido's journey began with the production of his first foot-operated cowbell at a local hardware store in 1952, a momentous event that would shape the future of percussion.

In 1999, New York's heavy-oriented salsa radio station *La Mega* became the first Spanish-language radio station in the country to take the number one spot in the area's Arbitron ratings.

Pianist Charlie Palmieri was the musical director of the Alegre All-Stars.

Carlos Gardel

Carlos Gardel, born Charles Romauld Geardes (1890-1935), was not only a tango singer but a sensation on a global scale. His music resonated with people worldwide, making him the most famous and beloved tango singer ever. Despite the controversies surrounding his birthplace, the consensus among top scholars is that he was born in Toulouse, France. His immense contributions to Latin music were recognized posthumously when he was inducted into the International Latin Music Hall of Fame in 2000.

Felipe Rodríguez was an amateur boxer during his youth. He used to search for young boxing talent and occasionally served as a referee for amateur boxing matches. Alongside four other individuals, Rodríguez was one of the founding organizers of the Puerto Rican Boxing Commission.

Cándido Camero was a highly skilled musician who played the *tres* with Chano Pozo's *Conjunto Azul*. During his tenure with this band, he crossed paths with Mongo Santamaría, who played the bongós at the time. At 14, in 1935, Cándido began playing the *tres* for El Conjunto *Gloria Habanera*. He also played the instrument on vocalist Alfredo Valdés's album, *Pionero del Son*.

Miguel Rafael Companioni Gómez was born on July 29, 1881, in Sancti Spíritus, Cuba. He was a composer and guitarist with a vast repertoire of travadoresque works, including boleros, criollas, guarachas, and songs totaling around three hundred. Many of his works are recognized worldwide. He lost his sight at the age of 11 and began to pursue music. He worked in a bakery store and sold pharmaceutical products. At the age of 29, he traveled to New York in 1911 to evaluate his eyes and was diagnosed with permanent blindness. There, he pursued his music studies and worked as a pianist in movie and stage theaters.

The Society of Cuban Authors awarded him a medal for fifty years of creative activity. Miguelito, as he was affectionately known, passed away on February 21, 1965, in the province of Havana at the age of 84. After a long life of triumphs between guitars, pianos, and orchestras, which he directed, he left us with a legacy that is treasured in Sancti Spíritus rich heritage culture that continues to be heard to this day. Some of his famous songs include "Por Qué Latió Mi Corazón," "A Le Le," "Juana," "La Fé," and "La Lira."

Did you know that in 1908, a group of four talented musicians from Cocula, Jalisco, made history by becoming the first-ever Mariachi band to record phonograph recordings? As they were known, the Cuarteto Coculense or Mariachi de Justo Villa recorded around 60 songs for Edison, Victor, and Columbia labels during the autumn season. These recordings were produced in Mexico City using primitive recording equipment that was available at that time. It's incredible to think about these musicians' impact on the world of music, paving the way for generations of Mariachi bands to come.

Merengue is a lively dance style that is often associated with the Dominican Republic. However, its history is deeply rooted in various Caribbean locations. Puerto Rico and Cuban marching bands introduced the music in the mid-19th century, which eventually evolved into the merengue we know today. Despite common misconceptions, merengue has a diverse and rich history in the Caribbean. Its fascinating and complex origin story deserves to be celebrated and acknowledged. By recognizing the true roots of merengue, we can better appreciate its cultural significance and impact across the Caribbean.

When Celia Cruz was just five years old, she fell ill with a rare and unknown disease that almost took her life. Her family and friends prayed for her recovery, and fortunately, Celia began to improve and started to sing. This behavior frightened her mother, who believed it was a bad omen. She pleaded with young Celia to stop singing, but Celia continued to sing and eventually fully recovered.

It has never been possible to create a complete and definitive discography that lists all of Tito Puente's recordings and their dates. However, it is estimated (although not confirmed) that Puente had over 450 compositions and more than 2,000 arrangements to his name, in addition to his 118 LPs. This number does not include his recompiled recordings, work done for other labels and artists, and some of the early 45s and 78s.

It is believed that Tito Puente performed live more than 10,000 times in his career, which spanned more than 50 years. When all these numbers are considered, it is clear that Puente was a truly prolific and talented artist. He averaged a new composition every 5 1/2 weeks and an arrangement every nine days and performed live about 200 times yearly.

Tito Puente's grandfather, Antonio Puente, was born in 1880. Tito's father, Ernesto, was born in San German, Puerto Rico, in 1896. On March 5, 1920, his grandfather and father left Puerto Rico on the SS Coamo, an old ship that carried thousands of Puerto Ricans on the three-day voyage to New York. They first settled at 111 West 134th Street in upper Manhattan, but according to a television interview with Tito, the family initially lived in Brooklyn. Depending on the day, Tito would tell a different story. During the early days, most Puerto Ricans settled near the port of Brooklyn upon their arrival.

Manuel Corona Raimundo (1880-1950) was a Cuban trova musician who wrote such fine tunes as "Mercedes," "Nubes de Ensueño," "Longina," "Santa Cecilia," "Aurora," and "La Alfonsa." He fell in love with a whore, and as soon as her pimp found out, he was on his trail. He came after him with a knife and cut his hand severely enough to prevent him from ever playing the guitar again. From that moment on, he earned his living from his compositions; however, he died in poverty.

Bény Moré learned to play the guitar as a child, and by the age of six, he had made his first instrument from a piece of stick and a sardine can that served as the sound box.

Joe Hernández

Edyie Gormé achieved her first hit in 1953 with the jazz song "Frenesi," featuring English and Spanish lyrics.

The Mexican American singer Selena Quintanilla-Pérez (1971-1995), known mononymously as Selena, became the first Tejano artist to earn a gold album with her 1990 release of *Ven Conmigo*. In 1994, her album *Amor Prohibido* went multi-platinum and was nominated for a Grammy. In 1995, at the age of 23, she was tragically murdered.

The world mourned the passing of Celia Cruz, the most famous Cuban singer of all time, except in her native Cuba, where it went unnoticed as the official Cuban media barely mentioned it. However, her death was quickly spread through "radio bemba" (the people's radio via the grapevine). Despite her music being banned for more than forty years and living in exile, she had never been forgotten by the Cuban people who loved her.

The recording of "El Manisero" in New York City in May 1930 by Don Azpiazú and his Havana Casino Orchestra is notable for the improvised trumpet playing by Remberto "Chino" Lara. In response to vocalist Antonio Machin, Lara used a Harmon mute without the stem, giving his playing a more human vocal quality. This call-and-response style was a hallmark of early son groups in Cuba, and it marked the first time American audiences were exposed to this tradition.

Bény Moré sang for the first time professionally on the radio with *Septeto Fígaro,* under the direction of Lazaro Cordero on the station CMZ.

According to Ray Barretto, his first recording as a conga player in jazz was in April 1958 when he recorded the LP *Manteca* with bassist Paul Chambers and drummer Arthur Taylor for the veteran of soul-jazz Red Garland.

Miguelito Valdés studied guitar, solfeggio, and voice with female bandleader María Teresa Vera. For a brief spell, he sang with María's *Sexteto Occidente.*

Dick Gilbert was the first Latin-music English-speaking disc jockey in Harlem in the early 1940s. He would come on the air at 10 PM on WHN 1050, right after the Dinah Shore Records show, and play until 10:45. The Harry James Records followed his show. This was the schedule for Saturday, December 25, 1942.

According to Daniel Santos in his autobiography, in the early days, when he was earning $17 a week, barely enough to live, he decided to become a pimp. Not to give the whores protection but to take their money. He talks about his good looks and how the whores wanted to be with him. He had five women where he was working. Come midnight, after the girls had been hustling their Johns, they would arrive at the lounge, sit with him, drink, and slip the money to him under the table. He would then pick one to go to bed with, sometimes two, and sometimes all five.

He claims to have given up this lifestyle when Cugat's agent offered him $85 weekly to sing at the Waldorf Astoria.

On March 22, 2014, Celia Cruz became the first Latin artist to be honored with a place on the Walk of Legends at New York's Apollo Theatre.

In 1938, Celia Cruz's cousin Serafin convinced her to take part in a radio talent show contest called Los Reyes de la Conga (The Kings of the Conga). At the time, Celia was only 13 years old. Despite tough competition from other contestants, Celia won the competition with a unanimous vote and was crowned the Queen of Conga. The contest judges were renowned figures in the Cuban music industry: popular singer Rita Montaner, famous composer Miguel Matamoros, Cuban music pioneer Gonzalo Roig, and author, composer, and musicologist Eliseo Grenet. This win marked Celia's first-ever public performance as a singer.

Cachao & Joe Hernández

Israel "Cachao" López, along with Arsenio Rodríguez, Antonio Arcaño, and Oreste Lopez, created the Mambo. He was raised in the home of Cuba's national hero José Martí, the grandfather of the actor César Romero, who played the Joker in the Batman series.

The Tito Puente Restaurant, located on City Island, New York, was owned by a group that also owned several other popular restaurants on the island. Tito's name was part of an endorsement deal, but he invested no money in the partnership.

Orestes López started playing with the Havana Symphonic Orchestra when he was just 13 years old.

Joe Hernández

Noro Morales

Pianist Noro Morales lived in an apartment on 116th Street between Fifth and Lenox Avenues. His neighbors on the floor above him were Rafael Hernández and his sister Victoria. Whenever Rafael had a new musical idea, he would quickly run downstairs to Noro's apartment, use his piano, and work on the composition. One of Rafael's earliest compositions was "Ahora Si Somos Felices." As a goodwill gesture, Rafael would offer his new tunes to Noro and his singer Davilita for recording. On June 15, 1938, they recorded this tune for Columbia Records.

Ernesto Lecuona, a Cuban musician, composed a song called "Siempre en mi Corazón" (Always in My Heart) that many famous artists have sung. Bobby Vinton included it in his third album, *Roses Are Red,* and Plácido Domingo, a Spanish tenor, performed it in 1983.

Domingo's rendition won him a Grammy Award for Best Latin Pop Performance in 1985.

In the early 1920s, there were very few recording facilities in Puerto Rico, and the existing ones needed development. When Francisco López Vidal recorded for Victor, he did so in the studios of radio station WKAQ. To avoid disturbances, they would wait until midnight when the trolleys stopped running.

Larry Harlow's father, Buddy Kahn, changed his stage name to Buddy Harlow when he started performing as a musician at the Latin Quarter in New York City, also known as the LQ. The name change occurred when Mr. Kahn was involved in a car accident in Washington, D.C., and was saved by a doctor named "Dr. Harlow." In honor of the doctor, Buddy Kahn changed his name to Buddy Harlow. This tradition was later carried on by his son, Larry Harlow.

Celia Cruz did nine albums with Tito Puente. Together, the Cuban & Puerto Rican duo performed over 600 times.

Early in their lives, Mario Bauza, Miguelito Valdés, and Machito had trained to become mechanics for the Dodge automaker.

Joe Hernández

The late Julio Jaramillo, a renowned Ecuadorian singer and recording artist, recorded over 2,200 songs during his career. At his funeral, over 250,000 Ecuadorians paid their respects to him. He is said to have fathered over 30 children.

Ray Barretto fired Pete Bonet as a singer from his charanga band because he could not play the guiro. To replace him, Ray hired a Cuban guiro player Cuban Osvaldo Martinez, nicknamed "Chihuahua." This made Pete angry, but he made the best of it and bought a guiro. He then hired Chihuahua to teach him how to play the instrument. Pete became exceptionally good at playing the guiro, and Chihuahua told him Mongo Santamaría was looking for a guiro player who could also sing.

One evening, Pete went to "La Campana" in the Bronx, where Mongo was playing. He introduced himself to Mongo and asked about his need for a guiro player who could sing. Mongo asked Pete to play the next set. Pete was nervous because he had not rehearsed with the band and did not know Mongo's repertoire. However, the bass player, Victor Vinegas, overheard the conversation and saw the panic in Pete's eyes. He took Pete outside the club and began to rehearse with him by imitating the music using his mouth. Victor told Pete what to do and took him back inside the club for the next set.

Pete successfully played the guiro and got a look from Mongo, who assured him he was now part of the band. And so, Pete became a member of Mongo Santamaría's band.

Arsenio Rodríguez

Arsenio Rodríguez experienced moments of melancholy and depression in his life. In 1948, he recorded "Me Siento Muy Solo" (I Feel Very Alone), which was probably partly inspired by his brother Quique's imprisonment for manslaughter. Arsenio was visually impaired, so hearing was his primary source of inspiration for his lyrics. This sensitivity and inspiration resurfaced in 1950 when his brother was released from jail, and he composed "Vuelvo A La Vida" (I Come Back to Life) to express his joy.

The Cuban trumpeter and Bandleader, Felix Chappottin, was the half-brother of Chano Pozo through their mother.

Daniel Santos recorded 308 LPs throughout his career and died of a heart attack on his farm in Ocala, Florida, on November 27, 1992.

Cuban Pete, Barbara Craddock & Joe Hernández

Pedro Aguilar, a.k.a. Cuban Pete, was a boxer before becoming a dancer. It was Miguelito Valdés, who was also a boxer at one time, who suggested to Pete that he switch to dancing after witnessing a fight where his opponent severely beat his face.

During the turn of the twentieth century, a wave of Latin immigrants to the north created a market for the products of record magnates such as Edison, Victor, Columbia, and others. The record companies, sensing the opportunity, swiftly responded, sparking a fierce competition to secure authentic recordings from all nations. In cases where local talent was scarce, the record companies would venture to the source, primarily Central and South

America. However, they initially focused on recording the nationals of those countries who lived in New York. A notable example is the Cuban singer Rosalía "Chalía" Herrera (1864-1948), who was the first singer of Latin origin to record commercial cylinders. She made 40 selections for the Bettini label from 1898 to 1900, a testament to the intense competition among record companies during this period.

Joe Cuba, Mr. Boogaloo, was a licensed paralegal.

In 1931, Marion Sunshine sang "The Peanut Vendor" at a Royal Command Performance for the first Buckingham Palace ball since 1924 at the request of Queen Mary.

Mexican music recorded in the United States from both sides of the border predated African American and Appalachian recordings.

The original 1958 recording of "Ti Mon Bo," arranged by Tito Puente, was reissued on a CD by Ralph Mercado on July 18, 2000, and retitled "El Puente Mundial."

Pedro Flores was a beloved Puerto Rican composer. He was born Pedro Flores Cordova on March 9, 1894, in

Naguabo, Puerto Rico. He worked as an office worker, train inspector, tax collector, and painter and served in the United States Postal Service. Pedro Flores passed away on July 14, 1979, in San Juan, Puerto Rico, and was buried in Santa Magdalena de Pazzis Cemetery in Old San Juan.

Headquarters of Laboratorios Vieta-Plasencia

Mario Bauza's upbringing has been described as raised by his wealthy white godparents, who were childless, with the consent of his parents. His godfather recognized his talent and enrolled him at the Havana Conservatory. By age sixteen, he was playing for the Havana Philharmonic Orchestra as a clarinet prodigy.

However, other musicologists and historians, such as Miguel Angel Duque, have discovered information contradicting this narrative. According to them, Mario Bauza, the creator of Afro-Cuban jazz, was born Prudencio Mario Bauza Cardenas on April 28, 1911. His father, Don Elario, was a traveling baseball player and coach, and not much is known about him. Mario was

The Latin Music Trivia Book

the youngest of six children, and his mother, Dolores Rodríguez Elario Bauza, was severely ill. After his birth, she used a wheelchair, and by the time he was two, she was bedridden.

Mario's family reached out to a family they knew for help. The family consisted of 12 adopted children and was headed by a Spaniard named Sofía Domínguez and her Cuban husband, Arturo. Arturo's family was an important family of high social standing in the community and was financially well-off. The Domínguez family took Mario in, and Arturo became his stepfather. They were a musical family, and with sixteen instruments in the household, everyone learned to play at least one. Mario began playing the piano at age five and showed signs of being a child prodigy. With the help of the Domínguez family, he received an excellent musical education. By the age of nine, he was a member of the Havana Philharmonic Orchestra, playing the clarinet.

Miguelito Valdés' path to success was paved at a remarkably early age. At 11, he embarked on a career as an auto mechanic, earning a modest $2.00 weekly. However, his talent and passion extended far beyond the workshop. He proved his mettle as an amateur boxer, inspired by the featherweight boxer Kid Chocolate at the age of 16. Valdés' skills led him to clinch the amateur welterweight championship in Cuba, a testament to his determination and hard work that would later define his success in the music industry.

Valdés' entry into the world of music was a spontaneous and courageous one. Following his twenty-third victorious fight, he was interviewed by the radio program *Casa del Deporte*. In a moment of daring, he asked if he could sing a tune. The program, intrigued by this unexpected request, granted his wish. This impromptu performance was a turning point in Valdés' life, sparking a passion for music that would shape his future. A performance by the Mexican vocalist José Mojica further fueled his musical aspirations, and by 17, he had joined the *Sexteto Habanero* as a vocalist, embarking on a successful music career.

Ray Barretto's influence on popular music was not limited to jazz, as he left his mark as a skilled conga player in numerous recording sessions for iconic pop, rock, and R&B artists. His contributions can be heard on albums for artists such as the Bee Gees, Average White Band, and even the Rolling Stones, where his conga playing added a unique flavor to their hit song "Sympathy for the Devil."

Tito Puente was honored in 2007 with the U.S. Post Office at 124th Street, between Lexington and Third Avenues, named after him.

The song "Son De La Loma" by musician Miguel Matamoros and his group *Trío Matamoros* became an international hit, reaching the same popularity and fame as "Guantanamera." The song's inspiration came from Matamoros's experience with his cousin, Alfonso del Río, in 1922. They sang under the windows of a

Santiago sanatorium when a woman and her young daughter opened a window to listen to them. The young girl asked her mother where the musicians were from, as she wanted to meet them. This encounter led Matamoros to create the tune.

Cándido Camero Guerra

Cándido Camero Guerra, also known as Cándido, was born on April 22, 1920, in the lively neighborhood of "El Cerro" in Havana. He began his music career playing bass, guitar, and *tres* (a mandolin-like instrument) before ultimately transitioning to playing the bongó and conga. His uncle, Andrés, was a professional bongósero for the *Septeto Segundo Nacional* in Cuba.

In 1939, Tito Puente, age 16, was drumming for Johnny Rodríguez, brother of Tito Rodríguez, in his *Stork Club Orchestra*.

Oscar Muñoz Boufartique, the composer of the famous song "Burundanga," was Celia Cruz's piano teacher. However, she would anger him by refusing to trim her long fingernails, which made playing the piano difficult.

The Corso

The Corso had humble beginnings as a restaurant that served the local German American community. After World War II, it transitioned to featuring 'Continental music,' primarily European music, until Tony Raimone took it over in the mid to late 1960s. Despite introducing renowned acts like the Glenn Miller Orchestra led by Buddy DeFranco and Lionel Hampton's band, the Corso struggled to draw a significant crowd.

However, a turning point in Corso's history came when Tony Raimone struck a pivotal deal with Pete Bonet, which marked an important transformation for the venue.

The deal shifted its focus to promoting Latin dances, ultimately redefining its success. The collaboration between Tony Raimone and Pete Bonet breathed new life into the venue, turning it into a haven for Latin music lovers.

As Mayor of Ponce, Carlos Eusebio de Ayo outlawed "La Borinqueña" in 1892, sparking a public outcry.

Doña Amalia Paoli

Doña Amalia Paoli (1861-1941), the first Puerto Rican soprano and diva, was the sister of tenor Antonio Paoli, the first Puerto Rican to achieve international fame in music.

By 1904, the label Zonophone recorded approximately 234 songs on cylinders. Edison was just a little behind, with 205 songs in Havana in 1905, and the Victor label recorded about 150 songs in the same year.

—⚯—

Despite the Great Depression, sales of Spanish-language records flourished among Puerto Ricans in New York City during the 1930s. Although not reaching astronomical numbers, the music provided solace for homesick Boricuas.

—⚯—

"La Paloma," which means "The Dove" in English, was the first habanera song exported from Cuba. It was composed in 1860 by a Spanish Basque composer named Sebastián Iradier (Yradier) while he was visiting the island. The song's lyrics, which speak of love and longing, reflect the composer's emotions during his stay in Cuba. Although the composer died in obscurity, his song became a widely known standard in the United States and Europe and has been recorded in many parts of the world.

With over one thousand versions, "La Paloma" is considered one of the most-recorded songs in music history, alongside the *Beatles'* "Yesterday." Its popularity can be attributed to its universal appeal, with artists from various genres and cultures interpreting and recording the song. The song has been featured in several movies, including the 1974 release of *The Godfather Part II*, in which the opening scene of the New Year party in Havana begins with the band playing the song. Dean Martin also interpreted it and sang Elvis Presley in the

1961 movie *Blue Hawaii* as "No More." Additionally, it was featured in one of Max Fleischer's famous cartoons with "Follow the Bouncing Ball" sing-alongs in 1930, a technique he pioneered originally for "Ko-Ko" Song Car-Tunes (1924-1927 and revised in 1929-1938) for Paramount.

The popularity of' La Paloma' reached its peak when the largest choir, consisting of over 88,600 people, sang it in the city of Hamburg on May 9, 2004. This monumental event placed the song into the Guinness Book of World Records, a testament to its enduring legacy. The global recognition and appreciation of 'La Paloma' are a tribute to its composer, who unfortunately never lived to see the extent of his song's popularity.

One of Miguelito Valdés's closest friends from his youth days in the barrio of Cayo Hueso was Chano Pozo.

"El Canario" recorded his final album in Puerto Rico in 1968 despite being blind and having both legs amputated due to diabetes. He passed away in 1975.

In 1957, Bény Moré visited the United States to attend the annual Oscar Awards in Hollywood. During his visit, he was highly praised when he performed with the orchestra of the renowned Mexican composer Luis Arcaraz. On another occasion, he sang at the well-known Palladium Ballroom in New York for 17 consecutive

Joe Hernández

days, accompanied by *Machito's Orchestra and his Afro-Cubans,* with Tata Guines as a special guest on congas.

―⚊―

In 1940, Machito suggested that Miguelito Valdés replace Desi Arnaz in the Xavier Cugat Orchestra. Valdés recorded "Babalú" with Cugat and became known as Mr. Babalú.

―⚊―

José Melis

José Melis (1920-2005) was a Cuban American bandleader and television personality. He graduated from the Juilliard School of Music and was the musical director for the USO's New York City branch. While there, he met Jack Paar, and they became close friends. Melis was also the pianist for *The Morning Show* on CBS, which Parr hosted. When Paar moved to The

The Latin Music Trivia Book

Tonight Show, Melis followed him and became his musical director.

—⁂—

In high school, Cal Tjader played drums for a Dixieland band with the then-unknown media mogul Merv Griffin as the pianist.

—⁂—

The creator of "La Pachanga" Eduardo Davidson (1929-1994) real name was Claudio Cuza.

—⁂—

During his mid-teens, Machito learned to play the maracas by seeing the virtuoso and ambidextrous maraquero Champito Rivera, who played for conjunto *Estrellas de Pogolotti* then. Machito's first professional debut was at 17 at a local theatre with the group *Union de Rendención* after playing with Teresa Vera.

—⁂—

Javier Solís was a Mexican singer and actor born as Gabriel Siria Levario in 1931. He faced abandonment from his parents at an early age and was raised by his uncle. He left school before his teens and could only complete the first five years of primary school to support his family. He tried his hand at several jobs and even tried to become a boxer, but after several defeats, he realized his talent for singing. He began taking part in singing competitions under the pseudonym of Javier Luquin and quickly became known for his talent. Eventually, he was barred from competing since he always won. Solís had an extensive discography and starred in over 20 films. He died at the youthful age of 34 in Mexico City due to complications that arose from gallbladder surgery.

Erasmo Lasalle, a barbershop proprietor, was a phenomenal singer who was the first Puerto Rican to record music from his country in New York City.

Cuba established its first radio station in 1922, becoming the first country outside of the United States to do so and the fourth in the world overall.

Gloria Estefan's mother, Gloria Fajardo, took part in an international contest during her childhood and emerged victorious. As a result, Hollywood offered her a job to dub Shirley Temple's films in Spanish. Unfortunately, her father, Leonardo García, did not allow her to pursue this opportunity. Nevertheless, she went on to obtain a Ph.D. in education in Cuba.

Don Rafael Cepeda Atiles, also known as "El Roble," was a Puerto Rican composer, musician, writer, folklorist, and a prominent figure in the "Bomba y Plena" music genre. He was born in Puerto de Tierra, San Juan, in 1910, and passed away in 1996. Don Rafael was a prolific composer who produced over 300 songs recorded and celebrated worldwide. His contribution to the music industry earned him a certificate of recognition from the former President of the United States, Ronald Reagan. He was widely acknowledged as "The Patriarch of the Bomba and Plena."

Tito Puente received six Grammy Awards, and he was nominated twelve times. In 1969, he was awarded the key to New York City.

Mario Bauza

In 1930, Mario Bauza left Cuba to pursue his love for jazz music and settled in the Sugar Hill area of Harlem, Manhattan. During this time, he stumbled upon a fortunate opportunity when he discovered that Antonio Machín needed a trumpet player for his recording session. Machín's current player, Remberto Lara, had already left for Cuba with Don Azpiazú. Bauza took advantage of the situation and convinced Machín to buy him a trumpet and replace Lara for the gig.

Joe Hernández

Puerto Rico's radio history dates to the fall of 1922 when WKAQ in San Juan became the second radio station outside the United States and the fifth in the world. It took twelve more years for the island to get another radio station, and as of 1940, only five stations were operational. However, today, there are over sixty-one radio stations on the island.

Celia Cruz and Olga Guillot sang for Conjunto Siboney, led by Isolina Carillo

---

In 1933, Miguelito Valdés contracted to sing with a Cuban band to play in a carnival in Panama. When the contract was over, he stayed in Panama until 1936. There, Valdés fell in love and married Vera Eskilssen-Tejada. with whom he had a son. Valdés worked washing dishes, waiting on tables, and singing at El Moderno Cubano Restaurant. One night, as he was singing, the famous Panamanian bandleader Lucho Azcarraga heard him, and as Valdés was taking his order, Azcarraga offered him a job. Valdés accepted and sang with the orchestra from 1934 to 1936 at the Union Club of Panama.

In 1957, the Cuban government invited artists from all over the world to return home and join in the celebration of the most excellent Cuban musicians of the previous fifty years. Despite not being a Cuban, Tito Puente was invited to the event due to his enormous contributions to Cuban music. The Cuban government formally recognized Puente during the ceremonies. Mario Bauza was crucial in ensuring Puente's inclusion in this affair.

Graciela Rivera y Padilla made history by becoming the first Puerto Rican singer to perform at the New York City Metropolitan Opera House on February 4, 1951. She sang "Lucia di Lammermoor."

Myrta Silva

The Puerto Rican singer Myrta Silva was the first woman to join the musical collective of Cuba's *La Sonora Matancera*.

Joe Hernández

Olga Guillot was the godmother of Mexican pop singer José José.

—⚬—

Desi Arnaz was given his first starring in the 1946 Universal Production of *Cuban Pete*. This low-budget black-and-white musical ran for barely an hour and was filmed in under twelve days.

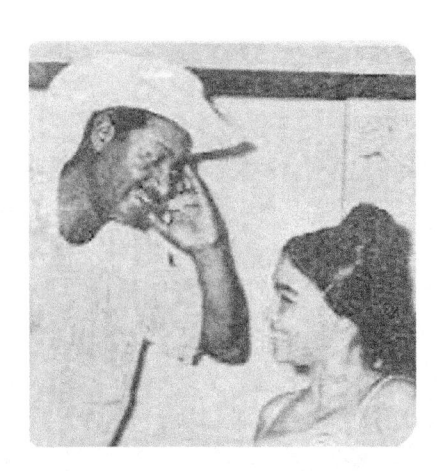

—⚬—

Bény Moré and La Lupe

La Lupe started her career at a small nightclub called *La Red* in Havana in the early 1960s. She had a devoted following of foreign fans, including Ernest Hemingway, Tennessee Williams, Jean-Paul Sartre, Simone de Beauvoir, and Marlon Brando.

—⚬—

During the turn of the twentieth century, Havana became a popular destination for artists worldwide to perform, especially opera singers. Many famous opera singers of that era went through Havana, including Titta Rufo, Lucrecia Bori, Beniamino Gigli, Tito Schipa, Scotti, Lauro Volpi, and others. By 1920, even the great Enrico Caruso had performed operas in Havana, charging an unheard-of sum of ten thousand dollars per performance, the highest fee he had ever received. This amount is equivalent to nearly $160,000 in 2021.

Antonio Poli

Antonio Poli, born on April 14, 1871, in Ponce, Puerto Rico, was a renowned Puerto Rican tenor who earned the titles "The King of Tenors" and "The Tenor of Kings." He was considered one of the greatest opera singers of all time, and his voice was believed by many to be more lyrical and powerful than that of his contemporary, Enrico Caruso. Antonio Poli passed away on August 24, 1946.

Joe Hernández

Francisco Hilario Riser Rincón, born in 1910 and passed away in 1988, was a renowned Cuban singer known for his soulful performances of boleros. Interestingly, his musical name, "Panchito Riset," was derived from a misspelling of his last name in one of his early recordings, where "Riser" was accidentally recorded as "Riset."

Carlos Gardel had a marvelous voice and good looks. However, he admitted having to watch his diet as he tended to gain weight quickly.

Pedro Flores

Among his many jobs during his lifetime, Pedro Flores was also a sportswriter in the 1920s for the publication *El Tiempo*.

Tite Curet worked at Tico Records and had the opportunity to meet various artists there. One of the most notable artists was Guadalupe Victoria Yolí, also known as La Lupe, who was a member of Tito Puente's orchestra at the time. Tite Curet wrote the bolero "La Tirana," originally intended for Roberto Ledesma but ended up being recorded by Puente and La Lupe. This began Tite Curet's successful career as an international composer. Following "La Tirana," he wrote "Puro Teatro," "Carcajada Final," and many other compositions that were also recorded by La Lupe, known as "La Yi Yi, Yi' Yoli."

During World War I, all European opera houses were closed, which led to opera singer Antonio Paoli finding work as a professional boxer. He was successful in his first five fights but unfortunately broke his wrist during his sixth match, ending his boxing career. Shortly after, he also lost his voice. However, with the help of medical and vocal exercises, he regained his voice. He returned to the international stage, receiving the same level of glory and accolades as before.

"Guantanamera" is a composition that has gained worldwide popularity despite its controversial origin. At one point, it was unclear who the song's composer was, with some attributing it to Herminio "El Diablito" García Wilson's pen. However, in 1993, the Tribunal Supremo Popular (People's Supreme Court of Cuba) ruled in favor of Joséito Fernández Díaz, officially recognizing him as the original and sole composer of the song.

Despite its origins, "Guantanamera" has managed to transcend language barriers and borders, with numerous artists recording it in various languages. It has even been adopted as the signature song for Salsa diva Celia Cruz, and the English version by The Sandpipers in 1966 was a commercial success. The song's universal appeal is further evident in its renditions by artists such as Joan Baez, The Fugees, Jimmy Buffet, José Feliciano, and Julio Iglesias.

Agustín Lara

Agustín Lara, a Mexican pianist and composer, was born as Angel Agustín María Carlos Faustino Alfonso del Sagrado Corazón de Jesús Lara del Pino in Veracruz, Mexico on October 30, 1900. He was a gifted child who showed his musical talents at an incredibly early age and had learned to play the piano by the time he was seven.

Mario Bauza played lead trumpet and contributed to the arrangement of Chick Webb's signature tune, "Stompin' at the Savoy," in 1934. Edgar Sampson composed the song based on Bauza's tune, "Lona."

Guillermo Portables, a Cuban musician born as José Guillermo Quesada Castillo (1911-1970), wrote a song called "El Carretero." The song imitated the sound of a horse walking on a country road and became famous worldwide. Unfortunately, after finishing a performance in Isla Verde, Portables was hit by a car while crossing the street and died at the age of 59.

When Olga Guillot became a solo performer, her emotional and mellow style of interpreting lyrics earned her the title "Cuba's Judy Garland."

Often, Cuban songs were composed with double entendre or other "hidden" messages. The technicians sent to Cuba to record the local talent did not speak or understand Spanish, allowing the artists to record whatever they wanted without fear of censorship. Many of the songs were of "protest" in nature, such as against Yankee interference in their country, as when the North Americans occupied Cuba for four years (1898-1902).

Joe Hernández

Singer Willie Torres, Puerto Rican actor Henry Silva, and singer Jose Feliciano grew up on East 103rd Street.

The Miami Herald (2004) reported that declassified documents from the US State Department revealed Celia Cruz's association with Cuba's Pre-Revolution communist party as early as the 1940s. Due to her suspected communist affiliations, the US Embassy in Havana once denied Celia a US visa.

Daniel Santos

Daniel Santos led a tumultuous life marked by a series of unfortunate events, including tumultuous relationships with women, bouts of violence, substance abuse, and multiple stints in prison. Despite his troubled life, he was a gifted musician and songwriter. One of his most famous songs, "El Preso" (The Prisoner), was written during one of his stays in jail. When the song was released in 1968, it did not attract attention. However, it gradually gained recognition over time and became one of Santos' most beloved and celebrated songs, resonating with audiences worldwide.

Don Azpiazú's sister-in-law, Marion Sunshine, was an actress and songwriter who married Azpiazú's brother, Eusebio Azpiazú. She played a crucial role in the success of her brother-in-law's orchestra, Havana Casino. She wrote the lyrics in English for Azpiazú's hit song "The Peanut Vendor" and even went on tour with the group to sing it. Her contributions helped propel the orchestra to tour the country from coast to coast.

In 1952, Bény Moré collaborated with *Orquesta Aragón*, playing gigs at dance halls and helping the group break into the Havana music scene.

Carlos Gardel was the first Argentine to make a talking picture movie in his country and went on to create ten more.

Rita Montaner aided Chano Pozo's early career by securing him a job as a doorman and bodyguard at RHC-Cadena Azul radio station.

Joe Hernández

Israel López Valdés, also known as Cachao, is ranked 24th on Bass Player magazine's list of "The 100 Greatest Bass Players of All Time."

The Victor Talking Machine, founded in 1901, was bought by the Radio Corporation of America in 1928; hence, it became known from then on as RCA Victor.

Marion Sunshine, a successful vaudeville actress and part of the Tempest and Sunshine duo, left an indelible mark on the music scene. She is best known for providing English lyrics to many Latin songs, including the first samba to gain widespread popularity in the U.S., "Amor, Doce Veneno" (Brazilian Night), and the first conga to make it to the U.S. shores," La Conga." Her versatility shone through in her collaborations with Chick Webb and Ella Fitzgerald, where she composed several jazz-oriented tunes, such as "I Got a Guy" and "When I Get Low, I Get High."

Antonio Paoli, a tenor from Puerto Rico, is the first opera singer to record an entire opera. He was part of the recorded performance of Ruggiero Leoncavallo's Pagliacci in Italy in 1907. Paoli's primary role was Otello by Verdi, in which he performed an impressive 575 times worldwide.

Rita Montaner, whose full name was Rita Aurelia Fulcida Montaner y Facender, was born in Guanabacoa, Havana, in 1900 and passed away in 1958. She was a multilingual artist who could speak English, Italian, and French fluently. In October 1922, Rita performed on one of the earliest radio broadcasts in Cuba at the PWX radio station, where she sang alongside Marino Méndez.

Celia Cruz briefly sang and toured Venezuela with the all-female Castro Sisters' orchestra Anacaona.

Don Azpiazú

The month after Don Azpiazú's Havana Casino Orchestra debuted the groundbreaking "The Peanut Vendor" at the Palace Theatre in New York City, in the heart of Midtown Manhattan, at 1564 Broadway, they recorded the tune for RCA Victor. However, Victor feared it was too alien for the American audience; the record was released in November after considerable pressure. Even Guy Lombardo predicted a doomed future for the song, saying it would never become a popular dance number. The American public felt different, making it a national blockbuster hit by early 1931, becoming the first Cuban 78 rpm selling over a million. It was called the "AT&T hit" because of all the calls by the public seeking to buy the sheet music, which sold over a million copies.

Vocalist and pianist Joe Bataan, born Bataan Nitollano Jr., had a difficult start in life. At the age of 17, he was caught driving a stolen car and was sentenced to serve five years in the state prison in Coxsackie, New York. During his time in jail, he found solace in music and learned the basics of music from Mark Francis. After two years, he was released on parole, but unfortunately, he violated his parole and was sent back to Coxsackie. However, while in prison, he reconsidered, and his outlook on life improved, leading to his release just one year later. After getting married and having a child, he formed a band and approached Federico Pagani for work, which paid well.

The father of Johnny Rodríguez, Tito Rodríguez's older brother, wanted him to study law, but his only interests were music and singing. Once back in New York, he worked as a dishwasher at the McAlpin Hotel to earn money.

In 1952, Tito Puente recorded 37 fantastic tracks for Tico Records. He would buy pre-written arrangements from Cuban musicians and add his touch to create more swinging tunes.

Eddie Palmieri, a pianist; Joe Quijano, a vocalist; Chickie Pérez, a percussionist; and Orlando Marín, a timbalero, all grew up in the Longwood neighborhood of the South Bronx, NY. When they were kids, they formed a band and performed at schools and Sunnyside Gardens.

Joséito Fernández

Joséito Fernández Díaz, a shoemaker born in Cuba, is credited with writing the famous Cuban folk and patriotic song "Guantanamera" in 1928. The song's lyrics were based on a poem by the Cuban nationalist and poet José Martí. Fernández popularized the song on the radio as early as 1929, and it was first recorded and released by *el Cuarteto Canéy* on April 18, 1938. He was born on September 5, 1908, in the district of Los Sitios, Havana, and passed away in Havana on October 11, 1979.

Before making a name for himself, Machito had mentioned to Cuban Pete that he was not dancing in Clave (beat). This revelation was a total surprise to Pete, but he listened to what Machito had to say and his explanation of the subtleness of the Clave. Pete incorporated this wisdom into his dance and became a better dancer.

Eddie Palmieri played for Vicentico Valdés for two years, starting in 1956, on the recommendation of his older brother, Charlie Palmieri. After playing for Valdés, he spent two years playing with Tito Rodríguez.

Initially, the song "El Watusi" did not appeal to Ray Barretto, partly because it was not danceable. The tune was created as a "filler" by Puerto Rican singer Wito Kortright in the studio to complete a side of an LP requiring twenty-one minutes. One evening, at the insistence of Pete Bonet's wife, Ray Barretto played the song at a gig. To his surprise, the audience loved it and created a novel dance step. The tune became a significant national hit. Although Wito recorded the song, he had left the band before its release. It was Pete Bonet who sang it live all over the world.

Rita Montaner made her New York debut at the Apollo Theater, performing with Xavier Cugat in the Schubert Follies.

Frank Grillo, also known as Machito, arrived in New York in 1937 and served as a vocalist for La Estrella Habanera.

Author in Tito Puente's Old Apartment

Contrary to widespread belief, when Tito Puente lived at 53 East 110th Street in East Harlem, he lived on the

4th floor and not on the 2nd floor, as mentioned on the day he was honored with the Street being renamed Tito Puente Way. Tito told this author how he remembered the difficulty of bringing his piano up four flights of stairs. On the day of the street inauguration, this author, along with Oscar Rivera, manager of the Tito Puente Restaurant in Long Island City, managed to get through security and enter the old apartment of Tito Puente on the fourth floor.

The history and significance of the song "La Cucaracha" are multifaceted and intricate. However, it is worth mentioning that it won an Oscar in 1935 for Best Comedy Short Film under the direction of producer Kenneth Macgowan. Ironically, despite its Mexican roots, only one member of Macgowan's crew, Don Alvarado, was of Mexican descent.

In 2014, Brett and Jennifer Griswold, the epitome of perseverance, embarked on a monumental challenge. They set out to perform the longest Argentine tango ever recorded, a grueling task that would test their endurance and commitment. Despite facing camera issues during their first attempt, which cost them two precious hours, they refused to be deterred. They restarted their performance and danced on, ultimately succeeding in their audacious endeavor. They danced the longest Argentine tango ever, a staggering 38 hours and 38 minutes.

Eusebio Delfín y Figueroa

Eusebio Delfin y Figueroa, a celebrated musician and composer, was born in Havana, Cuba, in 1893. His musical journey was marked by his pioneering introduction of arpeggio to Cuban popular music and his composition of numerous famous songs. His best-known classic, "¿Y Tú Que Has Hecho?" was featured in the 1997 Buena Vista Social Club, which Rolling Stones Magazine considers one of the all-time best and most important selling albums. Eusebio Delfin y Figueroa's personal life was equally intriguing, having married Amalia Bacardí y Cape, the daughter of Emilio Bacardi, a senator and mayor of Santiago de Cuba. His career was also marked by collaborations with several famous singers, including Rita Montaner.

During the early 1930s, Mario Bauza used to play his trumpet in people's homes for just 50 cents.

Joe Hernández

René Touzet

The Cuban-born American composer, pianist, and bandleader René Touzet y Monte was born in Havana on September 8, 1916. He was a child prodigy, playing classical piano from the age of 4, and went on to study at the Falcon Conservatory in Havana, studying under the tutelage of the most outstanding teachers; in 1953, he was awarded the Gold Medal as Cuba's great composer. Touset led his 16-piece band at the Hotel Nacional in Havana. His best-known compositions are "No Te Importe Saber" (Let Me Love You Tonight), "Tu Felicidad" (Made For Each Other), and "Mi Musica Es Para Ti" (My Music is For You). His songs have been interpreted by Bing Crosby, Frank Sinatra, Dean Martin, and others. He died of heart complications in 2003 in Miami, Florida, at age 86.

Pedro Flores entered the music world in 1928 when he met the "Cumbanchero" Rafael Hernández.

Miguelito Valdés stated that RCA in Cuba contracted him to make recordings at El Montmartre Night Club with Casino de la Playa. For three years, they recorded eight records every two weeks and were paid $20.00 a week, with no royalties. According to Miguelito, the exposure he gained from this opportunity was invaluable.

History of La Cucaracha

The song "La Cucaracha," over a hundred years old, is not actually about a cockroach that loses its legs and can't walk, although that's what it has come to represent. It was initially about a revolution. Specifically, it was about the women who followed their men into battle. These women, known as "las cucarachas" or "camp followers," were gritty, resilient, and often looked down upon. Yet, their bravery and courage in adversity testify to their strength.

During the Mexican Revolution of 1910, a folkloric song of the corrido genre was composed to honor these women warriors. The song became a source of inspiration for revolutionaries like Pancho Villa, who gave it a comedic twist. The song eventually made its way to the United States, entering American pop culture, appearing in Looney Tunes cartoons in 1937, and gaining the attention of jazz greats like Louis Armstrong, singer Charo, and pianist Liberace.

However, the song's origins go back even further, adding to its historical significance. Some of the earliest versions of the lyrics refer to the confrontation between Spanish and Moroccan troops during the Hispano-

Moroccan War of 1859 to 1860. The song even appears in a novel written in 1819 titled "La Quijotita y su Prima" by José Joaquin Fernández de Lizardi, a Mexican writer and political journalist. This rich history of the song deepens our understanding and connection to Mexican history.

Among the most popular versions of the song with Pancho Villa's soldiers, which had hidden political meanings, the cockroach represented President Victoriano Huerta, a notorious drunk who took part in the death of the revolutionary President Francisco Madero and was considered a villain and traitor for his role. This political symbolism adds a layer of intrigue and depth to the song, inviting us to delve deeper into its meaning.

Miguelito Valdés was born in Havana, Cuba, on September 6, 1912, with the full name Miguel Angel Eugenio Lazaro Zacarias Izquierdo Valdés Hernández. Unfortunately, he passed away on November 9, 1978, while he was performing on stage at the Hotel Tequendama in Bogota, Colombia. The cause of death was a fatal heart attack.

Rubén Blades served as Panama's Minister of Tourism from 2004-2009 under President Martin Torrijos.

When Joe Cuba was a teenager, he had no interest in Latin music.

Millie Donay and Cuban Pete

The Latin dance duo of Cuban Pete and Millie Donay performed extensively across North and South America and Europe. They were invited to perform privately for Presidents Eisenhower and Johnson and gave a command performance for Queen Elizabeth II of England.

Vocalist Johnny Rodríguez's favorite composition, "Libertad" (Liberty), was written when he was 14. Despite his belief in and desire for Puerto Rico's independence, he never published the song.

Pedro Flores served in the United States Army for eight years, including the period of World War I.

Eddie Palmieri & Joe Hernández

Eddie Palmieri began to learn to play the piano at age 8. However, when he was around ten, his grandfather and mother decided to get him a set of timbales because young Eddie was destroying the house by using any surface to play with the sticks. And since everyone wanted to be like Tito Puente, timbales were the choice. At 15, Palmieri decided to get back to the piano, so he sold his timbales to his uncle and never looked back.

Rafael Ithier, the founder of *El Gran Combo* de Puerto Rico, has ten children from multiple marriages.

The Cosmopolita orchestra was founded in 1938, the same year as the Riverside orchestra, by drummer Vicente Viana, who committed suicide in 1944.

The Latin Music Trivia Book

Bristol-Myers Ipana toothpaste was promoted in Cuba with the jingle "Las Perlas de Tu Boca," which had the lyrics *"those pearls that you keep with care..."* sung by Eusebio Delfin. Interestingly, Eusebio married Amalia Bacardí y Cape, the daughter of rum tycoon Emilio Bacardí.

Selena's popularity grew after she won the Tejano Music Award for Female Vocalist of the Year in 1987. She holds the record for most wins, winning 11 of her 12 nominations.

During the early 1920s, many Puerto Rican musicians received a well-rounded music education. As a result, recording companies quickly recruited them to play in recordings of Greek, Polish, or Ukrainian music. These musicians were valued for their ability to read sheet music and promptly play the songs with minimal rehearsal. However, most listeners and record buyers of that time were unaware that Latinos, particularly Puerto Ricans, were primarily playing the ethnic music they were enjoying.

The Tales of the Song Linda

The notion that Daniel Santo composed the song "Linda," which was a huge hit and remained Santo's signature song in his extensive repertoire, is a total fabrication. Santos claimed he wrote the song as one of many inspired by the women who crossed his path. Santos was known to misrepresent and fabricate stories of events in his life.

In another version, according to the composer Pedro Flores, the truth of how the song came about was that he had an engagement in Santo Domingo with his *Cuarteto Flores,* of which Daniel Santos was the lead singer. While in Santo Domingo, his eyes saw this beautiful and voluptuous mulata. Immediately, Flores fell in love and engaged her in a conversation. She reciprocated, and they talked for a while. Finally, Pedro Flores suggested that she fly to New York, and she could stay in his apartment. When his engagement in Santo Domingo was completed, he would fly to New York and meet up with her. Flores gave Linda a telephone number that belonged to a friend. He told her to call him, and he would provide her with access to the apartment. She agreed, and they parted.

Pedro Flores flew to New York after he fulfilled his contract, only to not find Linda and learn that she had gone away with his friend. He never heard from her again. This experience inspired him to write one of the greatest boleros he had ever written.

Another account by Pedro Flores on the song's origin was that one summer Sunday afternoon, Flores was in the Luis Muñoz Rivera Park in San Juan, Puerto Rico, when he saw a young child sitting on one of the park's benches, supposedly gazing at the Atlantic Ocean. This child inspired Don Pedro to write the song. The story continues, and he tries to see her again after that first encounter. He tried asking all who may have known her about her whereabouts. No one knew. Then, somehow, he received the sad news that Linda had left unexpectedly for New York. There is another video where Daniel Santos gives this version of Pedro Flores's account, but it is slightly different!

It doesn't take rocket science to see some of the holes in this version of the story. A child? Who could he have possibly asked about where she was and when? Then, he learns that she left for New York. With whom, if she was a mere child?

Composers need to create a "story" behind every song they write when, often, it is nothing more than the result of their creativity and imagination.

In another interview, Santos said that Pedro Flores, while lying on his deathbed at the Veterans Hospital in Puerto Rico, finally met his Linda. According to Santos, Pedro's daughter brought Linda, now a gray-haired old lady, into his hospital room.

Nevertheless, "Linda" is and remains a great song and has been interpreted by many, including Johnny Albino and Ruben Blades. However, Daniel Santos's interpretation of the song, in which he was the first to sing it, still is the most popular.

Selena is among the best-selling female Latin music artists, selling over 18 million records worldwide.

Orquesta de la Luz released their debut album, *Salsa Caliente del Japón,* in 1990. It was the first Salsa album to sell over 30,000 copies in its first month of release.

—⚿—

Joe Hernández, the founder and former president of the International Latin Music Hall of Fame, organized its first inaugural induction ceremony in 1999 at New York's World-Famous Birdland. The celebration was followed by a performance at the exquisite La Maganette nightclub, where *Orchestra Broadway* performed, featuring a special guest performance by José Fajardo.

—⚿—

Tito Puente

In 1942, Machito's drummer, Tony Escolies, was replaced by Tito Puente, who was only nineteen years old. However, shortly after joining the *Machito Orchestra,* Tito, along with Chino Pozo, left to join the *Jack Cole Dancers.* Tito returned to Machito within a month, but unfortunately, he had to go again as he was drafted into the United States Navy.

When performing live, the *Cuarteto Victoria* consisted of four musicians. However, during recordings, the group expanded to include between nine and ten musicians.

Johnny Rodríguez began singing at an early age, but not professionally. However, his reputation as a serenader was firmly established. He was paid a dollar for each serenade he performed, equivalent to $18 in 2024. He mentioned that he had to jump countless fences to earn that sum. When he gave an unforgettable serenade, the price included an empanada with French fries at the end of his performance. At that time, it cost thirty-five cents, approximately $6.50 in 2024.

Pedro Flores composed his first two songs, "Toma Jabón Pa' Que Te Laves" and "El Jilgüero," in 1926.

After divorcing her first husband, Eulogio Reyes, La Lupe sang as a soloist at *Cabaret La Red* in Havana. She performed ten sets daily, each lasting 45 minutes, for a weekly salary of $28.

Olga Guillot had one daughter, Olga María Touzet-Guillot, whose father was the Cuban-born American composer, pianist, and bandleader Réne Touzet.

Rafael Hernández is known as Puerto Rico's most proud jibaro, having written hundreds of songs. However, despite this reputation, he rarely incorporated indigenous Puerto Rican instruments or folklore music into his compositions, other than an occasional Aguinaldo. Instead, he spent most of his life in urban centers, traveling the world, and hardly spent any time in the countryside as a jibaro.

Puerto Rican percussionist Willie Bobo, born William Correa, was delivered by a midwife in an apartment on New York City's 115th Street and Lenox on February 24, 1934.

In December 1958, Tito Rodríguez performed at the Riviera in Las Vegas. During his act, he wore a cowboy hat and guns while singing "Hopalong Tito." His wife, Tobi, also performed wearing a Japanese Kimono and sang "Poor Butterfly." Unfortunately, their performance was poorly received, and they were forced to return to New York by January 1959.

Rafael Hernández's first girlfriend was named Nicolasa Cruz. She was a lovely Puerto Rican.

Louis Moreau Gottschalk

Louis Moreau Gottschalk passed away at the age of 40 due to peritonitis on December 18, 1869, while performing in Río de Janeiro. Ironically, he was playing his composition, "Morte," which means death, when he collapsed at the piano and died three weeks later.

Celia Cruz recommended La Lupe to Mongo Santamaría in 1962, after La Lupe was exiled to Mexico and left unemployed.

La Lupe's most famous song, "Que te Pedí," is featured in the 2006 film El Cantante, which stars Marc Anthony as Héctor Lavoe.

Rita Montaner

From 1927 to 1929, Rita Montaner recorded over fifty songs for Columbia Records. Her hits included "Ay, Mamá Inés," "Siboney," "Lamento Esclavo," "Noche Azul," and the first recording of the son sensation "El Manicero."

Rubén Blades' journey to success is a testament to his unwavering dedication. After completing his law degree in Panama, he moved to New York and started working as a mail clerk for the Fania label. Despite facing challenges, he found a place to stay on Larry Harlow's brother Andy's couch. During this time, Blades began to write songs, including the popular hits "Las Esquinas" and "Ciprianos." His talent and hard work soon led him to collaborate with renowned musicians such as Larry Harlow, Joe Cuba, Ray Barretto, and Willie Colón. As the saying goes, the rest is history.

Trío Matamoros

In 1926, *Trío Matamoros* went to Havana to find work. Even for some of the best musicians, performing full-time wasn't enough to make ends meet. The group leader, Miguel Matamoros, had to work as a chauffeur to pay the bills. Despite this, he kept writing songs, including the bolero "La Droga Milagrosa" and his big hit "El Que Siembra Su Maíz! Que Se Coma Su Pinol." His boss recognized his incredible talent and let him go as a driver, telling him it would be unfair to keep such an extraordinary talent in his employment. Matamoros returned to his love of music with no other alternative and dedicated his time to performing and composing.

In the meantime, he wrote another hit, "La Mujer de Antonio."

The first sound film in Argentina, *Tango*, featured the renowned Argentinian singer Libertad Lamarque in 1932.

Tito Puente was a dedicated musician who sharpened his arranging and musical skills while serving in the band of the USS Santee during World War II. He learned a lot about arranging techniques and compositions from a pilot who he remembered playing the tenor saxophone. This pilot served as an arranger for the big band Charlie Spivak and was a Navy lieutenant named Sweeney. Tito Puente was also part of the ship's band.

Before becoming a global obsession, the "nuevo ritmo" (new rhythm), known as the 'Mambo' was considered too African for the danzón crowd that attended the Havana salons. That radio banned the rhythm from their stations for six months.

According to Pete Bonet, the Puerto Rican singer Wito Kortright was the "inventor" who recorded "El Watusi" but never got the credit for this tune; Ray Barretto took the credit.

In the 1950s, Mambo music was the rage, and Latin music percussionists were highly sought after by recording studios. In 1952, William Correa was nicknamed Willie Bobo by the renowned pianist Mary Lou Williams while they were working on a recording session together.

Bény Moré recorded in the rhythm of bolero, guaracha, son, mambo, chachacha, merengue, batanga, guajira, afro, plena, porro, drum, danzón mazumba, guaguancó, changui and bahion. In total, 17 musical genres led him to sing with pride and with anyone.

Arturo "Chico" O'Farrill (1921-2001) earned his nickname "Chico" while working as an arranger for Benny Goodman. Goodman had trouble pronouncing his name correctly, so he started calling him "Chico." Chico wrote "Undercurrent Blues" for Goodman.

In 1931, Rita Montaner traveled to New York City's Broadway under contract to Al Jolson for his musical *Wonder Bar.*

Nat King Cole Español was recorded in Havana in 1958 with arrangements made by Armando Romeu.

Joe Hernández

The famous Puerto Rican composer Pedro Flores played professional baseball like Augusto Coen and Mon Rivera.

Roberto Roena (1940-2021) was a gifted dancer from his early days. He started his career as a dancer and singer in *Myrta Silva's Revue.* Later, he learned percussion from Cortijo, who also helped him enhance his dancing skills. Roberto's uncle, Anibal Vázquez, was a renowned salsa dancer.

In 1930, Pedro Flores recorded his first songs, "Adelita," "Nieves," "Contigo," "Palomita," "Azucena," "En Secreto," and "El Retrato."

It is rumored that Tito Rodríguez, a famous musician, was severely beaten by an unknown Puerto Rican boxer during the early 1970s. At least one musical historian has confirmed this. The reason for the beating and the identity of the boxer is still unknown. Tito was known for his popularity among women, leading to speculation about a possible motive for the attack.

Héctor Lavoe's most famous hit and his eventual signature song was "El Cantante." When Johnny Pacheco and Willie Colón searched for a song for Lavoe to record, they approached Rubén Blades to see if he could provide anything. Blades mentioned that he had already written a song called "El Cantante." Although the song was not initially intended for Lavoe, Colón convinced Blades to give it to him.

Rita Montaner was known to have a nasty disposition. During Ernesto Lecuona's show, while singing a duet with the lead tenor, she began to tear his clothes off on stage.

Eddie Palmieri has performed in over 2,500 concerts worldwide.

It was a common occurrence for Puerto Ricans, whether living in New York City or on the mainland, to enjoy the music of groups like *Cuarteto Victoria*, oblivious to the fact that these were Cuban musicians. Rafael Hernández, a staunch advocate of the 'Cuban' sound, was adamant that improvisations should be handled by someone other than a Puerto Rican. He often turned to Cuban musicians like Alberto Socarras on flute or Mario Bauza on trumpet to bring his vision to life.

In his teens, Daniel Santos lived alone in a tiny room. He supported himself by shining shoes, selling ice and coal, and picking up whatever menial jobs he encountered.

The clave is a fundamental and crucial rhythmic pattern that consists of two bars. This rhythm is the foundation of Cuban, Puerto Rican, and Dominican music. The clave originated from West and Central Africa and comprises five attacks divided into either 3 + 2 or 2 + 3, depending on the melody's rhythmic content. Two distinct clave patterns represent two different but related forms of Cuban music: the son and the rumba. It is worth mentioning that rock and funk rhythms also have their roots in the clave.

Ernesto Lecuona y Casado (1895-1963), a celebrated Cuban composer, initially honed his piano skills under the guidance of his sister Ernestina, a maestro in her own right. His musical education continued at the prestigious Peyrellade Conservatory (1904-1907) in Havana, Cuba. Despite his youthful age, Ernesto was already composing dance pieces at eleven and teaching piano and singing at fifteen. However, tragedy struck with the sudden loss of his father, forcing him to take up work as a silent film pianist. It was during this challenging period, between 1908 and 1909, that he premiered a few of his musical comedies.

In 2007, Olga Guillot was honored with the Latin Grammy Lifetime Achievement Award.

José Melis Guiu, a musical prodigy, was born in Havana, Cuba, on February 27, 1920. His journey into the world of music began at the tender age of three, and his exceptional virtuosity was evident even then. By the age of six, he had already entered the prestigious *Havana Conservatory of Music,* where he graduated just four years later. Recognizing his extraordinary talent, the Cuban government awarded him a scholarship to further his education in Paris. In the City of Lights, he triumphed in a competition that granted him the opportunity to study under the renowned French pianist Alfred Cortot.

After completing his studies in Paris, Melis returned to his native Havana and performed in concerts, including performances with the *Havana Symphony.* He then went to Boston, where he continued his studies with the harpsichordist and concert pianist Edwin Brodky. Three years later, he received another scholarship to study under Joseph and Rosa Lhévinne at Julliard Graduate School in New York.

After serving in the Army during World War II, José Melis Guiu embarked on a new chapter in his musical journey. He toured the United States, leaving a lasting impact as a musical director for the USO Camp Shows. His dedication and talent shone through, earning him the respect and admiration of all who witnessed his performances. Tragically, his life was cut short by a respiratory infection on April 7, 2005, in Sun City, Arizona, at the age of 85.

During his time in Los Angeles, Xavier Cugat formed a friendship with Rudolf Valentino, who played a crucial role in creating a tango orchestra. This encouragement led to the establishment of *Xavier Cugat and His Gigolos.* The orchestra debuted on a night of musical firsts, which coincided with Bing Crosby's debut at the

Coconut Grove in Los Angeles. In a surprising turn of events, Crosby also sang some tango with the group, adding a unique dynamic to the evening.

Sylvia Rexach

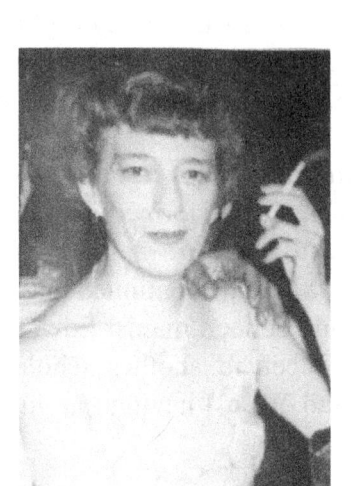

Sylvia Rexach was a famous composer from Santurce, Puerto Rico, born on January 22, 1922. In the mid-1930s, while she was attending a high school outing at the Escambrón Beach Club, she played one of her early compositions called "Di Corazón" ("Tell Me, Heart") on the piano. At that time, Rafael Muñoz, a bandleader taking a break from rehearsals for an evening performance at the same club, overheard the song and was impressed. He approached Rexach and asked her who had written it. Shortly after, her father signed a contract with the publishing company Peer International on her behalf, and Muñoz recorded the song before Rexach finished her junior year. Unfortunately, Sylvia

Rexach passed away on October 20, 1961, at the age of 39, due to stomach cancer.

Libertad Lamarque and Eva Duarte (Perón) starred in the 1945 film *La Cabalgata del Circo*. However, their strained relationship would later impact Lamarque's life.

While performing in Paris, Rita Montaner also appeared in Josephine Baker's Revue.

Tito Puente's first Latin music arrangement, which he sent to Machito, was "El Bajo de Chapotín," he wrote this piece while at sea on the U.S.S. Santee.

Louis Moreau Gottschalk, a pianist who performed throughout Cuba, spent some time recovering from malaria on a plantation near Cienfuegos. During his recovery, he enjoyed listening to the enslaved people singing in the evenings.

Celia Cruz met and became friends with Esther Buenaventura while attending Teachers College in Cuba. Esther fell in love and married the famous Cachao. Celia met Cachao at the dances at Jovenes del Vals, where he performed.

Joe Hernández

In his first competition appearance at radio station CMQ in the early 1940s, Bény Moré was *booed* off stage when he began to sing. However, on his second competitive appearance, he won first prize.

María Teresa Gertrudis de Jesús Carreño García (1853-1917) was a Venezuelan piano virtuoso, soprano, composer, and conductor. She made her debut at the Irving Hall in New York at the tender age of eight in 1862. Her mother was the cousin of María Teresa Rodríguez del Toro y Alayza, who was the wife of Simón Bolívar, the founding father of South America. At the age of ten in 1863, she performed at the White House for President Abraham Lincoln. Later, in 1916, she performed for President Woodrow Wilson at the White House. She passed away on June 12, 1917, at 63 years old in her apartment in New York City.

Eduardo Davidson, a renowned Cuban vocalist, is credited with creating the music style known as pachanga. He coined the term and choreographed the original form of the pachanga dance. However, the dancers at the Triton Ballroom further developed the steps to this popular dance. The song "La Pachanga" was first performed on May 21, 1959, on Havana's CMQ television's musical program *Casino de la Alegria,* and it was later recorded on August 5, 1959. For a brief period in history, pachanga became a craze.

The Panamanian singer Rubén Blades inherited his English name from his paternal grandfather, who hailed from the British West Indies (St. Lucia).

Rafael Hernández and brother Jesús

Following World War I, there was a decrease in demand for Puerto Rican musicians in New York City. Consequently, many Puerto Rican veterans, including Rafael Hernández and his brother Jesús "Pocholo" Hernández, were forced to seek work in factories. While working at a bedspring factory, Rafael, who had little experience, accidentally got his thumb caught in a machine, losing a portion of his thumb.

Charlie Palmieri was a City College of New York professor who taught Puerto Rican Studies and Latin Folkloric Musical Heritage.

Celia Cruz had two siblings who died. The first one was a boy who died while an infant named Japón. Then, a sister called Norma passed away at an early age.

―⟁―

Contrary to popular opinion, the great hit "La Tirana" sung by La Lupe was not written by her. Nor was the song initially a message to empower women or any of the psychological and sociological nonsense attributed to the song by those who have a feminist agenda. The prolific Puerto Rican composer Catalino "Tite" Curet Alonso composed the tune for the well-known male Cuban singer Roberto Ledesma. After some consideration, Ledesma decided that the song was not a good fit for him. Tite Curet then made minor changes to the original composition and gave it to La Lupe.

―⟁―

Arsenio Rodríguez & His Orchestra

Arsenio Rodríguez (Ignacio Loyola Rodríguez Skull) was born in Guines, near Matanzas, Cuba, on August

30, 1911. Arsenio had seventeen siblings. He lost his eyesight at a youthful age due to an illness, and not as is widely believed, at the age of twelve, by getting kicked by a mule. Many years later, in 1947, the singer Miguelito Valdés brought him to New York to see an eye specialist. After the examination, he learned there was no cure, forcing Arsenio to lose hope. Consequently, he wrote the sad bolero "La Vida Es Un Sueño" ("Life is a Dream").

Little is known about his childhood. Historians and musical experts affirm that the Cuban archives preserve some data about who would be recognized as one of the most influential musicians on the island. From these same historians, it is discovered that his civil registry name was Ignacio Arsenio Travieso Scull. Still, artistically, he used Arsenio Rodríguez Scull, the name under which he registered all his compositions.

This name change has undoubtedly made searching for data and information about him difficult. Despite this, it is known that his parents were of Congolese descent, the first generation of free descendants, day laborers on a farm that produced food, fruits, and legumes in the Guines region.

His illiteracy and blindness did not prevent him from developing self-taught musical training. As a Tresero and percussionist, he cultivated a love for records from an early age to keep up with what was happening in Cuban music. His enormous contributions revolutionized Cuban music. Arsenio died on December 30, 1970, in Los Angeles, at 59 from pneumonia.

Tito Puente won his first Grammy Award in 1978 for recording *Tribute to Bény Moré,* which Jerry Masucci produced.

Vernon and Irene Castle's dance team made the Argentinian tango a nationwide Latin dance craze in the US. By 1914, they commanded $1,000 for a one-hour appearance, equivalent to nearly $31,000 in 2024 dollars.

Pedro Flores's first musical formation was *El Trío Galon* with Piquito Marcano and Burgues and later *El Cuarteto Flores*.

Tito Rodríguez's father, Don Juan Rodríguez, was Puerto Rican from San Sebastian, not Dominican, despite earlier publications that claimed otherwise. The confusion arose due to Tito's father working as a land developer for the Dominican Republic. Tito's mother was Cuban from Holguin.

In 1922, Daniel Castellanos, a Spaniard, set up a record shop in the South Ferry area of lower Manhattan that sold Spanish-language records. By the decade's end, he had opened two additional branches in Harlem. Castellanos may have been the first person to own a Latin music store in New York City.

Bény Moré turned down an offer to record with *La Sonora Matancera* because he believed they needed better sound quality.

Victoria and Rafael Hernández

In 1927, Victoria Hernández, the sister of Rafael Hernández, one of Latin America's most celebrated composers, bought a storefront from a Jewish owner for $500 and opened Almacenes Hernández (Hernández Music Store) at 1735 Madison Avenue, located between 113th St. and 114th St. in El Barrio. This was the first Puerto Rican-owned music store in New York City, although not the first Spanish-language records shop. Her small store's success prompted her to move to a more prominent location at 1724 Madison Avenue. Later, a local businessman named Luis Cuevas bought the store, and as the business flourished and expanded, he founded the Verne Record label.

Joe Hernández

In the summer of 1961, a little-known bandleader visited Charlie Palmieri's home in the Bronx, NY, to compose new music. During this time, the charanga and pachanga genres of music were popular, but there needed to be more clarity between the two. The public needed to differentiate between the charanga as music and the pachanga as a dance. In his second year of leading his band, the bandleader kept this in mind as he sang out lyrics while Palmieri played the melody on his piano. The result was the song "La Pachanga se Baila Asi," performed by Joe Quijano and his *Conjunto Cachana,* recorded under the Columbia label, which would become a huge hit. Joe Quijano passed away in 2019.

Nilo Menéndez and Alberto Socarras earned up to $150 weekly as studio musicians for Columbia Records in the late 1920s, which is equivalent to $2,700 in today's market.

Xavier Cugat was a Spanish-born band leader who immigrated to Cuba with his parents sometime between the ages of three and five. By age eight, he was playing the violin in cafes throughout Havana.

The original Mexican Latin song, "Cuando Vuelva a Tu Lado," was later adapted into the famous song "What a Difference a Day Made." It was composed by Mexican songwriter Maria Grever in 1934.

According to the people at Fania, the movie *"Our Latin Thing"* was prepared almost spontaneously with just a few days of preparation. However, this seems highly unlikely as it would take many months to get all the musicians together, hire a film crew, write a script, etc. Interestingly, the cover of Vol. 1 of the LP, which Izzy Sanabria designed, bears his signature with the date 7/71. Since the movie was filmed on August 26, 1971, this suggests that the producer, Jerry Masucci, had been planning the film for at least a month, if not longer. Larry Harlow later confirmed in an interview that the movie was not spontaneous and that it took some time to plan.

In the 1920s, playing music in theatres that showed silent films was considered a good training ground for young musicians in Puerto Rico. In larger towns, musicians could perform six or seven evenings per week and earn anywhere from $1.00 to $2.50 per night of play.

Even though Johnny Rodríguez's mother was a talented singer and his father often played guitar to accompany her, his father did not want Johnny to pursue music. Instead, he wanted his son to become a lawyer. However, at the age of sixteen, Johnny began performing on the *West Indies Advertising Company's* noon show, a major sponsor of early radio in Puerto Rico. Johnny's father had no idea that his son had dropped out of school and was pursuing a career in music until someone congratulated him on his son's success as a radio star.

Joe Hernández

"Aquellos Ojos Verdes" (Green Eyes) is a song composed by the Cuban songwriter, orchestra leader, and actor Nilo Menéndez Barnet in 1929 in cooperation with Adolfo Utrera. It gained immense popularity when Jimmy Dorsey recorded it in the early 1940s. The song was inspired by Utrera's sister, Conchita Utrera.

—⚞—

At nine, Xavier Cugat played in a trío that performed at a silent movie house with Moisés Simons, the famous composer of the "Peanut Vendor."

—⚞—

In 1943, Ernesto Lecuona gave his first concert of Cuban music in North America at Carnegie Hall.

—⚞—

Enrico Caruso played a crucial role in launching Xavier Cugat's secondary career as a cartoonist. Cugat's caricatures were published in the Los Angeles Times and later syndicated nationally. Enrico's older brother, Francis, was also a talented artist who painted the cover art for F. Scott Fitzgerald's novel, *The Great Gatsby*.

—⚞—

Miguel Faílde (1851-1922) was a young multi-instrumentalist from the small town of Guamacaro. In June 1877, he created the first danzón, "La Altura del Simpson" (The Heights of Simpson), with his Traditional Group. However, the bourgeoisie initially criticized the danzón, viewing it as a "lascivious, devilish black dance." Despite the negative feedback, the tune gradually gained popularity, and even the upper class began dancing to it. Over time, the danzón continued to prevail and became increasingly popular.

Celia Cruz with parents (center) and family

Celia Cruz's mother seemed to have had a "premonition" on her daughter's future when she named her Celia Caridad. The name Celia is derived from St. Cecilia, the patron saint of music.

Puerto Rico's radio station ranks among the worst offenders in the illegal practice of payola.

Bény Moré recorded historical duets with Lalo Montane, Pedro Vargas, Tony Camargo, Alfredo Sadel,

Siro Rodríguez, Olga Guillot, and Kike Mendive, also accompanied by the Gaona Sisters, the Bermúdez Brothers, and the Anacaona Sisters. Titles by great bolero composers such as Ernesto Lecuona, Agustín Lara, Juan Bruno Tarraza, Miguel Matamoros, José Carbo Menéndez, Tony Fergo, Frank Domínguez, Emma Elena Valdelamar, Julio Brito, Osvaldo Farres, Pedro Flores and Consuela Velázquez, were part of his extensive repertoire.

Pablo Casals

In 1963, the Puerto Rican cellist, composer, and conductor Pablo Casals wrote and dedicated the song "Ven a Mi" (Come to Me) to Ruth Fernández.

Rafael Hernández composed the song "Preciosa" in 1937 while living in Mexico.

During the 1960s Charanga craze, New York City had twenty-two Charanga bands.

Mon Rivera

The Puerto Rican musician Mon Rivera spent over forty years working as a janitor and handyman at the University of Puerto Rico-Mayagüez, where the campus staff greatly loved him.

La Lupe suffered from one tragedy after another. Her husband suffered from severe mental problems; she lost her home in a fire, had an accident that led to a broken spine, and died in abject poverty, having to go on welfare to survive.

Joe Hernández

Bény Moré is widely regarded as the most outstanding Cuban vocalist of all time.

James Reese Europe Infantry Band

James Reese Europe (1881-1919) was born in Mobile, Alabama, and was an important ragtime and early jazz bandleader who recruited many black Puerto Ricans into his band, including Rafael Hernández. In May 1919, Europe was fatally stabbed in a quarrel by his drummer, Herbert Wright. Wright stabbed Europe in the neck with a penknife. Europe walked away with the wound, thinking it was superficial, but he died hours later at the hospital when the doctors could not stop the bleeding. He was only 38 years old. Herbert Wright was convicted of manslaughter and served eight years in prison.

Alberto Socarras, a Cuban flutist, was one of the few Latin musicians who started a genuine Latin sound in the U.S. during the late 1920s. In 1928, he became the first musician to record a flute jazz solo on Clarence William's QRS label recording of "Have You Ever Felt That Way?"

Did you know over fifty talented singers have graced the stage with *La Sonora Matancera?* From legendary performers to up-and-coming stars, this iconic Latin band has collaborated with some of the most renowned voices in the music industry. It's no wonder their music continues to captivate audiences worldwide!

Pedro Flores Quartet became an Orchestra, and Cándido Vicenty, Antonio Machín, Plácido Acevedo, Panchito Riset, Julito Rodríguez, and many more passed through it.

The Mexican composer Agustín Lara wrote the bolero "Impossible" as a teenager. He was employed as a pianist in a house of prostitution, where he fell in love with a prostitute who did not reciprocate his feelings.

It is widely believed that the tango was initially a dance performed mainly by men. However, this is just a myth. Men used to practice with each other because there were more men than women in Uruguay and Argentina at the time. At dances, men compete for women's attention, and to stand out, they must show off their dancing skills. Since there were so many men, the only way to practice was for them to dance with each other. Today, the tango enjoys global popularity and competes worldwide in international dance tournaments by couples from many countries.

The Puerto Rican megastar Marc Anthony began his musical start as a six-year-old kid hanging around Johnny Colón's music program in Harlem. Colón was among the first to be awarded a "Special Recognition" award by the International Latin Music Hall of Fame for his enormous contribution to developing and nurturing young musical talents.

In the mid-1970s, when Héctor Lavoe was the first voice for the Fania All-Stars, Johnny Pacheco composed the popular tune "El Rey de la Puntualidad" for him because he was always late to rehearsals and gigs. Ironically, according to the Fania sound engineer, Irv Greenbaum, Pacheco was always late to rehearsal.

La Sonora Ponceña was established in 1954 by pianist Enrique "Quique" Lucca Caraballo and is considered one of Puerto Rico's most influential bands, along with El Gran Combo. The band still exists today, with Quique's son, Papo Lucca, who joined as the pianist when he was twelve. Papo has been directing the band since, celebrating their 70th anniversary in 2024.

During the 1940s, the father of Willie Colón played the trumpet alongside Manny Oquendo.

Graciela, her parents & Machito

Machito (Frank Grillo) was not Graciela's Pérez brother by blood. Graciela's parents raised him as a teen, so he was an older adoptive stepbrother. Hence, Mario Bauza was not legally his brother-in-law. He was Graciela's brother-in-law because he married Graciela's sister Estela.

Rita Montaner's brother was a policeman who was killed in a drive-by shooting. The culprits were never found. Rumors were that it was an act of revenge for her talking on the air about how the President of Cuba, Ramón Grau, tried to bribe her during his second term in office.

―ᴧᴧ―

Pedro Flores was a house painter and did the back-breaking work with pick and shovel to construct the new Eighth Avenue subway line.

―ᴧᴧ―

Tito Puente had the opportunity to play alongside the renowned Machito when he was just 17 years old.

―ᴧᴧ―

Celia Cruz

Celia Cruz began recording with *La Sonora Matancera* at the age of twenty-five. She became the orchestra's first black frontwoman.

―ᴧᴧ―

At the age of 16, Tito Puente played with legendary pianist Noro Morales at New York City's Stork Club.

La Sonora Matancera has recorded over 4,000 songs in its 79-year history, averaging almost one song per week.

In 1983, Pérez Prado's brother, Pantaleo Pérez Prado, a musician known professionally by the same name as his brother Pérez Prado, died, and the press erroneously reported it as the death of Pérez Prado, The Mambo King.

In 1961, Al Santiago released the album *Alegre All Stars Volume I,* a jam session LP that, although it sold less than ten thousand copies, started a trend that would later materialize in the *Tico All Stars* and *Fania All-Stars*. With this production, Al Santiago, anticipating the future, commercially opened the path to the sound of salsa that would facilitate the birth of Fania Records.

Rafael Hernández, aged 23, arrived in New York in 1918, and his family joined him the following year. They lived at 1735 Third Avenue.

"El Arroyo Que Murmura" is the title of the very first guajira song, composed by Jorge Ankermann in 1899.

The Guajira dance is a flamenco style resulting from the combination of Spanish and Central American cultures. It is known for its cadent melody, slow rhythm, and joyful, sensual, and seductive character.

Celia Cruz & Myrta Silva

La Sonora Matancera was formed in 1924 and led by guitarist/singer Rogelio Martínez for over fifty years (He joined the group in 1926), who featured nearly one hundred singers from the Caribbean and Mexico. Among them were the legendary Puerto Rican singer Daniel Santos and the Cuban Celia Cruz, who replaced another legendary vocalist, Myrta Silva. The group took its name from the town of Matanzas, Cuba. The group existed for 79 years, until 2003, making it one of the longest-lasting groups in Latin music history.

Tito Rodríguez's future wife was a beautiful young Japanese American woman named Takeku Kunimatzu.

She was born in Washington state on January 23, 1925. To overcome discrimination during World War II, she changed her name to Tobi and pretended to be Chinese to secure a job. She landed a position as a dancer at a new nightclub called the China Doll, opening on Fifty-first Street and Broadway, where the Conga room had once been.

Tito Puente

In March 1949, after spending two years as musical director with the Pupi Campo Orchestra, Tito Puente left Campo and formed his first musical band, the Picadilly Boys, a name given by dance promoter Federico Pagani. He debuted with his seven-piece orchestra at El Patio Club in Atlantic Beach on July 4, 1949. The band's first record, a guajira entitled "Encanto Cubano," sung by Alfredito Valdés, was a hit. Anthony Benedetto (Tony Bennett) was on the bill that evening.

The massive popularity of the *son* music genre is largely attributed to the contributions of Nicolas Guillen, Miguel Matamoros, and Ignacio Piñeiro."

Joe Loco was the uncle of Louie Ramirez.

Oreste Aragón Cantero established *Orquesta Aragón* on the island of Cienfuegos in 1939, originally named *Rítmica 39* and later *La Rítmica Aragón*.

The bolero "El Canto Lastimero de una Tortola Sola" (The Plaintive Song of a Lonely Turtle) was recorded by the duet Peronet e Izurieta with the name of "Cuando Vuelvas" (When You Return) with the authorship of the Puerto Rican composer Rafael Hernández when its actual title is "Desde Que te Fuiste" (Since you left). Its author is Don Felo (Felipe R Goyco).

By September 1932, E.B. Marks, a music publisher, had already amassed an astounding catalog of nearly 600 Latin American songs. This achievement was even more impressive considering the company's youth, having been established four months earlier on May 9, 1932. E.B. Marks continued to operate for fifty-one years before dissolving on December 9, 1983, only to be re-established as the Marks Music Company.

Rafael Hernández was aware of the influence of his song's lyrics and how to use them to attract different audiences. In 1928, Trío Borinquen, led by Hernández, renamed their recording of "Linda Borinquen" to "Linda Quisqueya" to honor the Dominicans, even though it was the same Cuban habanera.

Victoria Hernández

Victoria Hernández had plans to expand her business, but unfortunately, she had to scale back after losing $5,000 of her hard-earned profits due to the failure of her bank in 1929. This amount was significant, particularly for a small merchant in Harlem. Today's currency would be equivalent to $88,000 in 2024.

Ruth Fernández was named "The Singer of the Century" in Puerto Rico during the last century.

In 1928, *La Sonora Mantancera* moved to Havana and recorded their first songs for RCA-Victor. They went on to record under thirteen different labels throughout their career.

Victoria Hernández, sister of Rafael Hernández, claimed to have been the first to record Latin music in New York in 1927 when she founded the Disco Hispano label.

Damaso Pérez

Damaso Pérez Prado was known as "Cara'e foca" (seal face) and "Cuello Duro" (Stiff Collar) because he walked uprightly.

Enrique Jorrín was inspired by the mambo created by Cachao and Orestes López and developed a new rhythm. His *Orquesta America,* introduced the first chachacha to New York with a tune called "La Engañadora." He unveiled this unique sound at a dance hall at the corner of Prado and Neptune in Habana in 1949.

The tune "Soul Drummer" on the Ray Barretto "Acid" LP was not written by Ray Barretto. Pete Bonet composed and sang the music.

Celia Cruz was the godmother to Linda Caballero, a.k.a. "La India."

Victoria Hernández had an exclusive dealership with Victor Company that covered a radius of several blocks. This "territorial protection" gave her a significant competitive advantage over other emerging record establishments trying to establish themselves in the densely populated areas of Harlem.

Celia Cruz was renowned for being punctual and well-prepared for all her engagements. Even when she fell ill, she continued to perform. There was one instance where she was performing in Spain, and she fractured a toe, but even that did not stop her. She refused to disappoint her fans by canceling the show and went on to sing and dance as if nothing had happened.

Joe Hernández

—〰—

Johnny Colón founded and directed the East Harlem Music School.

—〰—

Fania claimed that the musicians were unaware they were being filmed on August 26, 1971, at the *Fania All-Star* concert at the Cheetah nightclub. This story needs to be corrected. In the film *Our Latin Thing*, you can see camera operators standing before the musicians, walking around them as they film. Not to mention that five or six camera operators were in full view.

—〰—

Felix Chappottín

Felix Chappottín Lage, a towering figure in Cuban music history, was born on March 31, 1907, in Cayo Hueso, Havana. His father, Julio Chappottín, was a member of the renowned *son* group *Los Apaches*. Felix, one of eleven siblings, including his brother Chano Pozo who was raised by their parents after Chano's parents' passing, left an enduring legacy in the music industry. He was a member of three extraordinarily successful Cuban bands: Septeto Habanero, Arsenio Rodríguez's Conjunto, and Conjunto Chappottín, which he directed. His talent also led him to play for various conjuntos, including Conjunto Azul, directed by Chano Pozo. Felix Chappottín's musical journey concluded on December 21, 1983, at the age of 76, but his impact on the industry continues to resonate.

The record shows that in 1946, Joséito Róman played the first merengue at the Palladium (Alma Dance Studios) in New York City.

Andrea Brachfeld achieved the distinction of being the first female flutist to play for Charanga 76.

Louie Armstrong, Cab Calloway and Duke Ellington were among the first African American bandleaders to incorporate Cuban music into their repertoire.

The romantic female voice that sings the bolero "Cómo Todos" by Rafael Hernández (lyrics by Bernando Sancristóbal) is the Colombian Esther Forero. The record label says *Los Universitarios,* who had nothing to do with said recording.

Joe Hernández

Rafael Hernández was forced to dismiss Manuel "Canario" Jiménez from his band, *Trío Borinquen*, because he could not consistently fulfill his performance obligations. Canario was a singer and a merchant marine who needed to fulfill his job responsibilities and support himself.

Panchito Riset was a renowned Cuban singer who joined the *Antobal Orchestra* in 1933 to replace Antonio Machín. In the 1930s, he went on to sing with some of the top orchestras of his time. Unfortunately, he had diabetes, which led to him losing his vision, and eventually, his legs were amputated. Despite his health issues, he continued pursuing his artistic endeavors until the end. However, it is a sad irony that Panchito passed away blind and without his legs, in the confines of an asylum - a far cry from the romanticism of his famous song.

Celia Cruz (1925-2003), the *Queen of Salsa*, recorded over seventy albums, twenty-three of which were certified gold and a few reaching platinum.

Willie Colón and Rubén Blades' Siembra is the best-selling Latin Caribbean album of all time. In Caracas, Venezuela, it sold 500,000 copies.

Daniel Santos was absent from the military without leave (AWOL) for thirteen days. As a result, he was sentenced to six months of restricted confinement in his court martial. However, he was eventually honorably discharged as a first staff sergeant.

Julio Iglesias is an icon of Latin music who has achieved unmatched success. He holds the record for selling the most albums in history, with over 80 record productions and performances in at least 12 languages. His global appeal is evident because he has sold over three hundred million copies worldwide and has been awarded over 2,600 gold and platinum records. He has performed approximately 5,000 live shows, captivating audiences across five continents, with approximately 60 million attending his concerts. In 2013, China honored him with an award for being the first and most famous international artist to have performed in that country. The same year, he received the Guinness record for being the Latin artist with the most records sold in music history. In 1999, he was inducted into the Latin Songwriters Hall of Fame and the International Latin Music Hall of Fame, a testament to his enduring influence on the music industry.

In the early 1900s, charanga orchestras became popular and replaced the brass-oriented danzóneras as the standard instrumental line-up for the danzón. These orchestras were initially referred to as charangas francesas despite having no connection to France. Orquesta Cervantes was one of the first charangas and was the first to include a piano in their group.

Joe Hernández

Nico Saquito

Nenito Antonio Fernández Ortiz, also known as Nico Saquito, was a prolific guarachas composer. Some of his most famous compositions include "Cuidadito Compay," "María Cristina," "Adios Compay Gato," "Al Vaiven de Mi Carretera," "Camina Cómo Chencha," and "Amarrao Compe." Though he had promising futures in baseball and car mechanics, at 15, he already drew attention to his songwriting skills and decided to pursue that path. His first hit was in 1936 when the Trío Matamoros recorded his guaracha "Cuidadito Compay Gallo." He later founded Los Guaracheros de Oriente and made many recordings for RCA.

Rafael Hernández, a Puerto Rican composer, was an honored soldier in the 369th Infantry orchestra during World War I. The unit, also known as the *Harlem Hellfighters*, gained worldwide recognition for their bravery. The Regiment, established on June 2, 1913, in the New York National Guard, was a testament to the diversity of the war effort. It was primarily composed of African Americans, men from various other countries, including Puerto Rico, and a small number of white officers—the French highly esteemed the Regiment for their valor in fighting in the trenches.

In 1927, a famous Mexican composer named Agustín Lara, who was also known as El Flaco de Oro, was performing as a pianist at the Cabaret de Santa María la Redonda. During his stay there, he met a woman named Estrella (although some sources claim her name was Marucha), and they fell deeply in love. However, at the time, Lara may have been involved with another woman, which made Estrella extremely jealous. In a moment of rage, she attacked him with a razor, leaving a deep and permanent scar on his face.

Machito & Mario Bauza

When they were starting, Machito and Mario Bauza were members of the *Los Jóvenes de la Rendención* band.

One of the first timbaleros of significance in the United States was the Cuban Antonio Escollies, a.k.a. "El Cojito."

Pérez Prado was the first pianist and one of the earliest arrangers of La Sonera Matancera in 1936.

Joe Loco

As a young man, pianist José Estevez, a.k.a. Joe Loco, was groomed to be a Vaudeville dancer and danced for the Chick Webb band as a teenager. Joe Loco died in San Juan in 1988, two years after having a leg amputated.

The Latin Music Trivia Book

During the mid-to-late 1930s, Victoria Hernández, the sister of the renowned Puerto Rican singer and composer Rafael Hernández, offered piano lessons to two future superstars, Tito Puente, and Joe Loco. Tito expressed his interest in playing the drums to Victoria, requesting that she inform his mother about his preference for drums over piano.

—∞—

Celia Cruz's beloved nephew, John Paul, passed away unexpectedly due to hemophilia.

—∞—

The Puerto Rican violinist and composer Julian Andino composed one of the best-known danzas ever written in 1870, "Margarita." Years later, in 1910, he wrote "El Seis Chorrea'o," later to become "El Seis de Andino."

—∞—

In the early 70s, television executives banned La Lupe from appearing on the airwaves in Puerto Rico after she went into a frenzy and tore her clothes off during a nationally televised awards ceremony, revealing more of her breast than was allowed.

—∞—

Celia Cruz's husband Pedro had type 1 diabetes, while Celia herself suffered from near-sightedness.

—∞—

Joe Hernández

In the September 1947 issue of *Dance Mania* magazine, it was reported that Gabriel Cansino, the cousin of the famous actress Rita Hayworth, and his partner and wife Lita, performed the first merengue dance at the Saint Moritz Hotel, which is now known as the Ritz-Carlton New York, located at 50 Central Park South.

With the aid of others, Mario Bauza discovered and was able to introduce this shy young singer to Chick Webb, and she became a significant figure in jazz history. Her name was Ella Fitzgerald.

Joe Quijano

Joe Quijano was born in Puerta De Tierra, San Juan, Puerto Rico on September 27, 1937. At seven, his family settled in the Bronx, New York City. At age 13, Joe joined the quintet *The Mamboys from Banana Kelly Street* in the Bronx as a bongócero (bongó player) and singer organized by Orlando Marín and pianist Eddie Palmieri.

Arsenio Rodríguez is regarded as the most important and influential musician in developing the conjunto style and instrumentation of the son montuno.

Chico O'Farrill, the legendary composer, musician, and band leader, married the beautiful Mexican singer, Guadalupe Valero.

Tito Rodríguez

Tito Rodríguez was born Pablo Rodríguez Lozada on January 4, 1923 in Barrio Obrero, Santurce, Puerto Rico. In 1939, he moved to New York to live with his brother Johnny Rodríguez; after singing for a short while with his brother, he went to work with Xavier Cugat and Noro Morales. Tito then did a brief stint with José Curbelo in 1946, during which he first played at the Palladium, before embarking on forming his band, the Mambo Devils, then the Mambo Wolves, and finally the Tito Rodríguez Orchestra.

―⟩⟩⟩―

Joe Cubas' song "Bang Bang" was the first boogaloo to sell a million copies and reached No. 63 on the US Billboard Hot 100 and No. 21 on the R&B chart.

―⟩⟩⟩―

The musical arranger for the tune "El Manicero" was Alfredo Brito (1896-1954).

―⟩⟩⟩―

In 1922, Cuba marked its first commercial radio station, PWX, operated by the Cuban Telephone Company. Initially, there were only 40 radios available for the public to listen to. However, the number of radio stations increased rapidly, and by 1924, the island had 24 stations with tens of thousands of listeners. Eventually, by 1939, the number of operating radio stations in Cuba reached 85.

―⟩⟩⟩―

Like his father, Ismael Rivera learned bricklaying from a vocational school. He was proud of his skills.

―⟩⟩⟩―

Ignacio Piñeiro Martínez (1888-1969) was a gifted musician, bandleader, and songwriter who composed over 327 numbers, mostly sones and a few rumbas. He learned to play the double bass from the renowned trovadora María Teresa Vera and was a member of her band, Sexteto Occidente, which recorded in New York City in the mid-1920s. In 1927, he formed the Sexteto Naciónal de Ignacio Piñeiro, which later evolved into the Septeto Naciónal. Some of his most popular songs include "Suavecito," "Mayeya, no Juegues con los Santos," "Échale Salsita," "Guaguancó Callejero" and "Lindo Yambú."

Tito Puente and Joe Hernandez celebrating Tito's 70th birthday.

Tito Puente

Tito Puente had a remarkable career, performing worldwide in various venues. He had the honor of performing at the White House multiple times.

Eddie Palmieri learned about the musical structures of Cuba at an early age from Manny Oquendo, who

Joe Hernández

scientifically and intuitively inspired Eddie to become a serious music student by studying the Schillinger System of Music (developed by Russian musical theorist Joseph Schillinger) with guitarist Bob Bianco.

Pedro Knight, the husband of Celia Cruz, played the lead trumpet for the *Sonora Matancera* between January 6, 1944 (Three Kings Day), and April 30, 1967.

Edmundo Ros

Edmundo Ros, a famous Latin band leader from Britain, was born in Venezuela to parents of Venezuelan and Scottish mulatto descent. He made his final performance at the age of 83 on January 8, 1994. Sadly, he passed away on October 21, 2011, just six weeks before his 101st birthday.

Graciela shared with this author that when she was six years old, a family friend who was a well-known singer told her father, "That child is going to be a singer; she is gifted with natural talent." The singer in question was none other than María Teresa Vera.

Mario Bauza played a significant role in launching Dizzy Gillespie's career in the Cab Calloway Orchestra. When Bauza was an orchestra member, he pretended to be sick so that Gillespie, a struggling young trumpet player with innovative musical ideas, could replace him and showcase his talent. This move helped Gillespie gain recognition and established himself as a prominent musician.

Pedro Flores collaborated with the Cuban pianist Peruchín to record "Si No Eres Tú," "Le Doy Mil Gracias," and "Botaron La Pelota" early in their careers.

Rafael Hernández composed his first song, "Virginia," when he was just 13 years old. He was deeply inspired by the beauty of Mexican theater actress Virginia Fabregas. Rafael had met her while working as a member of the orchestra that accompanied her during a performance in Aguadilla, Puerto Rico. However, it is worth noting that the waltz's lyrics and music do not hold any artistic significance.

It was Al Santiago, the man with an ear for talent, who first discovered Willie Colón. As a young trombonist and an employee at Santiago's record company, Colón would often take part in the Jam Sessions that Santiago promoted. Santiago was so captivated by Colón's musical prowess that he saw the potential for an album.

The album never became exposed. However, Johhny Pacheco, who had also heard Willie when Pacheco worked for Santiago, signed him up as soon as he founded Fania Records. "He was a rough diamond," Pacheco said on one occasion.

Moisés Simons

Moisés Simons, the composer of "The Peanut Vendor," spent two years in a German concentration camp because his last name was mistaken for a Jew. Moisés Simons died in Madrid, Spain, in 1945.

The authorship of the bolero "En la Orilla del Mar" (On the Seashore) was wrongly attributed to José Barros on some record labels. However, it belongs to José Berroa Riveras, a Cuban composer and violinist. This song was a massive success for Bienvenido Granda.

Cuban flutist Alberto Socarras-Estacio was born on September 18, 1908, in Manzanillo, Oriente, Cuba. At seven, his mother, Dolores, known as "Lolo," began to teach him how to play the flute. Years later, his mother, grandfather, two sisters, four uncles, and three cousins made up *La Familia Socarras Orchestra*. The band was hired to play at all the social and town functions, including the town's only silent movie house.

Eliseo Grenet

Way before Desi Arnaz did the conga dance during the New Year week of 1937-1938, Eliseo Grenet's "La

Conga" had already been published with a tune called "Havana is Calling Me." Also, British "Latin" musician Maurice Burman had composed another conga song two years prior. It originated in the festivities carried out by enslaved Black people. At the beginning of the Cuban Republic, it became an element of political propaganda used by the candidates in the pre-electoral period to move the popular masses behind their rhythm and songs, in which the politician's victory was advocated.

However, Desi Arnaz popularized the Conga in the United States. Desi formed a band in Miami and claimed it was the first and only "Típica" (typical) Cuban band in Florida, despite the band having two Italians, two Jews, and one Spaniard who never played Latin music.

During the first set of their debut performance, they were a disaster. During the second set, Desi has a moment of inspiration, grabs the Conga, and teaches his band a simple beat consisting of 1, 2, 3, and a kick. The dance is reduced to marching to the beat of the characteristic rhythm; alternately, in all the even measures, a syncopation stands out that the dancers emphasize by slightly raising one leg and marking the beat with a sudden body movement. It was an enormous success that made Desi famous, and soon, he had all of Miami dancing the Conga.

He then went to New York to play in a club named Conga in his honor. It was there that Roger and Hammerstein discovered Desi and brought him to Broadway. Broadway, in turn, opens the doors to Hollywood and the big screen.

The Cuban tres player "Mulaton" popularized the *tres* in the United States in 1930.

Initially, Daniel Santos was sympathetic to the *Fidelistas* in the Sierra mountains of Cuba. He composed "Sierra Maestra," a song that became the hymn of the Cuban Revolution. For this, the FBI "haunted" him for the next twenty years.

Al Santiago introduced Hector "Lavoe" Pérez to Willie Colon, but Lavoe initially didn't want to sing for Willie's orchestra because he thought Willie was a "thug."

Xavier Cugat understood Americans knew little about Latin music. He would put a beautiful woman at the forefront of his band to appeal more to their visual senses. In 1932, Cugat discovered Rita Hayworth, who was just thirteen years old at the time, and she seemed to be a perfect fit. Later, he hired Rosario and Antonio, a Spanish flamenco dancing team.

The first large-scale evening Latin dance in El Barrio was held in 1930 at the Golden Casino on 110th Street and Fifth Avenue, sponsored by a Puerto Rican civic association.

In 1939, at age sixteen, Tito Puente dropped out of Central Commercial High School, which later became the Norman Thomas High School for Business and Commercial Education, which closed in June 2014.

In 1947, Rafael Hernández returned to New York from Mexico due to issues with another woman named Celia Luna, who was jealous of him. After staying with his sister for a month, he left for Puerto Rico. In Puerto Rico, Rafael continued to work and eventually retired. During his last days in 1962, after being diagnosed with terminal cancer, Rafael confided in his sister Victoria that the only woman he had ever loved was Juanita, the woman he had lived with for 15 years in Puerto Rico.

Carmen Miranda

In 1939, Carmen Miranda (1909-1955) found herself in esteemed company as she made her American debut.

She appeared in the finale of the Broadway *Show on the Streets of Paris,* a revue that featured the comedic duo Abbott and Costello and the renowned French singer Jean Sablon. Carmen's unique style, including her trademark six-inch heels and fruit basket headdress, was a standout in the performance, catapulting her to instant stardom.

María Luisa Lecompte was an exceptionally talented Puerto Rico musician specializing in classical music. She was also the mother of Luis Carlos Varona, a pianist who played for Machito. At her music school, 112 East 116th Street in New York City, she taught piano to many aspiring musicians, including Tito Puente and Joe Quijano, who became famous percussionists. Lecompte, born in Puerto Rico into a family of professional musicians, held a prestigious position in the opera orchestra of Puerto Rico. She was married to Luis Humberto Varona, a Cuban concert violinist, and they both lived at 234 West 114th Street, just a few blocks from her music school.

Carlos "Patato" Valdés was the cousin of Francisco Fellove, a prominent Cuban songwriter, singer, and composer of the *Feeling* generation, also known as "El Gran Fellove."

One of Ismael Rivera's most famous songs is "Las Caras Lindas" (de mi gente negra...of my black people), written by prolific Puerto Rican composer Tite Curet Alonso.

Joe Hernández

Spike Jones & Pérez Prado

Dámaso Pérez Prado was born on December 11, 1916, in Matanzas, Cuba. He began his career in the 1940s, playing with legendary musicians like Arsenio Rodríguez and Miguelito Valdés. He worked as a pianist and arranger for the *Sonora Matancera*, a dance orchestra that gained international success from his hometown. Pérez became the most recognizable pianist and bandleader of the 1950s mambo craze and is credited with introducing the mambo to audiences in the U.S.A. Sadly, he passed away on September 14, 1989, in Mexico City, Mexico, due to complications from a stroke at the age of 72.

While in Mexico, Bény Moré learned that his nickname, Bartolo, meant "donkey," so he changed it to Bény.

In the late 1930s, Machito met Hilda Torres, a beautiful Puerto Rican girl. They married on January 17, 1940.

Shortly after their marriage, Machito changed his nickname from "Macho."

The renowned series of descargas, *Cuban Jam Sessions in Miniature*, was recorded for the Panart label in 1957. The album was subtitled *Cachao y Su Ritmo Caliente*. It was done in less than five hours, from 4 to 9 a.m. All the musicians had finished their contractual gigs before recording.

In the early to mid-1930s, Julio Roque, a successful dentist and part-time musician, operated the first radio Latin music show in Spanish Harlem called *Revista Roque* (Roque's Revue). He broadcasted over Radio WABC, which became independent under the CBS banner. Julio Roque was the son of a wealthy white family from Aguadilla, Puerto Rico. Despite the Depression, he played a vital role in the flourishing of Latin music in El Barrio.

La Lupe, the famous Cuban singer, was known for her unique musical style, blending Latin, African, and American music elements. She was born in Cuba and was partially of French descent, which added to her diverse cultural background and influenced her artistic expression. La Lupe's music was adored by many, and she is still remembered as a legendary figure in the Latin music industry.

Joe Hernández

In 1949, the Latin music scene witnessed a significant event. Two famous Latin musicians, Tito Rodríguez and Tito Puente, decided to leave *José Curbelo's Orchestra*, a well-known Latin band, to pursue their own musical careers. This amicable split not only allowed each of them to form their own bands, but also set in motion a new era in Latin music. Their bands went on to achieve enormous success, and this decision became a significant turning point in their careers, solidifying their legacies as influential musicians in the genre.

During the 1930s, Jewish theaters in East Harlem became Latin nightclubs, and their names changed to reflect this transformation. For example, the Photoplay Theatre became the San José, and the Mount Morris at 116th and Fifth Avenue was renamed the Campoamor.

Augusto Cohen (1896-1970) was the first director and organizer of the first Puerto Rican orchestra in New York. He also founded and became the first director of the Music Band of the Public Parks and Recreation Administration in San Juan.

Ernesto Lecuona's melodious bolero, originally titled "Si No Puedo Yo Quererte" (If I Cannot Love You), underwent a significant transformation. Its journey to success began when it was featured in the movie Always in My Heart. Lecuona altered the song's title to better resonate with the American audience, giving birth to the iconic "Always in My Heart."

Bola De Nieve

Bola de Nieve was a renowned Cuban singer, pianist, and songwriter. He was born as Ignacio Jacinto Villa y Fernández in 1911 in Guanabacoa, La Habana. Initially, he worked as a chauffeur, but he also played the piano for silent films. He gained recognition when his friend Rita Montaner invited him to play as an accompanist in the early 1930s. During his school days, one of his classmates gave him the nickname "Bola de Nieve" to tease him about his round black face. At one of his concerts, Montaner introduced him as "Bola de Nieve" jokingly, and the nickname stuck ever since. Unfortunately, he passed away while visiting Mexico in 1971 when he was only 60 years old.

Joe Hernández

Rita Moreno

Rosa Dolores Alverio, a.k.a Rita Moreno, was born in Humacao, Puerto Rico, on December 11, 1932. She was the first Hispanic actress to win an Oscar and made the Guinness Book of Records for being the first person to win show business's four major prizes: the Oscar, the Grammy, the Tony, and the Emmy. By age 11, she earned money by imitating the actress and singer Carmen Miranda. She once had a toxic Romantic relationship with Marlon Brando that lasted eight years, over whom she attempted suicide in his home. Marlon also had Rita abort their child.

Manuel "Canario" Jiménez received his professional nickname from a merchant marine captain who caught him singing while he was supposed to be painting. The captain reprimanded him, saying, *"You are always singing like a canary, and you don't work!"* The nickname" Canario" has stuck with him ever since.

Armando Manzanero Canche (1935-2020) was a Mexican musician, singer, composer, actor, and producer. In 1950, at fifteen, he composed his first Melody, "Nunca en el Mundo" (Never in the World). This song has been recorded in twenty-one different versions and languages.

Olga Guillot, at the age of 20, performed with Edith Piaf, France's most popular and famous singer and one of the most celebrated performers of the last century.

Noro Morales

The Puerto Rican pianist Noro Morales, who was twenty-four when he emigrated to New York City in 1935, began his first gig in El Barrio in the pit at the Teatro Hispano on 116th Street and Fifth Avenue. He

Joe Hernández

then played with Alberto Socarras and Augusto Cohen before he and his brothers Humberto and Esy created the *Morales Brothers Orchestra* in 1939.

On May 16, 2011, the United States Postal Service issued a commemorative stamp featuring the legendary Cuban American singer, Celia Cruz. The stamp was part of the USPS's Music Icons series, which honors musicians significantly contributing to American culture. Celia Cruz, also known as the "Queen of Salsa," was a prominent figure in the Latin music industry for over five decades, and her music influenced countless artists worldwide. Through this stamp, the USPS sought to celebrate her life and legacy and recognize her as one of our time's most influential and iconic musicians.

Vikki Carr is a renowned Mexican American singer born Florencia Bisenta de Casillas Martinez Cardona. She has significantly impacted the music industry with her soulful voice and won numerous awards throughout her career. Born on July 19, 1941, in El Paso, Texas, Vikki Carr began her career in the music industry in the early 1960s. She has released over 60 albums in her career, with many of her songs reaching the top of the charts. Her full name, Florencia Bisenta de Casillas Martinez Cardona, reflects her Mexican heritage and family background.

Morris Levy, the impresario, requested Tito Puente be the backup orchestra for Rafael Cortijo and Ismael Rivera's album *Bienvenido Cortijo y Rivera*. Both Cortijo and Rivera had returned from jail on drug-related charges, and Tito's involvement was a way to help them jumpstart their careers. However, the copy of the LP does not mention Tito Puente's orchestra.

Pérez Prado's rendition of "Cherry Pink and Apple Blossom White" is this tune's most widely recognized version. It topped the U.S. Billboard charts in 1955 as a lively mambo. Other versions include "Cerezo Rosa" (original title), "Ciliegi Rosa," and the English version "Gummy Mambo." The song's original title is "Cerisiers Roses et Pommiers Blancs," written in 1950 by Louis Guglielmi, who used the pen name Louiguy. Guglielmi was a Spanish-born French musician of Italian descent.

In 1962, Tito Rodríguez released an album titled *Tito Rodríguez Hits* under United Artists, which included three phenomenal hits, "Vuela La Paloma," "Cuando, Cuando," and "Cara De Payaso."

Johnny Segui suggested Mongo Santamaría to Tito Rodríguez, but Tito disliked Mongo's bongó playing and instead chose to hire Chino Pozo.

Pedro López, Cachao's father, played as a flutist with *Tata's Pereira charanga* band in the early 1930s alongside Anselmo Sacasas. Tata's charanga orchestra was among the first to introduce a saxophone and a trumpet into this type of band arrangement as early as 1933.

In 1952, Mongo Santamaria became a sideman for Pérez Prado during a tour of Texas and Brazil. While traveling through Texas in a bus, the driver fell asleep at the wheel and crashed into the side of a bridge. As a result, Mongo's right ankle was almost severed by a jagged piece of metal. However, he underwent immediate surgery, which saved his leg from amputation.

Larry Harlow & Joe Hernández

Larry Harlow, a legendary salsa musician known as "El Judío Maravilloso," was born on March 20, 1939, in the Brownsville neighborhood of Brooklyn. His mother, Rose Sherman, was an opera singer who used the same stage name, and his father, Buddy Kahn, was a bandleader at the Latin Quarter in New York for over twenty years, performing under the name Buddy Harlow.

The Cuban songwriter and composer Osvaldo Farrés, best known for having written the famous song "Quizás, Quizás, Quizás," dedicated the song "Madrecita" to his mother in 1954, which then became the anthem of the Mothers of Cuba. However, there is something very paradoxical in all this since she could never hear the song because she was deaf. It is still sung in Latin America on Mother's Day.

Federico Pagani (Center)

Federico Pagani (1907-1987) started the *Los Happy Boys* band in 1936. He had previously worked for Vicente Sigler as his band boy. Later, he became a successful promoter and convinced the owner of the Dreamland Dancing Academy (also known as Alma Dance Studios), located on 53rd and Broadway, to let him promote Latin nights. This boosted the business and eventually led to the academy's transformation into the famous Palladium

Joe Hernández

on March 15, 1946. The Palladium became home to New York's big band mambo.

―∽―

In 1930, four musicians from Cuba sailed together to New York. Each one of them, in their unique way, would influence the development of Latin music in the United States. These four musicians were "Mulaton," a *Tresero*, Don Azpiazú, a singer named Antonio Machín, and Mario Bauza, who played the clarinet, saxophone, and trumpet.

―∽―

In 1967, Willie Colón, an unknown 17-year-old, sold 30,000 copies of his first album, El Malo. These numbers rivaled those of many established salsa artists of his day.

―∽―

While imprisoned at "The Tombs," Ismael Rivera fell into a deep depression. His friend and composer, Bobby Capó, wrote the song "Las Tumbas" (The Tombs) for Rivera.

―∽―

On May 10, 1960, the *Trío Matamoros* gave their final, bittersweet performance. They bid farewell on the *Partagas Thursday* program, one of the most popular Cuban TV shows and a stage where they had witnessed their musical journey. Miguel Matamoros, a man torn between his love for music and his political beliefs, did not support the Cuban revolution. He could not bear to represent a communist country through his music. As a result, he made the painful decision to stop playing, choosing silence over compromise.

—∞—

Mario Bauzá's musical journey is a testament to his exceptional talent and unwavering dedication. He first arrived in New York City to record with *Antonio María Romeu's charanga orchestra,* then returned to Cuba. In a remarkable turn of events, he found himself back in the Big Apple in 1930, this time recording with Antonio Machín's *Cuarteto Machín* as a trumpet player. What's more astonishing is that he had only picked up the trumpet two weeks prior, teaching himself by listening to the likes of Louis Armstrong, Phil Napoleon, and Red Nichols. This rapid learning process is a testament to his innate musicality and passion for his craft. However, there is evidence that he had been playing the trumpet earlier in his career in Cuba, having taken lessons in Havana in 1928 with Lazaro Herrera, who was part of *Ignacio Piñeiro's Septet.*

—∞—

Johnny Ventura was a well-known singer, bandleader, lawyer, and politician. Born as Juan de Dios Ventura Soriano on March 8, 1940, in Santo Domingo, Dominican Republic, he was considered the "Elvis of Merengue." During his career, he released over 100 albums and won six Latin Grammys. Ventura served as a legislator of the Lower House from 1982 to 1986 and later became the vice mayor of Santo Domingo from 1994 to 1998. He was then elected as the mayor of the same city and served from 1998 through 2002.

—∞—

Joe Hernández

José Fajardo

José Antonio Fajardo, a Cuban flutist, was a highly regarded bandleader in Latin music. He recorded more than forty albums for various recording labels, half of which were made as guest players. After moving to Havana in 1936, he briefly served as a policeman and then as a soldier in the Cuban army.

The influential trumpeter and bandleader Tony Pabón almost died early on New Year's Day in 1976. Pabón performed at St. Joséph's Hall in New Jersey in front of a packed house of dancers celebrating the New Year. As soon as Pabón hit a high note as his orchestra played the mambo "El Capitán," he fell to his knees in excruciating pain. After a few minutes, Pabón regained his composure and continued the night's performance.

Later that night, he awoke to blood pouring from his nose and mouth. Immediately, he went to the hospital, where he was diagnosed with a ruptured vessel, causing his pancreas to burst, and causing heavy internal bleeding. Skillful hospital personnel closed the ruptured artery, pumped the remaining blood from his stomach, and saved his life. After several months of recovery and back to normal health, Pabón retired as an active musician and became a distributor for Ritmo Records in South America and the Caribbean.

In February 1932, George Gershwin took a two-week vacation to Havana, Cuba, a trip that would inspire one of his most celebrated works. It was during this trip that he was introduced to Ignacio Piñeiro, a musician whose hit song "Echale Salsita" would have a profound impact on Gershwin's music. The opening motif of Gershwin's Cuban Overture was a direct result of this influence. Gershwin composed the piece in July and August of 1932, and it premiered as "Rumba" at New York's Lewisohn Stadium on August 16, 1932. The performance was a sensation, with over 18,000 people in attendance and over 5,000 unable to get in. This overwhelming response was a testament to the immediate impact and appeal of Gershwin's work. To prevent the piece from being perceived as a mere novelty, the title was changed to "Cuban Overture" three months later at a benefit concert at the Metropolitan Opera.

Bola de Nieve grew up in Guanabacoa, Cuba, with thirteen siblings. During his youth, he would play at silent movie houses with his friend, Cachao López.

Don Azpiazú

Don Azpiazú hired black and white musicians in 1930, breaking the color barrier in Cuban bands.

The Puerto Ricans Luis Wito Kortright and Pete Bonet were the first singers in Ray Barreto's *Charanga La Moderna* band.

In the late 1950s, Cheo Feliciano worked as a band boy for Tito Rodríguez. When Willie Torres left the *Joe Cuba Sextet,* Tito recommended Cheo Feliciano as a replacement. This turned out to be a wise decision, as Cheo Feliciano, whose real name was José Luis Angel Feliciano-Vega and was born in Ponce, Puerto Rico, on July 3, 1935, played a significant role in the success of the *Joe Cuba Sextet*. On October 5, 1957, the day Cheo was getting married to Socorro 'Coco' Prieto, he started playing with the sextet. He went straight to the dance hall where the sextet had a gig, played until 5 a.m., and then returned to his new bride to leave for their honeymoon.

Olga Guillot began her singing career in 1938 on a radio show titled *La Corte Suprema del Arte*. On the show, she performed the song "Lluvia Gris" (translated as "Grey Rain"), a rendition of "Stormy Weather." The radio show was top-rated and served as a platform for many emerging talents at the time. Interestingly, the show was like the United States Gong Show, where a bell would ring if the talent did not impress the audience.

Daniel Santos

Daniel Santos started as a singer in his teens in an unconventional way. One day, he was taking a shower down the hall from the little room where he lived alone. As the young Santos was showering, he began singing one of two songs he knew, a guaracha from Rafael

Hernández. Santos got a knock on the door in the middle of his inspiration. He opened the door to be greeted by one of the members of the *Trío Lirico*, a local musical group. The fellow complimented him on his singing and asked Santos to meet the other group members.

Following an informal audition, Santos was warmly received by the group members, who were impressed by his talent. They extended an invitation for him to perform with them at a local gathering, which took place on September 13, 1930. For each song he sang at such local social events, Santos was paid a humble sum of one dollar. This modest start marked the birth of Santos's illustrious singing career.

Armando Peraza was a childhood friend of Mongo Santamaría. During a difficult period, he resorted to becoming a loan shark to make ends meet. In 1964, he collaborated with Cal Tjader to produce the album *Soul Sauce*. The single "Guachi Guara" from the album was awarded a Grammy in 1965.

114th Street and Fifth Avenue were commonly referred to as "congueros corner" because it was a popular gathering spot for many percussionists, including Willie Bobo, Pupi Torres, Negrito Pantoja, Chonguito, Patato Valdés, Santos Miranda, and Gilberto Calderón.

The impresario Al Santiago loved music so much that he named two of his four children Melody and Clef.

When Marc Anthony was a young teenager starting his career as a singer, he used to wear his hair loose and long. One day, his friend and producer "Little" Louie Vega took him to meet the famous salsa singer Héctor Lavoe. According to Anthony, upon meeting him, Lavoe said, *"Ave Maria, what an ugly chick!"*

Victoria Hernández and María Luisa Lecompte were crucial in nurturing the musical careers of renowned artists such as Tito Puente, Charlie and Eddie Palmieri, Joe Quijano, Paquito Pastor, Héctor Rivera, and Art Azenzer.

In the early 1940s, Noro Morales, Joe Loco, Tito Puente, Tito Rodríguez, Arsenio Rodríguez, Ray Coen, and General Colin Powell lived within walking distance of each other in the Bronx.

Celido Faustino Curbelo y Valdés, a renowned pianist and orchestra director from Cuba, was born on February 15, 1911, in Havana. He was also the uncle of the famous pianist and music impresario José Curbelo (1917-2012). In 1937, Faustino joined Xavier Cugat's orchestra and then started his own. He lived in Miami, Florida, until his passing at the age of 112. Despite his age, he stayed mentally sharp and lucid until the end of his life.

Joe Hernández

El Niño Rivera

Andrés Echevarría Callava (1919-1996), known as Niño Rivera, was born in Pinar del Río, Cuba. By the time he was five years old, he was already a bongócero with the *Septeto Caridad*. By age nine, he was playing with the *Septeto Segundo Bologna* as a *tresero,* and at age eleven, he was the timbalero of *Nicomedes Callavas Charanga*.

Desi Arnaz began his career in the United States as a singer for Xavier Cugat.

Ray Barretto was a percussionist and Army veteran who became one of the first Latin musicians to achieve a successful crossover hit. In 1962, he recorded "El Watusi" under Tico Records, which became a popular tune on the American pop charts. It debuted on the Billboard Hot 100 singles chart on April 27, 1963, and remained there for nine weeks, peaking at No. 17. The song sold over one million copies.

Myrta Silva was known by many nicknames, including "The Queen of Guaracha," "Café con Leche," "La Gorda de Oro," and "Madame Chencha."

The Puerto Rican Casimiro Duchesne, born in San Juan in 1852, composed the zarzuela "Cada Loco con su Tema."

Patato Valdés (Left)

Carlos "Patato" Valdés, a Cuban percussionist, musician, bandleader, and composer, was born on November 4, 1926, in Habana. His real name was Carlos Valdés Galan. Valdés was not just any musician, but a highly regarded one. Tito Puente, a respected figure in the music industry, once bestowed upon him the title of *"The greatest conguero alive today."* This recognition speaks volumes about Valdés' talent and his significant contributions to Cuban music.

Valdés had several nicknames, some of which were not very favorable. Due to his small size, he was called "Potato" in school. In his boyhood neighborhood, he was named "Remache" and "Tampon de Banera," which were disrespectful. As a young dancer and boxer, he was called "El Toro" (The Bull). Because of his unique dancing style, he was also called "Pinguino" (Penguin). Valdés was also known as "El Zombie," "Zombito," or "Pequeño Zombie" (Little Zombie).

It's worth noting that "Potato" is also the Yoruba word for "tiny."

Promoter Catalino Rolón suggested Orchestra Broadway as the band's name, as most of the group's members lived near Broadway Avenue.

Xavier Cugat, a bandleader, would only hire Puerto Ricans to play in his orchestra if they had light skin color. He would never hire individuals with dark complexions. In the 1940s, when color restrictions in New York were relaxed, he refused to hire singer Bobby Capó, telling him, "What a pity you are so dark." This was a business decision, as Cugat did not want to upset or provoke a violent response from his patrons during his Southern tours. Noro Morales, a Puerto Rican pianist and bandleader, had a similar policy.

The Great Cuban bass player, Cachao, was also an excellent bongó player.

Lou Pérez

Lou Pérez was a renowned musician, best known for his composition "De Todo un Poco," featured in the popular 1987 movie Dirty Dancing, where Patrick Swayze and Jennifer Grey danced to his music. His charanga group was among the best in the early 1960s. Lou wrote over 300 compositions recorded by legendary musicians such as Tito Puente, Johnny Pacheco, Roberto Ledesma, Machito, Celio González, and others. Unfortunately, Lou passed away on May 27, 2005, due to injuries he suffered when he was hit by a car while crossing a street in New York City. Interestingly, this author had spoken to him on the phone just the day before his demise.

Peter Ríos, a commercial artist from Puerto Rico, founded the magazine Latin New York. From 1973 to

1985, it was led by Izzy Sanabria until it eventually folded.

Manuel Jiménez (center)

Manuel Jiménez, also known as "Canario," was born in 1895 in Barros, now called Orocovis. He is believed to be the first Puerto Rican to record music in New York City and played a crucial role in popularizing the plena music genre in the United States. Despite his success, he had an adventurous and often troubled life, frequently traveling the world by stowing away on ships. He also spent time in prison for failing to pay his debts.

The Bolero "Nosotros" has been sung by over 400 artists, including Plácido Domingo, Luis Miguel, and Sara Montiel. It was initially written by Pedro Junco as a farewell letter to his girlfriend when he was diagnosed with tuberculosis, an incurable disease at the time.

Tony Chiroldes first performed the song on the Pinar del Río CMAB radio station in February 1943. Unfortunately, Pedro Junco passed away on April 25, 1943, in Havana, Cuba, just a few months after he wrote the song.

Pedro wrote the song "Nosotros" shortly before his death when he was sick with tuberculosis. The song was dedicated to his great love, María Victoria Mora Morales, a beautiful young woman from high society in Cuba. However, María's family disapproved of Pedro's romance with her, as he had a reputation as a seducer. Her father even prohibited her from seeing Pedro, but they kept meeting secretly.

Shortly before he died, Pedro asked his friend Tony Chiroldes to perform the song "Nosotros" on a top-rated radio program. The song was received with enormous success by the listening audience. María Victoria was present at Pedro's funeral, and the attendees sang the song "Nosotros" in his memory.

Dave Valentín, a Puerto Rican Latin jazz flutist and Grammy winner, was born on April 29, 1952. He was known for carrying up to twelve diverse types of flutes to his performances. Jazziz Magazine readers voted him the "best jazz" flutist for seven consecutive years. He toured with the legendary Tito Puente and served as the music director of Tito's Golden Latin Jazz All-Stars for a few years.

Before his music career, Valentín was a junior high school teacher in the South Bronx for three years. Sadly, he passed away on March 8, 2017, due to complications of a stroke and Parkinson's disease in the Bronx, New York, at the age of 64.

Governor Luis Muñoz Marín

The Puerto Rican Governor, Luis Muñoz Marín, who at one time was a fierce independentist but became a staunch ally of the United States, had the word tirano (tyrant) officially changed to destino (destiny) in Rafael Hernández's composition "Preciosa." He did so sometime in the late 1940s with no apparent objection from Hernández, giving the impression that he favored the change. The public outcry was fierce, and Hernández fell into disgrace. However, Hernández formally reestablished the word tirano in the song.

However, both versions of the song have circulated to this day. Muñoz had also tried to delete several words from "Lamento Borinicano" on a prior occasion but was unsuccessful.

The dissolution of *Cortijo's Combo* gave rise to two great orchestras: *El Gran Combo*, founded by Cortijo's pianist Rafael Ithier, and *Los Megatones,* which later became known as *Roberto Roena y Su Apollo Sound,* founded by the bongócero Roberto Roena.

Xavier Cugat

Xavier Cugat (1900-1990) was born as Francisco de Asis Javier Cugat Mingall de Bru y Deulofeu in Girona, Catalonia, Spain. He married Rita Montaner as his first wife, followed by Carmen Castillo, Lorraine Allen, the voluptuous Abbe Lane, and the singer Charo.

―∽―

In the 1950s, Jose Fajardo was Cuba's most popular and famous personality.

―∽―

At the height of his popularity in Mexico, Pérez Prado was unexpectedly deported to Havana in 1953 because he lacked a work permit. Prado was arrested in his dressing room backstage. He was not allowed to return until 1964.

Celia Cruz

Celia Cruz's philanthropic work was not just about building homes but also about building futures. Her donations helped construct homes for underprivileged children in Nicaragua, Peru, Venezuela, Honduras, and Costa Rica. Moreover, her creation of The Celia Cruz Foundation has been instrumental in providing scholarships to young Latinos, paving the way for a brighter future in music education.

Although *La Sonora Matancera* was a well-established and popular band before Celia Cruz joined them, she provided the orchestra with the best years and catapulted their fame worldwide. In turn, *La Sonora* elevated Celia's fame throughout the world.

The Latin Music Trivia Book

In the late 1980s, Héctor Lavoe's mother-in-law, whom he loved like a mother, was murdered in Puerto Rico. She was stabbed multiple times as she was leaving her home. Shortly after that, his father died, and then his oldest son, Héctor Pérez Jr., was killed in an accident from a shooting.

In 1958, Eddy Zervigon, the musical director and flutist of Orquesta Broadway, was studying to be a meteorologist; one year later, he changed his mind and decided on a music career.

Charlie Palmieri initially hired Johnny Pacheco as a drummer. However, when Mario Cora, the trumpeter, left for Puerto Rico, Pacheco started playing solos on the flute.

The Puerto Rican singer Ismael Rivera joined the U.S. Army in 1952 but was quickly discharged because he could not speak English. Rivera perpetuated this fraud by pretending he did not know the language to get discharged.

The Puerto Rican musician and orchestra leader from Ponce, Augusto Coen (1895-1970), played professional

Joe Hernández

baseball before enlisting in the U.S. Army during World War I.

—⚘—

Juan Tizol Martínez

Juan Tizol Martínez (1900-1984) was a jazz trombonist and composer born in Vega Baja, Puerto Rico. He was a member of Duke Ellington's big band and is best known for composing several popular jazz tunes, including "Caravan," "Pyramid," "Moonlight Fiesta," "Jubilesta," "Conga Brava," and "Perdido." Tizol also played with other notable musicians, such as the Harry James Orchestra, Nelson Riddle, and Louis Bellson, and he even performed on Nat King Cole's television show. Unfortunately, Tizol passed away at the age of 84 due to a heart attack in Inglewood, California.

—⚘—

Celia Cruz received her Hollywood Walk of Fame star on September 17, 1987.

—⚘—

Sid Torrin

In the summer of 1948, the police raided the apartment of Sid Torrin (born Sidney Tarnopol 1909-1984), known professionally as "Symphony Sid," a long-time jazz and Latin music disc jockey. He was arrested on charges of marijuana possession. Despite this, he continued to broadcast while waiting for his trial, ending in a mistrial in late January 1949.

Despite the controversies surrounding Symphony Sid, the Rock and Roll Hall of Fame in Cleveland staff included him in a display featuring history's most influential disc jockeys.

Felipe Pirela, the Venezuelan interpreter of bolero music, was born as Felipe Antonio Pirela Morón in Maracaibo in 1941. Unfortunately, Pirela struggled with deep depression, which led him to use drugs and alcohol. Tragically, he was murdered in the early morning of July 2, 1972, in San Juan, Puerto Rico, by a local drug dealer named Rosado Medina. Medina confessed to killing

Pirela ten days later, saying that it was due to money owed to him by Pirela that was not paid. The police arrested Medina and brought him to justice for his crime.

Young Mario Bauza (Center)

Mario Bauza received an early education from private teachers and public bands. As a child, he played in the *Havana Symphonic Orchestra,* performing operas, ballets, zarzuelas, and other classical works.

Ricky Martin, whose birth name is Enrique Martin Morales, initially auditioned for Menudo twice without success before being accepted on his third try at 12. He became a child star pop singer in the group.

Celia Cruz refrained from excessive talking leading up to performances and limited communication on the day of her engagements.

In early 1943, Uncle Sam drafted several members of the *Machito Orchestra,* including tenor saxophonist José "Pin" Madera, alto saxophonist Johnny Nieto, pianist Gilberto Ayala, Tito Puente, and finally Machito himself.

During her fifteen-year tenure with *Sonora Matancera,* Celia Cruz recorded over 180 songs. However, her most famous song worldwide is "El Yerberito Moderno."

Tito Puente dedicated the tune "Guaguancó Arsenio" to Arsenio Rodríguez, a great Cuban composer, musician, and band leader. The song features an extended piano solo by Tito and the timbales.

At an early age, Xavier Cugat's family moved to Havana, a city that would shape his musical destiny. Their neighbor, a violin maker, gifted Cugat with a small violin for Christmas, a gesture that would ignite his musical journey. By the age of 10, Cugat's prodigious talent had already propelled him to the stage, where he played as a classical violinist in a symphony orchestra, a testament to his early success.

Joe Hernández

Jimmy Sabater co-wrote "Bang, Bang," which appeared on the 1966 hit album *Wanted: Dead or Alive,* making it one of the most significant top forty Latin hits since the rock and roll hit "La Bamba" by Ritchie Valens.

Tito Rodríguez and Tobi

During one of their early dates, Tito Rodríguez asked his future wife Tobi to meet him in front of the Roseland Ballroom one early afternoon. Tito never showed up despite waiting for over two hours in torrential rain. Later that evening, when they both met at the China Club workplace, Tobi asked him why he didn't show up. Tito responded with a look of disbelief, *"Didn't you notice it was raining…did you want me to get wet?"*

On May 1, 1966, The Palladium, a famous Latin music ballroom, closed its doors permanently. The last three groups to perform on the stage were Ricardo Ray, Eddie Palmieri, and *Orquesta Broadway*. The final song that echoed on the dance floor was "Pare Cochero" by Broadway.

Bobby Capó

Bobby Capó arrived in New York City in 1939 to study law but needed more resources to make his dream come true. With the Depression still lingering, he found it much easier to find work as a vocalist, so he shifted gears and pursued a music career.

Besides singing, Celia Cruz began acting in the 1950s in a soap opera broadcasted by *Radio Progreso* in Cuba, to which she won the best actress award. She went on to work on a variety of film and television projects during her career.

The famed Latin dance hall, the Palladium Ballroom, was closed in 1966 when a police detective had the place raided because of suspicions that drugs were being used and sold.

Gloria Estefan became the first Hispanic songwriter inducted into the Songwriters Hall of Fame in June 2023, recognizing her accomplished career as a composer.

Armando Manzanero was a prolific Mexican composer who created over four hundred songs. Over fifty of his songs gained international acclaim and were performed by some of the most celebrated singers in the world, including Tito Rodríguez, Elvis Presley, Frank Sinatra, Tony Bennett, Perry Como, Andrea Bocelli, Dionne Warwick, Christina Aguilera, Shirley Bassey, Luis Miguel, and Marc Antonio Muñiz. Manzanero's immense contribution to the music industry led to his induction into the International Latin Music Hall of Fame in 2000.

Monchito Muñoz was born as Ramón Muñoz-Rodríguez on June 6, 1932, in San Juan, Puerto Rico. At the age of seven, he began taking piano lessons from Alicia, Noro Morale's sister. His father, Rafael, had an orchestra that performed at the El Escambrón Beach Club in 1935. The orchestra featured Noro Morales on piano. On October 24, 1955, Monchito played the drums for Tito Rodríguez in a twenty-minute Universal motion picture named Mambo Madness. The movie was filmed at Palm Gardens, Fiftieth Street, and Eight Avenue.

Augusto Cohen and his Golden Conjunto Orchestra

Augusto Cohen, born in Ponce, Puerto Rico, in 1895, was a man of many talents. He had a Jewish father and an Afro-Puerto Rican mother. In addition to being skilled in playing multiple instruments, Cohen was an excellent pitcher and played baseball across the island. After finishing high school, he joined the United States Army as a lieutenant during World War I. Following the war, Cohen moved to New York and began working at the post office. He initially planned to study Law at Columbia University but later pursued music. Before starting his orchestra, he played with some of the most prominent musicians of his time, such as Duke Ellington, Noble Sissle, Fletcher Henderson, and Eubie Blake.

Joe Hernández

Gilberto Monroig joined the *Tito Puente Orchestra* in the early 1950s and had many successful hits with Puente, including "Malcriada," written by the Cuban pianist Facundo Rivera.

Catalino "Tite" Curet Alonso, a prolific composer from Puerto Rico, graduated from the University of Puerto Rico, where he studied journalism and sociology. His career was marked by his versatility, spending over twenty years at the United States Postal Service and working as a sports columnist for the newspaper Diario/La Prensa in New York City. Despite his varied career, he was best known for his creativity as a composer of both songs and poetry.

Many songs that made the airwaves had sexual double entendres or criticized the U.S. government for its political domination of Puerto Rico. Because the songs were in Spanish, they slipped past the censors. Of these, there were plenty by Rafael Hernández, Pedro Flores, and many other composers. Rafael Hernández's super popular hit, "Menealo Que Se Empelota" (Shake It, Stir It Up, It's Hardening), recorded several times by his group Trío Borinquen, was heard throughout New York City and in many other parts of Latin America. It would never have become exposed if this song had been in English.

The Latin Music Trivia Book

**Bárbaro Jiménez Alfonso
(Celia Cruz's brother)**

Celia Cruz's brother Barbaro was a surprisingly good singer. According to Celia, he was never allowed to develop his potential and pursue a career in music because he was related to Celia, who needed to be in better standing with the Cuban government.

—∞—

Before coming to New York City from Puerto Rico, Héctor Lavoe had an older brother who had died in the city due to an overdose of heroin.

—∞—

Louis Moreau Gottschalk, a Creole composer, traveled to Caribbean islands such as Cuba and Puerto Rico in the 1850s. After returning to New Orleans, he introduced tropical rhythms like the habanera, which led to a fusion of diverse musical styles in the city.

Joe Hernández

During the late 1920s to early 1930s, a popular song typically sold about 10,000 records across the United States, with a few hundred more sold in countries like Cuba, Puerto Rico, and Santo Domingo. There was little to no advertising or publicity for these songs except for playing them on the radio and waiting for the public to buy them.

Oscar D'León was born Oscar Emilio Leon Somoza on July 11, 1943, in Caracas, Venezuela. Before becoming a Salsa music superstar, he would alternate jobs as an auto mechanic, assembly line worker, and cab driver.

Doc Severinsen, the Grammy-award-winning jazz trumpeter and former bandleader of *The Tonight Show*, frequently played as a "house" musician on various Latin recordings.

Bobby "Dedo Gordo" Rodríguez, a famous Cuban American bassist born in 1930 and passed away in 2000, was a renowned musician who left a significant mark on the Latin American music scene. His versatility was clear in his collaborations with more than 50 orchestras, a testament to his wide-ranging musical influence. The nickname "Dedo Gordo" was bestowed upon him by Mario Bauza.

The Story Behind the Iconic Song

En Mi Viejo San Juan

Noel Epifanio Estrada Suárez

Noel Epifanio Estrada Suárez was born in Isabela on June 4, 1918, and passed away on December 1, 1979. He was famous for composing the well-known song "En Mi Viejo San Juan." Estrada was a World War II Army veteran who created his most famous work in 1942.

The song is recognized worldwide and considered a second national anthem by many Puerto Ricans, primarily those living outside Puerto Rico. Estrada received international acclaim for his works during his lifetime.

The story behind the birth of this incredible song is as follows: on August 2, 1942, Noel Estrada was waiting for some soldiers to arrive who would take him to a recording session at a friend's house. The album was made for Puerto Rican soldiers stationed in Panama. While waiting, he recalled a letter from his brother Eloy, who was in the United States Army. In the letter, Eloy requested him to compose a song that would raise the patriotic sense of the Puerto Rican soldiers. Noel then went out to the house's balcony, where he could see the city's colors, faded by time and the sea. It appeared more beautiful to him than ever, and at that moment, inspiration struck. In less than ten minutes, he had written the lyrics and music of "En Mi Viejo San Juan," which he later recorded without imagining the impact it would have.

However, some have claimed that the author wrote this song in New York City. Regardless, this bolero has been popular outside of Puerto Rico, replacing "Lamento Borincano" by Rafael Hernández.

The song's first recording was by *El Trío Vegabajeño* in 1943 under the RCA Victor label and later under Mar-Vela. It is considered a classic and has been performed by dozens of artists, including Celia Cruz, Rafael Cortijo, Ismael Rivera, Libertad Lamarque, Marco Antonio Muñiz, Trío Los Panchos, Javier Solís, and Felipe Pirela, among many others.

Something anecdotal happened with this song. The day *El Trío Vegabajeño* went to record it with three other songs, Felipe Casanova, who was the representative of RCA, flatly refused to do it, citing the fact that the theme of the song was very regional, and the records had Latin American circulation. Alvarez, the trío's director, refused to record the other songs if "En mi Viejo San Juan" was omitted. Casanova had no choice but to accept Alvarez's decision.

An interesting aspect of the song "En Mi Viejo San Juan" is its similarity to "La Bata de Ollá," sung by

Miguelito Valdés with *Orquesta Casino de la Playa*. "La Bata de Ollá" was recorded under the Victor label on or before April 3, 1939, which predates "En Mi Viejo San Juan." It is worth noting that this is the first time this observation has been made that "En Mi Viejo San Juan" seems to have incorporated some elements from "La Bata de Ollá." At the very least, the melody appears to have been plagiarized.

The song has been heard in over 50 Mexican and 20 Puerto Rican motion pictures and recorded in multiple languages, including Japanese, German, Russian, and French. More than 1,000 distinct recordings of the song have been made worldwide.

Promoter and businessman Ralph Mercado began promoting "waistline parties" in his teens. These were live music events in basements of apartment buildings in which women paid an entrance fee proportional to their waist size. Mercado was sure to be at the entrance to measure the women himself.

Tito Puente's "Machito Forever" composition was commissioned by the Newport Jazz Latino and initially titled "Mambo Adonis." The piece would be performed simultaneously by the Puente, Machito, and Tito Rodríguez Orchestras at the Palladium Ballroom at the stroke of midnight on New Year's Eve for them to have *a mega descarga* (jam session) to bring in the New Year. Puente renamed it to honor Machito upon his death in 1984.

For $1.75, the Palladium offered mambo lessons, an amateur contest, a show, and two bands to dance the night away.

Armando Manzanero, a Mexican singer and composer, passed away at the age of 85 on December 28, 2020, due to complications caused by Covid-19.

Trini López was born Trinidad López III on May 15, 1937, in Dallas, Texas. He formed his first band at the age of 15. By the time he was 18, he was working with his band at The Vegas Club, a nightclub owned by Jack Ruby, the man who assassinated President Kennedy's alleged killer, Lee Harvey Oswald.

On June 7, 1993, Louie Ramírez, Bandleader, composer, arranger, and timbalero, suffered a fatal heart attack while driving on Junction Boulevard in Queens, New York. He was 55 years old.

Noro Morales had a reputation for buying songs from other talented composers and claiming them as his own. For example, he bought "110th Street and Fifth Avenue" from the brilliant music arranger and Mexican trumpet player Paul López and bought "Ponce" from Rubén

Berrios for one hundred dollars but gave himself credit as the composer for both songs.

Tito Puente had a lifelong dream of becoming a dancer, but unfortunately, his ambitions were cut short due to a bicycle accident in the 1930s. The accident caused a tear in his ankle tendon, forcing him to give up his dancing aspirations. Despite this setback, he continued with his passion for music and went on to tour with the *Jack Cole Dancers* as a musician.

Tito Puente's 1958 LP *Dance Mania* is regarded as one of his greatest works. The album marked the debut of singer Santos Colón and was a commercial success, selling an impressive 50,000 copies. This feat was particularly noteworthy in the Afro-Cuban genre. Dance Mania's success also played a pivotal role in launching Ray Barretto's career. Barretto had taken over from Mongo Santamaria in Tito's orchestra and recorded his first album.

According to an interview given by his brother Johnny Rodríguez, Tito Rodríguez's father was Don José Rodríguez-Fuentes, a Puerto Rican musician from San Sebastian del Pepino, who married Severina Niña Lozado of Holguin, Cuba. She gave birth to Tito on January 4, 1923, while they lived in Santurce, Puerto Rico, near "La Parada 18." She died in 1932 after the birth of her tenth child. Tito's dad passed away six months later.

Joe Hernández

Toña La Negra

Toña La Negra, born María Antonia del Carmen Peregrino Álvarez in Veracruz, Mexico, on October 17, 1912, was discovered by Mexican composer Agustín Lares at a party in Mexico City.

Jacinto "Pupi" Campo, a Cuban entertainer, dancer, and bandleader, got married with Betty Clooney, an American singer who happened to be Rosemary Clooney's sister. Rosemary was widely known for the song "Mambo Italiano." José Ferrer, a Puerto Rican actor and director of stage, film, and television, also known as José Vicente Ferrer de Otero y Cintron, was married to Rosemary. The Clooney sisters, Betty and Rosemary, were the aunts of George Clooney, the famous American actor and filmmaker.

Julio Iglesias has achieved the remarkable feat of being among the top 10 best-selling music artists of all time.

1925 was a crucial moment for the recording industry when the Victor and Columbia labels put the first electrically recorded and reproduced records on sale. The Brunswick label brought the first electric phonographs to the market.

In a pivotal moment in Latin music history, conguero Mongo Santamaría and bongócero Willie Bobo left the *Tito Puente band* in 1957 to embark on a new journey with bandleader Cal Tjader. This departure led to reshuffling the musical deck, with Puente bringing in the formidable Ray Barretto on conga and Johnny Pacheco on bongó to fill the void.

Introducing radio in Cuba gave people who were poor and not professionally trained a chance to become famous by taking part in radio talent competitions. Bény Moré and Celia Cruz began their careers and gained recognition by winning such contests.

Trini López got his first big break from Frank Sinatra. Sinatra recognized his talent and signed him to an eight-year contract with his label, Reprise Records. Today, Warner Music Group owns the label.

Joe Hernández

Eddie Palmieri

La Perfecta was the first band founded by Eddie Palmieri, a Grammy Award-winning pianist, bandleader, musician, composer, and arranger of Puerto Rican descent in 1961. He started the band under the Alegre record label of Al Santiago during the charanga craze in New York. "Muñeca" was his first big hit from his third album. The band eventually disbanded in 1968.

Gilberto S. Valdés, a Cuban bandleader born in 1905 and passed away in 1972, moved to New York City in 1952 and created the first charanga band. He played a significant role in training Johnny Pacheco as a flutist. However, according to the singer Pete Bonet, Spanish flutist Joe Cornera taught Pacheco how to play the flute.

During the time that Celia was in the hospital recovering after the removal of her left breast, her husband, Pedro Knight, had to undergo colon surgery at the same facility. For a few days, they were both recovering and sharing the same hospital room.

Gloria Estefan's father, José Manuel Fajardo, was involved in the Bay of Pigs Invasion, which unfortunately failed. During the invasion, Fajardo was captured by a member of Fidel Castro's army, who happened to be his cousin. He was subsequently imprisoned for almost two years before he was finally released. After his release, Fajardo moved to the United States, joined the military, and fought in the Vietnam War.

It was during his visit to England to obtain the opinion of a renowned specialist that Tito Rodríguez's leukemia diagnosis was revealed. While awaiting the results, Tito contracted British musicians to record his newly established record company's first album, *Inolvidable,* under the TR label.

In 1959, the United States stopped producing 78 RPM records.

Joe Hernández

The Cuban singer Roberto Torres founded New York's *Orquesta Broadway,* a swinging and long-lived cooperative charanga band.

Sindo Garay

Sindo Garay, a renowned Cuban *trova* musician, was born Antonio Gumersindo Garay García in Santiago on April 12, 1867. He was a disciple of Pepe Sánchez, the creator of Cuban bolero, and the cousin of Miguel Matamoros. Despite being musically illiterate, he taught himself the alphabet at the age of 16 and went on to become an exceptional composer of *trova* songs. Many of his songs, such as "Adios a la Habana," "Mujer Bayamesa," "Guarana," "El Huracán y la Palma," and "Perla Marina," have been recorded multiple times and continue to be recorded to the present day. Sindo Garay traveled to Paris in 1926 with Rita Montaner and sang his songs there for three months. He was famous for saying, *"Not many men have shaken hands with José Martí and Fidel Castro."* He lived to the age of 101, but there are reports that he may have been even older, as he celebrated his 100th birthday several times, usually due to financial constraints.

Pupi Campo Orchestra

Charlie Palmieri, known as Carlos Manuel Palmieri, made his mark on the music scene when he joined the prestigious *Jack Paar's Today Show* on CBS in the 1950s. As the pianist for the television band under the direction of Pupi Campo, he showcased his exceptional talent. His career reached new heights in the 1970s when he took on the role of musical director for Tito Puente's television show, *El Mundo de Tito Puente,* a testament to his musical prowess and influence.

Ismael Rivera was performing with *Cortijo's Combo* in Panama when he got arrested upon his return to San Juan, Puerto Rico, for having illegal drugs. He took the fall, sparing his fellow musicians from jail time as he was sentenced to four years in Kentucky. After his release from jail, Rivera formed his successful group of eight years called Ismael Rivera and *His Cachimbos*. Rivera went to prison several times, straining his musical career.

Bény Moré was married four times and had seven children. His first child, Hilda, was with his wife and cousin, Inesita Moré Armenteros. However, he had no children with his second wife, Juana Bo Canegra Duran, whom he married in Mexico in 1946.

Bény had two children - Bebo and Bény Jr. - with his third wife, Norayda Castillo, and his cousin. Both have made vocal recordings, and Bebo has even recorded with Tito Puente's orchestra.

Bény's fourth and final wife, Iraida Valdivia, gave birth to four children—two girls and two boys. The youngest, Juan Roberto, uses the stage name Bény Moré Jr. and performs in Puerto Rico, where he has lived since 1981.

In 1970, Armando Manzanero's song "Somos Novios" was reissued with new lyrics by Elvis Presley's composer Sid Wayne as "It's Impossible." Perry Cómo performed it and was nominated for a Grammy.

Tito Rodríguez's 25th Anniversary Performance LP was recorded live in a nightclub in Peru a few months after the release of his hot-selling LP *Palladium Memories* and one month before his death.

The Cuban composer and tenor poet Adolfo Utrera, who penned the verses of the famous song "Aquellos Ojos Verdes" (Those Green Eyes), informed his friends and family that he would take his own life. He was suffering from a contagious and incurable disease and preferred death over enduring pain and agony. Adolfo wrote his famous song in 1929, which is considered the first bolero composed for the piano. He dedicated the song to his younger sister, Conchita's eyes, who spent time with him in New York. Adolfo was the eldest of ten siblings and died on December 3, 1931, at 30.

In late 1959, Charlie Palmieri, wandering through the kitchen of a nightclub, discovered Johnny Pacheco practicing the flute. Impressed by his talent, Palmieri made a spontaneous decision to hire him. This led to a momentous occasion on New Year's Eve of 1959-60, when Palmieri's *Charanga Duboney* made its debut, with Pacheco on the flute. This was a significant event as Duboney's sound, distinct from the prevalent brass and saxophones of Cuban-based music in New York, challenged the status quo and left a lasting impact on the musical landscape.

Eddie Palmieri began his career in 1958 when he joined *Tito Rodríguez's Orchestra*. He left the group two years later to start his own independent career. In 1961, he formed *La Perfecta* and released eight albums with the band before disbanding it in 1968.

The media reported that the popular recorded guaguancó by Tito Rodríguez, "Avisale A Mi Contrario" (Let my Rival Beware), was part of the ongoing "riff" between Tito Rodríguez and Tito Puente. However, the fact is that the tune was composed by the Cuban composer Ignacio Piñiero in the 1930s when both "Titos" were young and had not yet met each other. Perhaps Tito Rodríguez intended to continue the rivalry, but the song's origin predates his feud with Tito Puente.

Augie and Margo

Augie and Margo were a dance team that played a significant role in popularizing the mambo. Augustin "Augie" Rodríguez (1928-2014) and Margo Bartolomei Rodríguez (1929-2019) were both born in New York City. Augie's father came to the United States from Spain, and his mother came from the Dominican Republic. Margo's parents were originally from Puerto Rico, and her father was of Corsican descent. They married in 1950 and became a famous dance team at Roseland and Palladium Ballroom.

In 1955, they debuted with Harry Belafonte at the Waldorf Astoria. They were often the opening act in Las Vegas for celebrities like Sammy Davis, Jr, Frank Sinatra, Dean Martin, and many others throughout the United States and Europe. They were also frequent guests on The Arthur Murray Show, The Steve Allan Show, and The Ed Sullivan Show. Moreover, they were honored to dance for Queen Elizabeth II and Presidents John F. Kennedy and Richard M. Nixon at the White House.

The Cuban percussionist Carlos "Patato" Valdés Galan (1926-2007) played the tres for the *Sonora Matancera* between 1943 and 1945 before becoming the group's conguero.

In the 1940s, when Joe Cuba was a teenager, his father owned a candy store on the ground floor of their apartment building on 115th Street in East Harlem. This account contradicts the narrative that Joe's father abandoned the family when he was young.

The United States saw the birth of the first commercial gramophones in the 1890s. These marvels of technology were sold at a hefty price of around $25 to $30, equivalent to $850 to $1,000 in today's market. This cost was higher than the average yearly family income, making the ownership of a gramophone a significant investment. However, the rapid advancement of technology soon made these innovative devices more affordable, with the price dropping to approximately $10 by the early 1900s.

—⟨⟨⟩⟩—

The Stories Behind El Sonero Mayor

Ismael Rivera was known as "El Sonero Mayor," a nickname that has been the subject of much debate among music enthusiasts and historians. Over time, different versions of the story have emerged, adding to the mystery. In one version, Ismael Rivera claimed that the Cuban producer Angel Maceda, who owned the Bronx Casino in New York, gave Ismael the nickname as Maceda heard it from Bény Moré. However, later, Ismael changed his story and claimed that Bény Moré had given him the nickname at the Palladium Ballroom. Bény's cousin, Chocolate, who was present, clarified that Bény had called Ismael the "Sonero Mayor de Puerto Rico."

On December 10, 2010, Puerto Rican trumpet player Elías Lopés García shared his version of events in an interview on YouTube. According to García, who was 13 at the time, the pivotal moment occurred during the shooting of *La Taberna India*, a TV show in Puerto Rico in 1958. Ismael Rivera and Bény Moré were part of the show, and it was during the rehearsal that Bény Moré bestowed the nickname upon Ismael. The catalyst for this was a Cuban comedian named Americo Castellano, who began to dance. As they watched him, Ismael improvised the now-iconic line, *"Castellano que bueno baila usted."*

However, García's account differs from what others remember of that day. Moreover, García had never shared his story before, waiting 52 years to tell his version of events after everyone had passed away. No one else has ever confirmed García's version of events. In the same video interview, Shorty Castro claimed that Bény Moré gave Ismael Rivera the nickname but seemed surprised when García said he was there. It seems odd that Ismael never told this story or took credit for the famous chorus line improvised that day.

Others recollected that Bény Moré was on tour in Puerto Rico in July 1958. At the same time, they were rehearsing for the TV show *La Taberna India,* where El Combo de Cortijo was also scheduled to perform with Ismael Rivera on vocals. When Bény Moré saw the Cuban comedian Americo Castellanos dance, Bény improvised the song *"Castellano Que Bueno Baila Usted!"*

The term "Sonero Mayor" carries significant weight in Cuban and Puerto Rican music. It was a title bestowed upon performers with exceptional sonero skills, such as Orlando 'Cascarita' Guerra and Abelardo Barroso. Catalino 'Tite' Curet Alonso, a renowned Puerto Rican Salsa composer, also referred to Ismael, Cascarita, and Barroso as "Soneros mayores." This context is crucial in understanding the honor and recognition of the title, further adding to the intrigue surrounding Ismael Rivera's nickname.

The term "sonero mayor" has multiple meanings and stories behind its origin, suggesting that it is not unique or belongs to just one person like Ismael Rivera.

Regardless of the true origins of Ismael Rivera's nickname or who bestowed it upon him, one thing is clear—he was a musical legend. His immense talent and contributions to Puerto Rican music earned him the title of "Sonero Mayor de Puerto Rico." Whether Bény More baptized Rivera with this monicker or not, Rivera's fans and those who loved his music did think of him as El Sonero Mayor. This author opines that Ismael was a step beyond that, he was "El Cantante Mayor."

Gloria Estefan's father, José Manuel Fajardo, was a bodyguard for the Cuban dictator Fulgencio Batista. There are unconfirmed reports that he also served as a motor escort for the dictator's wife.

Rogelio Martínez, the director of Sonora Matancera, was born in Matanzas. He was the son of José Martínez, who was originally from Galicia. Rogelio started singing Spanish songs at eight and later became an apprentice in the culinary arts.

Mon Rivera was incarcerated in 1958 for possessing cocaine, an experience that inspired his hit song "Lluvia con Nieve."

Catalino "Tite" Curet Alonso (1926-2003) was a Puerto Rican composer known for composing over 2,000 salsa songs. Around 200 of these were hit songs, fifty of which became top hits. In addition to salsa, he wrote Sambas, with the Brazilian jazz drummer and percussionist Airto

Moreira being one of the interpreters of this genre and his songs.

Olga San Juan

Actress and comedian Olga San Juan, also known as The Puerto Rican *Pepper Pot* due to her vibrant and spicy personality, was a childhood friend of Tito Puente. Tito had a crush on her, as did Tito Rodríguez and Joe Loco, and so did Bobby Capó later on despite him being much older. Olga and Tito's mother were friends, and they all took part in many activities together.

The film *Our Latin Thing* has several inconsistencies that could have been avoided with better editing. In one scene, Johnny Pacheco plays a flute solo, and behind him, Cheo Feliciano is seen wearing a brown suit with a shirt and tie. However, the next moment, when the camera pans to the side in the same scene, Cheo Feliciano is behind Johnny Pacheco, wearing an orange shirt. There are also multiple wardrobe changes from many singers and musicians, while some, like Ray Barretto and singer Pete Rodríguez, remain in the same outfit. Even Johnny Pacheco begins the movie with a plain colored shirt, but as the film progresses, he wears a dark printed shirt. Izzy Sanabria, Héctor Lavoe, Ismael Miranda, and Adalberto Santiago have also changed their outfits.

Moreover, in another scene, Pete "El Conde" Rodríguez sings his solo on "Quitate Tú" while playing the maracas. Although the maracas can be heard in the film and on the LP, there are moments in the scene when they are not being played and are just held still.

―⁂―

Bobby Capó had been previously married, but his marriage ended in divorce soon after. In 1948, he married Irma Nydia Vázquez. She was Miss Puerto Rico and took part in the Miss America pageant that same year. However, her family disapproved of their marriage due to Bobby's humble background. This inspired Bobby to write the song "El Bardo" ("The Bard"), which became a massive hit for Felipe Rodríguez.

―⁂―

Pete "El Conde" Rodríguez, also known as Pedro Juan Rodríguez Ferrer, was born in Barrio Cantera, Ponce, Puerto Rico. At age five, he began playing bongós in his father's quartet, *El Conjunto Gondolero*.

―⁂―

Tico Records was founded in New York City in 1948 to help record up-and-coming Latin bands that were of no interest to the more prominent recording companies. It was initially owned by the Jewish entrepreneur George Goldner, a pioneer in Rock and Roll, and then bought by high school dropout turned successful businessman (gangster) Morris Levy, founding partner of the Birdland jazz club and subject of investigations into organized crime and the music industry. The name *Tico* was from the Brazilian song "Tico Tico no Fuba."

In 1939, at age sixteen, Tito Puente, while living at 53 East 110th Street, between Madison and Park Avenues, met sixteen-year-old Tito Rodríguez, who was living with his brother Johnny Rodríguez down the block at 65 East 110th Street. They met at a teenage hangout, La Casita María, in the same block. They were close friends, not only because they were on the same baseball team but also because of their love for music.

Celia Cruz's first recording with *La Sonora Matancera* was "Cao Cao, Mani, Picao" on December 15, 1950, under Seeco Records.

In 1955, Joe Cuba persistently asked agent Sid Sayre for work. Finally, he was offered a steady job at the Pines Resort with room, board, food, and a payment of fifty dollars per week per band member. Cuba accepted the offer and convinced the Rainbow label's management to record his Sextet and use the tune to promote the resort under the name "Mambo of the Pines." However, to avoid legal issues, the song's name was changed to "Mambo of the Times."

During the later stages of his life, Daniel Santos was faced with the challenge of being unable to control his bladder and bowel movements. As a result, he had to spend most of his time confined to his home, as going out in public became impossible. This condition, known as incontinence, greatly affected his daily life and made it difficult for him to engage in activities that he once enjoyed. Despite this, Daniel remained optimistic and found ways to stay occupied within the comfort of his own home.

In 1985, Julio Iglesia's father was kidnapped. Fortunately, after two weeks, he was found alive. This incident prompted Julio Sr. to move his family to Miami, Florida.

"To Be with You," Jimmy Sabater's most celebrated composition, is a testament to the universal language of music. Initially crafted in Spanish as "Nunca" by Nick Jiménez and Willie Torre, it was later reimagined in English, resonating with a worldwide audience.

In 1942, *La Sonora Matancera* formed a cooperative and distributed earnings equally among group members.

Tito Rodríguez enlisted in the U.S. Army but was discharged for unknown reasons after one year of service.

―――

"Vereda Tropical" is a famous bolero composed by Gonzalo Curiel in Acapulco in 1936. Lupita Palomera, the first singer to perform the song, tells us that the bolero became so popular in Mexico that some newspaper advertisements for domestic service requested employees who did NOT sing "Vereda Tropical."

―――

Hilton Ruiz was an American pianist of Puerto Rican descent, born in 1952. As a child prodigy, he performed Mozart at Carnegie Hall when he was only eight. Later in life, he went to New Orleans to shoot a promotional video for M27 Records to benefit the victims of Hurricane Katrina. However, on May 19, 2006, he was found unconscious outside a French Quarter bar on Bourbon Street. He had suffered severe head injuries, including a broken skull and several broken facial bones, from an apparent accidental fall. Despite being transported to the hospital, Ruiz suffered a heart attack, fell into a coma, and died on June 6, 2006, at the age of 54.

Although a video was produced showing that he fell face-down on a curb after leaving a club, many people believe that he was attacked first. Some witnesses at the scene claimed he was the victim of a severe beating, but police reports concluded otherwise. Sadly, he never regained consciousness and passed away a week after his birthday.

A lawsuit was filed, and the Latin music community in New York lobbied Congressional members of the Hispanic Caucus to petition for a re-investigation of the case. However, the case remains closed, and many believe the New Orleans Police Department was involved in a cover-up.

Mon Rivera, a well-known Puerto Rican *plenero*, was born Efrain Rivera Castillo in Río Cana, Mayagüez 1924. Before becoming a musician, he played professional baseball as a shortstop for *Los Indios de Mayagüez* from 1943 to 1945. Interestingly, he used to work as a bat boy for the same team in his younger days. Rivera holds two league records: the most triples in a game (three) and the most consecutive doubles in a doubleheader (five).

In late 1962, Trini López landed a steady gig at the nightclub PJ's in Los Angeles, where he developed a large following. Frank Sinatra, who had started his record label, Reprise Records, heard the young Trini and signed him. Subsequently, in 1963, he debuted his first live album, *Trini López, at PJ's,* which included a version of Pete Seeger's "If I Had a Hammer," which topped No. 3 in the United States but number one in 36 countries, selling over 4.5 million copies and awarded a gold disc.

In 1962, after leaving Cortijo, Rafael Ithier founded *El Gran Combo*. It has become an iconic salsa music group performing for over seven decades, making it Puerto Rico's most celebrated band.

Mon Rivera's most famous plena is called "Askarakatiskis." In this song, he tells the story of a gambler named Rafael who loses all his money by rolling dice. Consequently, Rafael's wife, Luz María, assaults him with a broomstick while their daughters laugh. Mon Rivera delivers this tale in the *trabalengua* style, a rapid-fire Puerto Rican tongue-twisting technique. This style is deeply rooted in Puerto Rican culture and adds a unique flavor to the song, making it a true representation of the island's musical heritage.

In the 1950s, the Cuban composer, arranger, bandleader, and trumpet player Chico O'Farrill joined the *Benny Goodman Orchestra* for a brief period.

Carlos "Patato" Valdés father played the *tres* for Los *Apaches* in 1915 and later for the *Septeto Habanero*.

Ismael Rivera's mother, Margarita Rivera (Doña Margot), composed the hit tune "Maquinolandera" for her son.

Joe Hernández

—⚉—

Willie Colón's musical journey started at the remarkably youthful age of thirteen when he formed his debut band, *Los Dandies*. A year later, he expanded his musical horizons with the creation of *La Dinámica*. While the trumpet was his first instrument of choice, it was the profound influence of Mon Rivera and the soulful sounds of Barry Rogers that led him to switch to the trombone, a decision that would shape his musical career.

—⚉—

The Mexican composer Luis Alcaraz claimed that the song "Always in My Heart" was the same as his bolero titled "Sortilegio." Both parties took the matter to court, and the court ruled that the royalties earned by the Lecuona song in Mexico would go to Alcaraz, while Lecuona would receive the royalties for the rest of the world.

—⚉—

In 1904, the double-face 10-inch record cost $1.50. Adjusted for inflation, that would equal $52.00 in today's market.

—⚉—

Pedro Bonet Harris, famously known by his stage name, Pete Bonet, was an exceptionally talented musician and vocalist who significantly impacted the music industry. Born in 1938, Bonet's love for music began at an early age, and he soon became a skilled singer and composer. Pete collaborated with over fifty bands throughout his career, showcasing his versatility and unique style. His passion for music was evident in every performance, and he quickly gained recognition for his exceptional talent. Sadly, Pete Bonet passed away in 2022, leaving behind a legacy that his fans and fellow musicians will forever remember.

Luis Kalaff

Luis Kalaff (1916-2010), a renowned Dominican composer, guitarist, and singer, has left an indelible mark on the music industry. His dedication to his craft is evident in the sheer volume of his compositions, which number nearly two thousand songs. Many of these have been performed by prominent Dominican singers like Alberto Beltran and Fernando Villalona. Singers from other countries, including Julio Iglesias and Rafa Galindo, have also performed Kalaff's songs. Despite his passing in 2010, his music continues to be celebrated and enjoyed by people all around the world.

Joe Hernández

The father of Paquito D'Rivera, Tito D'Rivera, played tenor saxophone with Benny Goodman.

The Bolero began to be danced as a bolero-son between 1927-29.

At the age of 17, Ismael Rivera, a.k.a "Maelo" or "El Sonero Mayor," sang "El Negro Bembón" in the first film of Puerto Rico, *Maruja* (1959).

In the late 1970s, the world-famous Studio 54 nightclub in New York City was the place to see and be seen. Celebrities, socialites, and the city's elite flocked to the venue to dance the night away. During this time, the *Tito Puente Orchestra* made history by becoming the first Latin band to perform at Studio 54. The Orchestra, led by the legendary musician and bandleader Tito Puente, brought their unique blend of Latin rhythms to the club's dance floor, leaving the audience in awe. Their performance was a testament to music's power to unite people and break down barriers. Today, the Tito Puente Orchestra's performance at Studio 54 is remembered as a milestone in the history of Latin music and a testament to the enduring legacy of Tito Puente.

Promoter Catalino Rolón named the Joe Cuba Sextet without Cuba's approval. Initially, the band was known as the *Cha-Cha Boys,* and they made their debut performance at El San Juan Club in 1953. Rolón convinced Cuba to change the band's name to his birth name, Gilberto Calderón, but the owner of the Starlight Ballroom in the Bronx disliked the name and asked Rolón to change it again. Rolón then renamed the band the *Joe Cuba Sextet.* Calderón later learned about the name change from a New York Post article about the Starlight attraction being Joe Cuba. He was upset and asked Rolón who Joe Cuba was. Rolón replied that Calderón was Joe Cuba, and the rest is history.

However, there is another version of the story, as reported by Max Salazar. According to this version, Joe Cuba still performed with the band as the *Joe Panama Sextet.* One evening, while the group was performing at the Bamba Club in midtown Manhattan, Joe Panama and his mother visited and informed Rolón that the band's name was a copyright infringement. Rolón ignored their warning, and they went to the musician's union, where the ruling favored Panama. As a result, Rolón renamed the group the Joe Cuba Sextet.

Band member Willie Torres, in stark contrast to the previously shared narratives, reveals a different version of events. He claims that Joe Panama's father visited Catalino's office and delivered the news that the name couldn't be used. In a moment of spontaneity, Catalino decided to change the name on the spot from Joe Panama to Joe Cuba.

The true story may be somewhere between these three versions, or there may be another version altogether.

Nonetheless, what is important is that the Joe Cuba Sextet became immensely popular and unstoppable.

The *Anacaona Septet* performed at the Waldorf Astoria Hotel in 1937 for President Franklin D. Roosevelt's birthday.

Miguel Matamoros, a latecomer to the music world, started his career at the age of 31. In 1924, he formed a duo with Rafael Cueto, a former baseball champion in Cuba, who played the cuatro and cornet. Their journey took a new turn in 1925 when they were joined by Siro Rodríguez, a blacksmith by trade but a fine baritone singer, to form the *Trío Oriental*. However, their path was not without obstacles. In 1928, while recording in Camden, New Jersey, they discovered another *Trío Oriental* led by guitarist Roberto de Moya, which forced them to rebrand as *Trío Matamoros*.

The *Sonora Matancera* group took its name from the town of Matanzas, Cuba. The group was active for 79 years until 2003, making it one of the longest-lasting groups in Latin music history. On January 12, 1924, in the Ojo de Agua neighborhood of Matanzas, at 41 Salamanca Street, a musical group was established by Valentín Cané, who played the *tres*. The group was initially known as *Tuna Liberal*, which had a political inclination, as its debut was in honor of Governor Juan Gronlier. With the addition of Carlos Manuel "Caito" Díaz, the group was called *Septeto Soprano*, and later, with the inclusion of Rogelio Martínez, they became *Estudiantina Sonora Matancera*.

In subsequent years, the group's name changed to *Sonora Matancera, Conjunto Sonora*, and *Matancera*. The *Sonora Matancera* entered the Guinness Record in 1996, after seventy-two years of existence, as the oldest orchestra in the world.

It's a testament to Tite Curet's genius that numerous renowned salsa singers have performed his compositions, and his work has sold millions of records. Tite, a prolific composer of some of Salsa's most iconic tunes, left an indelible mark on Latin music. However, the fact that he received almost no royalties from his work is a painful reality. Had he been compensated; his talent would have made him a wealthy man.

Due to contractual obligations with the Fania label, Cheo Feliciano performed for the Alegre label using the pseudonym Juanchu Feliciano Merceron.

William Correa, also known by his stage name, Willy Bobo, began his dance career at 12. He worked briefly as a bandboy for Machito before playing with Tito Puente. Later, Bobo joined the band of British pianist George Shearing, followed by a stint with Cal Tjader. However, at the age of 49, he passed away due to cancer.

Chico O'Farrill & Joe Hernández

Chico O'Farrill's father was an attorney who wanted his son to become a lawyer. In 1936, Chico joined the United States Military Academy in Georgia and graduated in 1940. He returned to Havana and enrolled in law school, but he continued to play the trumpet with pianist *Rene Touzet's Orchestra*. However, in 1941, he dropped out of law school and pursued a full-time music career. Although his father was initially unhappy with his decision, he eventually blessed Chico.

After an extensive European tour in July 1990, the renowned Cuban jazz trumpeter Arturo Sandoval found himself in Rome. Following a series of events, Sandoval decided to defect from his home country and seek refuge in the American Embassy. Accompanied by the legendary jazz musician Dizzy Gillespie, the two made the daring journey to the embassy and ultimately paved the way for Sandoval's musical career to flourish in the United States.

Daniel Santos had twelve children, one of whom tragically committed suicide.

Willie Torres was a widely recorded Latin music vocalist. In 1965, he appeared as a background singer on 17 albums, but he never released a solo album.

Willie Colón's album, Asalto Navideño, was a momentous change. It was the first salsa album to feature the *cuatro*, played by the legendary Yomo Toro. This musical innovation brought back Puerto Rican musical forms like the *aguinaldo* and *el seis chorrea'o*. It sparked a cultural revival among young second-generation Puerto Ricans in New York City, making them feel more connected to their roots.

In 1954, Bienvenido Granda departed from the Sonora Matancera and was subsequently replaced as the lead singer. This decision came after a dispute over salary with the band's director, Rogelio Martínez. Granda demanded a higher pay than his colleagues, but the band had a collective agreement in which all members received the same income.

Pete "El Conde" Rodríguez moved to the Bronx from Ponce, Puerto Rico, after his father passed away when he

Joe Hernández

was only 12 years old. In 1963, when he was 30, he sang and played the conga at a bar in the Bronx where Johnny Pacheco discovered his talent. Impressed, Pacheco invited him to participate in a recording of "Suavito" with Ray Barretto. After that, Pete became Pacheco's vocalist for the album *Cañonazo,* the first release under the Fania label.

—⚎—

Besides being one of the all-time Latin pop divas, Gloria Estefan earned a B.A. in psychology with a minor in French from the University of Miami in 1978.

—⚎—

In October 1947, Charlie Palmieri was recruited by Tito Puente, the musical director of *Fernando Alvarez's band* at the Copacabana Club, to replace Joe Loco. A year later, Palmieri recorded his first album with *Conjunto Pin Pin,* which was released on the Alba label.

—⚎—

In the early 1940s, the pianist Damaso Pérez Prado decided to pursue his musical career in Havana. He started performing at the Pennslyvania Cabaret, earning a salary of $1.45 per night. Later, he moved to the Kursall Cabaret located on the docks of the bay and then to Paulina Álvarez's orchestra, where he was contracted for $1.60 per night. Pérez Prado also began making muarrangements for Ernesto Roca of the Peer label, charging $2.00 for each arrangement. Some of his arrangements were played by the Casino de la Playa Orchestra, which Liduvino Pereira directed at the time. Cascarita, the orchestra singer, enjoyed Pérez Prado's arrangements, which led to him joining the Casino de la Playa orchestra.

María Teresa Vera & Rafael Zequeira

In 1916, the Cuban singer-songwriter María Teresa Vera met Rafael Zequeira, with whom she formed an extraordinary musical duet. Their music, which significantly influenced the Cuban music scene, resonated with audiences. Together, they embarked on five trips to the United States and recorded an extensive repertoire of songs with major record labels such as RCA Victor, Columbia, and Pathé. However, their partnership was cut short when Zequeira passed away in 1924. After his death, Vera continued to perform and sing with Miguelito García.

The Cuban conguero "Patato" claimed to have taught the Cuban Latin jazz percussionist Armando Peraza how to play the bongó in the mid-1940s when Peraza was around twenty years old.

—⚏—

The 1980 Mariel boatlift brought percussionists Daniel Ponce, Roberto Borell, Orlando "Puntilla" Ríos, and Ignacio Borrea to the U.S.

—⚏—

After completing his intense physical therapy and recovering from a car accident, Julio Iglesias briefly attended the Bell Educational Trust Language School in Cambridge before obtaining his law degree from the Complutense University of Madrid.

—⚏—

Ralph Mercado (1941-2009) founded the RMM label in 1987, representing over 130 artists. Universal bought the label for approximately $26 million in 2001. Mercado died at the age of 60 from cancer.

—⚏—

Rogelio Martínez Díaz joined the *Sonora Matancera* as a *coro* (chorus) member and clave player. He took up the guitar and eventually became the orchestra director in the 1930s when Valentín could not keep up with the demanding schedule due to his cardiac asthma. Rogelio's persistence and responsible leadership contributed significantly to the group's success as they toured the world for seven decades with their music.

—⚏—

Fernando Collazo was a Cuban singer who appeared in Cuba's first talkie film, Maracas y Bongó, with his musical group Septeto Cuba in 1932. After that, he went to New York in 1935 and recorded with Armando Valdéspi. However, on October 16, 1939, at the age of thirty-seven, he committed suicide in Havana under mysterious circumstances.

Myrta Silva

Myrta Silva, also known as "La Gorda de Oro," was born in Arecibo, Puerto Rico, as Myrta Blanca Silva Oliveras on September 11, 1927 (although some sources suggest 1923). She began her career in the 1930s at 10 with the *Ernesto Wilches Company*. At 12, she moved to New York City, where she was known for her singing and maracas playing skills. Later, she also learned to play the guitar, as well as the timbales. Her debut as a singer and entertainer was in 1939 at the Hispanic Theater in New York. Rafael Hernández discovered her when she was still in her teens. Before joining Rafael, Myrta worked as a dishwasher and chambermaid, performing 21 shows weekly at the Teatro Hispano for $25. Rafael made several tours to various Latin American countries with her. She also sang with another famous Puerto Rican composer, Pedro Flores, in his *Sexteto Flores,* where Daniel Santos and Pedro Ortiz Davila, a.k.a Davilita, joined her. She was also known as "The Queen of the Guaracha." In her later years, she had dementia. She died in Arecibo, Puerto Rico, on December 2, 1987, at 60.

Graciela Pérez

Graciela Pérez, then seventeen years old, replaced the singer and founder of the all-female group *Anacaona* in 1933. The group was founded in 1932 by Cochinta Castro with three of her sisters and four friends during the strike against Cuba's tyrant Machado when all the schools were shut down. The group was named to honor a legendary Cuban Indian princess of the Siboney tribe. Conchita was one of eleven sisters, and as the years passed, they all became part of the band.

In 1993, Willie Colón ran unsuccessfully as a Democrat for state representative in Westchester County, New York.

In the mid to late 1940s, Pérez Prado had been blacklisted in Cuba from working as an arranger because his charts were considered "too extreme." He caught a break when the famous Cuban singer Cascarita recommended him as an arranger-pianist for *Orquesta Casino de la Playa,* known for its swinging music.

Between July 1930 and November 1935, Antonio Machín and his quartet recorded over 150 songs for Victor and other labels. He possibly recorded more songs than anyone since Bing Crosby during the economic depression.

Eddy Zervigon, leader of Orchestra Broadway, suffered two horrifying experiences in the early 70s that led him to move out of New York City. The first occurred on New Year's Eve of 1972 when he was attacked by two muggers in the elevator of his apartment building at 36 Laurel Terrace in upper Manhattan. Eddie was slashed on the wrist during the scuffle as he attempted to fight off the assailants.

Then, in February 1974, his three-year-old son was at his babysitter's home when she answered a knock on the door. A man forced his way in at gunpoint and battered the older woman senselessly after the babysitter told him she had no money. The gunman then pointed the gun at the child's head and threatened to kill him unless she gave him all her valuables, which she did. Neither case was ever solved.

Charlie Figueroa

Charlie Figueroa, born Carlos Fabriciano Figueroa Rosario in 1921, was a Puerto Rican singer. Sadly, he passed away at the age of 34 due to liver cirrhosis. Despite his health condition, he recorded the bolero "No Pises Mi Camino" by José Barros while confined to a wheelchair. His son, Sammy Figueroa, is a well-known conguero.

In the early 1930s, during the Great Depression, Daniel Santos performed at the small nightclub Los Chilenos, located near Broadway in Manhattan. He was paid twenty dollars for his performances, equivalent to $400.00 in 2024.

Ray Barretto

Ray Barretto, a Brooklyn-born native of Puerto Rican descent, began to teach himself congas by using the back of a banjo as a substitute for a drum when he was in the U.S. Army stationed in Germany.

Due to the limited availability of space, the Puerto Rican singer Eladio Peguero, also known as "Yayo El Indio," was buried in the same tomb as his childhood friend Daniel Santos at the Santa María Magdalena de Pazzis Cemetery in Old San Juan.

Tite Curet Alonso's music, despite its immense popularity in the hearts of "salseros" worldwide, was banned from Puerto Rico radio stations for decades by the strong-arm tactics of the music publishing company ACEMLA (Asociación de Compositores y Editores de Musica Latinoamericana).

Alberto Socarras

The Cuban flutist, clarinetist, and saxophone player Alberto Socarras (1908-1987) was the musical director of the all-female *Anacaona Orchestra* during its tour of Paris in 1938.

In 1943, at 16, while still in high school, Charlie Palmieri made his professional debut as a piano player for the *Osario Selasie Band*. After graduating from high school in 1946, he immediately went to play for various bands. He made his recording debut with "Se Va La Rumba" as a member of the *Rafael Muñoz Band* in the same year.

In 1938, Daniel Santos worked at the Cuban Casino Cabaret in Manhattan, which Puerto Ricans and other Hispanics mainly frequented. His job responsibilities included singing, waiting on tables, and occasionally acting as master of ceremonies by introducing other acts. He received a monthly salary of thirty dollars, approximately equivalent to $640.00 in 2024.

One evening, while performing "Amor Perdido," he caught the attention of the composer Pedro Flores, who happened to be in the audience. Flores was impressed with Santos's performance and invited him to join his group, El Cuarteto Flores, which featured Myrta Silva and Pedro Ortiz Davila, also known as Davilita. Santos accepted Flores's offer and recorded many songs with the group, which helped him gain fame and recognition.

Francisco Flores del Campo

Francisco Flores del Campo, also known as Pancho Flores, was a Chilean composer, instrumentalist, and actor. He was born in 1907 and passed away in 1993.

Flores was not just a composer but a prolific one at that, having written more than 150 registered works. His repertoire included the emotionally charged song "Sufrir" (Suffer). He also left his mark in the film industry, collaborating with Carlos Gardel on the iconic film *El Día Que Me Quieras* (The Day You Love Me).

In 1970, the renowned singer Willie Torres left the nightclub circuit to work as a New York Transit Authority bus driver. He worked in this role until his retirement in 1991. Interestingly, his bus route included his childhood neighborhood on the M15 between First and Second Avenue.

Despite his career change, Torres remained in high demand as a background studio singer in his spare time. His love for music never faded away. Sadly, Willie Torres passed away on August 13, 2020, at the age of 90, at South Lake Hospital in Claremont, Florida.

In the early 1960s, a new music genre known as "boogaloo" emerged in the United States. Trumpeter Tony Pabón was the first to use the term "boogaloo" while playing for *Pete Rodríguez y Su Conjunto*. He wrote a song for Pete Rodríguez called "Pete's Boogaloo," which became the first Latin Boogaloo song to be broadcast on radio.

The birth of the Latin Boogaloo genre directly responded to the audience's desire for a soulful twist in their music. Inspired by Peggy Lee's "Fever," Tony Pabón combined the cha-cha-chá rhythm with 50s/60s R&B sounds, creating a unique fusion genre that resonated with audiences. Their most successful song, "I Like It Like That," topped the charts, cementing the Latin Boogaloo genre in the music industry.

While Joe Cuba is often credited as the "Father of Latin Boogaloo," Tony Pabón's "Pete's Boogaloo" ignited the craze. In 1967, Riche Ray & Bobby Cruz released *Jala Jala y Boogaloo,* followed by *Jala Jala Boogaloo Volume II*, which featured their international hit "Mr. Trumpet Man." However, "Mr. Trumpet Man" is a mambo/son montuno rhythm with exclusive English lyrics, fueling the ongoing debate about the true origin of the Latin Boogaloo. This intriguing and engaging debate adds another layer of depth to the genre's history. However, there is a growing consensus among many scholars that the origin of Latin Boogaloo as a musical style was with Mongo Santamaria's 1963 hit version of Herbie Hancock's tune "Watermelon Man."

―∽―

La Sonora Matancera was established in 1924 and led by guitarist and singer Rogelio Martínez for over fifty years, ever since he joined the group in 1926. The ensemble comprised nearly a hundred vocalists from the Caribbean and Mexico. Among them were renowned Puerto Rican singer Daniel Santos and Cuban singer Celia Cruz, who replaced the legendary vocalist, Myrta Silva.

―∽―

By the end of 1998, Tite Curet hosted a weekly program on the University of Puerto Rico's radio station. He continued to write for local newspapers and magazines until his death.

In 1951, Singer and Timbalero Jimmy Sabater met Gilberto Calderón, known as Sonny at the time (later, in the mid-1950s, he became Joe Cuba). This happened during a stickball championship game between the 112th Street Viceroys and the Devils. The Devils team beat the Viceroys by ten runs, and Calderón invited Jimmy to a party that evening. This was the beginning of a meaningful relationship between the two.

During the 1960s, a popular sound and dance called Boogaloo or Bugalú emerged in the United States. It was also referred to as Latin Boogaloo and Latin R&B. This new sound, born from the creative energy of teenage African Americans and young Puerto Ricans living in New York City, was essentially a chachacha or a son montuno with a backbeat. The mystery of its origins adds to its allure, with some arguing it started in Chicago in 1965 and others suggesting that Wilson Pickett's "Mustang Sally" and "In the Midnight Hour" were early forms of boogaloo. The Latin shingaling and jala jala were subsets of the bugalú. However, despite these intriguing speculations, the true origins of this musical style continue to elude us.

Some make the case that Willie Bobo and Mongo Santamaría were at the forefront of this musical movement.

Antonio "Tony" Pabón was inspired to study the trumpet at Harlem's Patrick Henry School from listening to Harry James, America's most popular bandleader in the 1940s.

Going back to his early days, Tito Puente's reputation as a sizzling arranger grew, leading to numerous assignments from prominent bandleaders. Even Tito Rodríguez hired Puente to arrange charts for four numbers he recorded with his Mambo Devils on Gabriel Oller's "Spanish Music Center" label on August 31, 1949, at the SMC Studios. The recordings were "Un Yemerico," "Mango del Monte," "Guararé," and "Frisao con Gusto."

Willie Colón was the godfather of Héctor Lavoe's first son.

Ray Barretto was known for mistreating his band members, which caused many of them to leave. Once, the band was hired to perform at the Hollywood Palladium and other clubs in California for a month. However, they were surprised when Barretto arranged for them to travel by Greyhound bus instead of taking a flight like they did the first time. When they arrived at the station, Barretto told them to board the bus and said he would catch the next one as he had forgotten something. Later, they discovered he had flown ahead of them and purposely made them take the bus.

Joe Hernández

Celia Cruz

In 1935, when she was ten, Celia Cruz won first prize on the amateur radio show *La Hora del Te* by singing the tango "Nostalgia."

People think Jerry Masucci produced albums one and two of the *Fani All-Star* at the Cheetah. This story is not valid; Larry Harlow produced it. Jerry Masucci was the producer and executive producer of the movie *Our Latin Thing*.

Mon Rivera was one of twelve children fathered by his father, Don Mon.

Carmen Miranda was born Carmo Miranda da Cunha in 1909 in Marco de Canavezes, Portugal, but raised in Río de Janeiro since infancy. If there ever was an overnight sensation, Miranda epitomizes the fast rise to stardom, becoming a massive star in Brazil by age twenty. By the late 1940s, she was the highest-paid woman in Hollywood. She suffered a heart attack in her Beverly Hills home in August 1955 while tapping an episode of *The Jimmy Durante Show.*

After Cuba and Mexico, Puerto Rico has produced the most bolero composers in Latin America.

Before the arrival of any significant wave of Puerto Rican migrants to New York, in March 1904, the Cuban composer, trovador, and guitarist Tata Villegas (1886-1989) singing with the group he founded, *Sexteto Manhattan,* was the first male Cuban to appear in Carnegie Hall. He died in Havana, Cuba, at the age of 103.

Many Latin musicians need to have a regular job to make ends meet. Machito, for example, used to work during the day at a rehabilitation center for drug users called Project Return, and he also helped older people at a senior center. Joe Cuba and Pete Nater were licensed paralegals, while singers Rafael DeJesús and Dave Valentín worked as full-time teachers in New York City Public Schools.

Joe Hernández

Odeón 78 RPM

In 1904, the Odeón label pioneered Europe in recording the record on both sides; North American companies followed.

Charlie Palmieri joined Tito Puente's conjunto in 1951, replacing pianist Gilberto López, who had gone to the Korean War. Charlie stayed with Tito Puente for several years.

The Puerto Rican aguinaldo "Si Me Dan Pasteles" comes from a melody written by the composer and pianist of Creole and Jewish descent, Louis Moreau Gottschalk that he composed in 1857 titled Souvenir de Porto Rico (Recuerdo de Puerto Rico) with the subtitle of Marche des Gibaros (La Marcha de Los Jibaros).

The Cuban composer Miguel Faílde (1852-1921), creator of the danzon, was highly active when the North American record companies recorded local talent in Cuba at the turn of the 19th century, producing hundreds of records. Yet, despite his orchestra being extremely popular and successful, he was never recorded.

The Afro-Cuban song "Babalú" was written by Margarita Lecuona, the cousin of composers Ernesto and Ernestina Lecuona. The song's title refers to the Santería deity Babalú Aye.

In 1965, Jimmy Sabater and Nick Jiménez wrote "El Pito" after listening to Dizzy Gillespie's recording of "Manteca". While Sabater was listening to a bass riff in the tune and heard Gillespie sing, *"I'll never go back to Georgia, I'll never go back,"* it inspired the song. Sabater did not believe it would be a hit and thought that the piece "Pruebalo" would be the one to top the charts. However, WLIB DJ Dale Shields gave "El Pito" airplay, and it ended up on the R&B charts, selling over a million copies.

Years after the song became an enormous success, Tito Puente told Joe Cuba that "El Pito" was out of clave. Cuba remained "troubled" about not being on clave despite the success. In another interview, Joe Cuba stated that he and Jimmy Sabater wrote "El Pito," taking inspiration from Tito Puente's "Oye Cómo Va." However, this later version seems like a stretch.

Joe Hernández

Throughout his life, Joe told different stories about how the song came to be.

—⚏—

The Puerto Rican Latin jazz percussionist Giovanni Hidalgo, who is known as "Mañenguito," had to undergo an amputation of the ring finger on his left hand in October 2016 following an infection caused by diabetes. Further finger amputations followed this. Despite the setback, he has kept playing music using a stick in his left hand.

—⚏—

La Anacaona Septet

In 1938, an all-female orchestra named *La Anacaona Septet* from Havana, Cuba, was the main attraction at *Les Ambassadeurs* in Paris. They performed alongside the legendary guitarist Django Reinhardt at *Chez Florence in Montmartre*. One of the group members was Graciela, who became Machito's lead female singer.

—⚏—

In 1950, Cal Tjader, while in his third year of college, was offered a job as a second drummer by jazz great Lionel Hampton; Cal turned it down.

Larry Harlow's music education in Cuba during the late 1950s was abruptly interrupted by the political upheaval of Fidel's Cuban revolution. In 1959, he was forced to leave the country, leaving his studies behind. Undeterred, he continued his academic journey, earning a B.A. in Music from Brooklyn College in the early 1960s and a master's degree in philosophy from the New School of Social Research in New York City.

Tito Puente and Charlie Palmieri performed as musical directors for Franc Peri's Roper label. They recorded under the names of The Latin All-Stars, Roper Dance Orchestra, and The Dancing Strings. Roper Records mainly distributed these high-quality LPs to dance studios throughout the United States and not to the general market.

Cal Tjader, whose full name was Callen Radcliffe Tjader Jr., was born on July 16, 1925, in St. Louis, Missouri. His parents were vaudevillian performers; his father was a tap dancer, and his mother was a pianist who frequently traveled up and down the West Coast for their performances. In 1927, they settled in San Mateo, California, and opened a dance school.

Teatro Puerto Rico

Pérez Prado moved to Mexico City in 1944 and formed his group, where he immediately earned the reputation of being the "Glenn Miller of Mexico." His first U.S. appearance was at Teatro Puerto Rico in the Bronx, New York during the months of April and May of 1941.

La Orquesta de la Playa's most memorable recording was Cristina Saladrigas' bolero titled "Ojos Malvados." Cristina, a young woman from high-class Cuban society, was determined to get the most famous orchestra in Cuba to record one of her songs. She convinced the orchestra's pianist and arranger, Anselmo Sacasa, to write the musical arrangement for this number. However, she faced another challenge in getting the orchestra's star singer, Miguelito Valdés, to sing the song. Miguelito, a good composer, reviewed the lyrics and melody but did not feel it suited him.

Cristina did not give up and approached the orchestra's second singer, Walfredo de los Reyes, to record her song. Although Walfredo was the first trumpet player in the orchestra and did not have a powerful voice, he recorded the number, and it went on to become one of the Casino de la Playa Orchestra's biggest hits.

Since then, many artists have covered "Ojos Malvados." Some notable interpretations include those by Chucho Avellanet, Barbarito Diez, Santos Colón, Felipe Pirela, Tito Rodríguez, and María Victoria. More recently, the Cuban singer of Buena Vista Social Club fame, Ibrahim Ferrer, also covered the song. Nonetheless, the original recording by the Casino de la Playa Orchestra remains the best version.

Justo Betancourt was supposed to perform his song "Pa' Bravo Yo" in the movie *Our Latin Thing*. He had received advance payment to buy a suit for the filming. However, when Betancourt arrived on the set, he was informed that the charts were unavailable for his song and was asked to sing along with the other singers. Betancourt refused and insisted on singing his song as per the contract. Massucci, the producer, urged him to stay, but Betancourt left, stating that he had no obligation to stay if he couldn't perform his music. He spent the rest of the evening drinking.

In the spring of 1934, *El Club Cubanacan* opened its doors at 114th Street & Lenox Avenue, with Alberto Socarras and his trumpet player Augusto Coen as the house band. The club was a popular spot for Latinos in New York who could listen to Afrocuban music broadcast every evening between 10 and 10:30 p.m. and 3 to 3:30 a.m. over radio WMCA. The owner, Marcial Flores, was a wealthy Puerto Rican. A few months later, Flores rented the vacant Mount Morris Theatre at 116th Street & 5th Avenue and renamed it *El Compoamor Theatre,* with Alberto Socarras's band backing up the stage shows. This kept Socarras busy doing what he loved.

In 1949, the Machito Orchestra became the first Latin band to record over the four-minute standard for 78 RPM recordings, with the extraordinarily successful tune "Tanga."

The original "To Be With You" by the Joe Cuba Sextet, singing Jimmy Sabater, was released in 1962. Eleven years later, in 1973, Cheo Feliciano sang the Spanish version of "Pensar en Ti."

Bebo Valdés, the father of Chucho Valdés, served as the house band leader at Hotel Tropicana in Havana in the 1950s. The orchestra was considered the most important one in the city at the time.

Trini Lopez's brother Jesse Lopez was also a singer. Strangely, they both died on the same day but two years apart.

Celia Cruz & Pedro Knight

At twelve, Celia Cruz's husband, Pedro Knight, became the youngest musician in the Matanzas municipal band of Cuba.

Morris Levy, the president of Roulette Records, was worth an estimated $75 million at the time of his death in 1990 (equivalent to $177 million in 2024).

Singer and songwriter Rubén Blades ran for the presidency of Panama in 1994, but he lost. He came in third place with 18% of the vote under the political party he formed, *Movimiento Egoro*.

Joe Hernández

The Argentine government decreed December 11 as National Tango Day. It is now celebrated globally. In 2009, UNESCO added the tango to its list of Intangible Cultural Heritage.

—∞—

Glenn Monroig, the Puerto Rican singer, and son of Crooner Gilberto Monroig made headlines with his recent legal victory. He sued Ralph's Mercado label RMM in a federal court for copyright infringement on one of his father's songs, which had been modified without permission or payment of royalties. The court's decision was not only a win for Glenn but also had significant financial implications. He was awarded a settlement of $ 7.7 million, a figure that grew to $11 million with interest, highlighting the economic impact of copyright infringement in the music industry.

Sonora Matancera

Valentín Cané, the founder of the *Sonora Matancera,* passed away on October 29, 1956.

Orlando Guerra, also known as Cascarita (1920-1973), was the first to sing guarachas backed by a Cuban jazz-style band.

In 1966, Tito Puente and Celia Cruz recorded eight albums at a pace of one album every six and a half weeks.

In 1974, Eddie Palmieri was awarded the first-ever Grammy for a Latin recording for his album *The Sun of Latin Music*. During the album's recording, sixteen-year-old Lalo Rodríguez made a remarkable debut as a *sonero*. Palmieri's initial choice for lead singer, Andy Montañez of *El Gran Combo*, declined to sing the entire album, agreeing to sing only one or two tracks. This prompted Palmieri to consider other options, ultimately leading to Rodríguez's impressive debut.

La Sonora Matancera departed Havana on July 15, 1960, to Mexico City, then resettled in New York City in 1962. The group continued performing their music style for the next 39 years.

Tito Puente's journey as a Santero is a testament to his deep connection with the Yoruba deity of creativity, Obatala. His initiation into the faith in adulthood reflects his unwavering commitment to spiritual growth and his willingness to embrace new experiences.

In the early 19th century, Puerto Rican musicians were in significant demand because of the musical training that many of them had. African Americans often recruited them for parts in Broadway shows because of their ability to read music, including musicians like Moncho Usera, Noble Sissle, and Rafael Escudero.

In 1948, Celia Cruz took over Rita Montaner's position at the Tropicana nightclub in Havana.

Embedded in the very soul of Cuba's cultural landscape are its six main genres of Afro-Cuban music, each pulsating with its unique rhythm and flavor. These include the vibrant Rumba, the melodious Bolero, the rhythmic Son, the heartfelt Canción Cuban, the graceful Danzón, and the earthy Punto Guajira. Despite its modest size, Cuba is a veritable powerhouse of nearly 70 musical rhythms, a living testament to its vibrant and diverse musical culture. This musical kaleidoscope has not only enriched Cuba but has also catapulted it to the forefront as a leading producer of musical genres in the Latin American region, underscoring its profound cultural influence.

However, not to be outdone, Colombian music has a rich and diverse cultural heritage. Every part of this fantastic country moves to a different sound; each region has its rhythms. There are more than 1,025 folk rhythms grouped into 157 genres. Colombia is known as "the land of the thousand rhythms.

"Abaniquito" was Tito Puente's second music recording featuring Vicentico Valdés. It was one of the earliest mambos that became a significant hit among non-Latin people. The song received a lot of *airplay* from disc jockeys such as Dick "Ricardo" Sugar from WEVD, Pedro Harris, and Symphony Sid Torin, who were musical trendsetters and had English-language radio shows.

Joseíto Mateo

In 1962, the legendary composer and Dominican merengue singer Joseíto Mateo (1920-2018) became the first lead vocalist of *EL Grand Combo de Puerto Rico.*

Joe Hernández

Since its inception in 1913, the old Apollo Theatre in Harlem, located at 253 West 125th Street, has regularly hosted Latin shows. 1918 the Cuban *trovadora* María Teresa Vera debuted in the United States.

—⚙—

Carmen Miranda, also known as the "Samba Queen," was a boutique designer of fashionable hats. She made her first recording with composer Josue de Barros in 1929. She was famous for her signature fruit hat outfit, which she wore in her American films.

—⚙—

Jerry Masucci passed away on December 21, 1997, at the age of 63, due to an aortic aneurysm, which resulted from a heart attack he had in Buenos Aires, Argentina.

—⚙—

The Merengue, now the national dance of the Dominican Republic, was banned in Puerto Rico in 1849 due to its scandalous nature.

—⚙—

The Tico Records company was sold to Fania Records in 1974 but stopped issuing new releases in 1981.

—⚙—

Here are ten songs that you may be surprised to learn were composed by Cubans:

"**Contigo en la Distancia**" was written by the Cuban composer, guitarist, and singer Cesar Portillo de la Luz in 1946 when he was 24, a house painter who would listen to jazz while working. Portillo debuted as a professional guitar player on the radio, and a weekly slot on *Radio Mil Diez* followed in the same year, increasing his popularity. This masterpiece has become one of his most celebrated compositions. It is considered one of the most acclaimed boleros in Cuban music. The song has been interpreted by a multitude of top singers, including Luis Miguel, Christina Aguilera, Il Divo, Plácido Domingo, Pedro Infante, Pablo Milanes, José José, María Dolores Pradera, Machito, Lucho Gatica, Joan Manuel Serrat, Belinda, Los Tres Ases, Olga Guillot, Dyango, Mina, Caetano Veloso, Pedro Guerra, and Eugenia Leon. It has appeared in at least ten movies.

"**Delirio de Grandeza**" is a bolero composed by the Cuban musician Carlos Querol. It was first performed by Justo Betancourt, another Cuban artist, in 1968 on his debut album *El Explosivo,* released under the Fania label. The song gained widespread popularity thanks to the efforts of Rosalía Vila Tobella, a Spanish singer who fused Spanish art styles based on folk music with hip-hop influences.

"**Quizás, Quizás, Quizás**" was a bolero composed in 1947 by the Cuban songwriter Osvaldo Farres (1903-1985), born in Quemado de Guines, Las Villas. The song became a big hit with the interpretation in the same year by the Puerto Rican singer Bobby Capó. Notable cover versions include Bing Crosby (1951), Nat King Cole

(1958) with his version of "Perhaps, Perhaps, Perhaps," Los Panchos, with Johnny Albino (1960), Cliff Richard and the Shadows on the *When in Spain* album (1963), Celia Cruz (1964), Doris Day (1965) in her album *Latin for Lovers,* later used in the 1992 movie *Strictly Ballroom,* CAKE (band) (1966), Mari Wilson for the television series *Coupling,* Hari Loren (2008) in her album *They Oughta Write a Song,* Andrea Bocelli with Jennifer López (2013), and Arthur Hanlon with Debi Nova (2022).

"Flor Palida" is a song by the Cuban singer and composer Polo Montañez in 2002. Polo Montañez's real name was Fernando Borrego Linares (1955-2002), and he was born on a farm known as El Brujito in Sierra del Rosario, Pinar del Río. Polo Montañez had no professional training or musical knowledge, but he would compose his songs while walking, driving a tractor, swimming, and even asleep. By 44, he had written over 70 songs as an autodidact. Unfortunately, he died on November 26, 2002, in a tragic car accident in his hometown. As for the song "Flor Palida," Marc Anthony's interpretation of it has over 880 million views on YouTube as of the end of 2023.

"Mambo #5" is an instrumental mambo that incorporates jazz elements. It was initially composed by Cuban musician Damaso Pérez Prado in 1949 and was released the following year. In April 1999, a German artist, Lou Bega, sampled the original song and released it as part of his album, *A Little Bit of Mambo.* However, the song became the subject of a lengthy seven-year legal battle between Prado's estate, the music publisher Peermusic, and Bega's producers. In 2008, the Federal Court of Justice in Germany ruled in favor of Peermusic and Prado's estate. The court declared that the song was a new composition co-written by Prado and Bega due to Bega's significant contribution in creating his version. On November 2, 1999, the song reached number three on the U.S. Billboard Hot 100 chart.

"**Una Palabra**" is a song by Cuban singer-songwriter Carlos Varela. He was born as Carlos Victoriano Varela Cerezo on April 11, 1963, in Havana. The song has been featured in the soundtracks of *Powder Keg* (2001) and *Man on Fire* (2004), which starred Denzel Washington. It was also used in Episode 3 of the Netflix series *The Night Stalker: The Hunt for a Serial Killer*.

"**Lágrimas Negras**" is a renowned Cuban bolero composed by Miguel Matamoros in 1929. That year, he traveled to Santo Domingo and stayed in a hostel owned by Mrs. Luz Sardana. One day, the musician heard the woman's constant crying in one of the rooms. As time passed and the crying did not stop, Matamoros asked Doña Luz what happened. There, he discovered the whole story: her lover had left her the night before for another woman. Listening to the suffering and desperation of the abandoned woman made him compose "Lagrimas Negras" (Black Tears).

The song has been interpreted by over forty singers of different nationalities, including Martha Catalina, Eliades Ochoa, Compay Segundo, Daniel Santos, Omara

Portuondo, Sara Montiel, Celia Cruz, Olga Guillot, María Teresa Vera, Astrid Hadad, Orquesta Aragón, Babarito Diez, Cuco Valoy, José Feliciano, Rubén Blades, Adalberto Santiago, Buena Vista Social Club, and Bebo Valdés with Diego El Cigala.

"Inolvidable," which means "Unforgettable" in English, was composed by Julio Gutierrez (1918-1990), a Cuban composer-pianist, arranger, and music director, in 1944. Gutierrez was born in Manzanillo and started playing the piano at six. By age 14, he was already directing his orchestra. The song tells the story of the protagonist kissing different lips and seeking new experiences while haunted by memories of a past love. It was one of the most popular boleros released during the Cuban musical movement led by pianists. In 1963, Tito Rodríguez, a Puerto Rican crooner, recorded the song *From Tito Rodríguez with Love* on his album, and it became a huge hit, selling more than 1.5 million LPs across the United States and Latin America.

The global appeal of the bolero was reaffirmed in 1991 when the song soared to the top of the Billboard Top Latin Songs chart in the United States with the version recorded by Mexican singer Luis Miguel. Many renowned performers have interpreted the song, and it has transcended borders and languages. From the Brazilian singer-songwriter Roberto Carlos to Danny Rivera, Eydie Gormé, Cuban pianist Bebo Valdés with Spanish flamenco performers Diego El Cigala, Fernando Trueba, and Paloma San Basilio, the song has touched hearts across the world. Tito Rodríguez's daughter Cindy paid homage to her father by recording the music, creating a beautiful duet using Tito's original soundtrack.

"**Quiéreme Mucho**" (known in English as "Yours") is a song composed in 1911 by Gonzalo Roig Lobo, a Cuban composer, pianist, violinist, and musical director. The song is unique, combining two genres, criolla (the first part) and bolero (the second part), for the first time. Roig and his partner, Blanca Becerra, wrote the lyrics after their marriage in 1911. The inspiration for the song came from some verses that they paraphrased from an obscure poet and journalist, Ramón Rivera Gollury. This version was never published, and the last version of the lyrics was written by Augustin Rodríguez, who wrote the lyrics to many other songs by Roig.

Initially, the song debuted as "Serenata Criolla" by tenor Maríano Ménendez at the Nicholas Hall in the Hubert de Blanck Conservatory of Havana. However, the song failed at first. In 1921, Roig published the music through a private enterprise with its definitive title "Quiereme Mucho" ("Love Me a Lot"), giving credit to Gollury. Unfortunately, Gollury did not receive royalties for the song as he had sold the rights for only Five Cuban pesos. Roig had not done any better because he sold his rights for three pesos.

In the twenties, many interpretations were recorded, starting with Tion Schipa, an Italian lyric tenor and one of the most famous tenors of the century. Other vocalists who recorded the song in the 1920s were Elena Ehlers, José Moriche, and Maríano Meléndez. The song's success led to its translation into English by lyricists Albert Games and Jack Sherr, published as "Yours." It became popular with the recording by the Jimmy Dorsey Orchestra, Vera Lynn, and Dick Contino. The song reached the Billboard Best Seller chart multiple times with different artists. Many versions were sung by various artists, including Lucie Arnaz, Bing Crosby, Xavier Cugat, Gene Autry, Vikki Carr, Ray Charles, The Del-Vikings, Plácido Domingo, The Duprees, Ibrahim Ferrer, Freddy Fender, Connie Francis, Benny Goodman, Eydie Goemé, Engelbert Humperdinck, Linda Ronstadt, Jerry Vale, Julio Iglesias, and many others.

Gonzalo Roig passed away in Havana on June 13, 1970.

"Sarandonga" is a song composed by the Cuban duo Los Compadres, consisting of Lorenzo Hierrezuelo and Francisco Repilado (Compay Segundo), in the late 1950s. In 1966, the song was first sung in Spain by Antonio González, known as 'El Pescailla,' who was the husband of Lola Flores and father of Lolita. Later, in 2002, Lola Flores' daughter, Lolita herself, sang her version of the song in her album *Lola, Lolita, Lola,* which made the song famous worldwide. Over the years, the song has been interpreted by several artists, including Adalberto Santiago and Johhny Pacheco, as well as, more recently, by Haila María Mompie and Pilar Boyero.

Jimmy Sabater started his music career as a timbalero with Joe Cuba's band. He also had experience in composing and performing background vocals. However, he didn't get a chance to sing until 1962. At that time, the lead vocalist of the band, Willie Torres, left to join the José Curbelo orchestra. Joe Cuba then decided to hire a young Puerto Rican singer named José "Cheo" Feliciano on the recommendation of Tito Rodríguez. The issue was that

Cheo had a strong accent while speaking or singing in English, but Jimmy did not. In the same year, Jimmy got to record his first song, "To Be with You," which became a big hit.

In 1948, Daniel Santos signed a deal with *Sonora Matancera,* and together, they produced twenty remarkable songs in one night, breaking the international recording record.

The beautiful Mexican movie star María Félix inspired Agustín Lara to compose the bolero "María Bonita."

The Colombian singer and composer Edulfamid Molina Díaz, born Jhojan Esteban Parra Cubillos, a.k.a. "Piper Pimienta," in Puerto Tejada, Cauca on August 4, 1939, was murdered on June 4, 1998, in his residence in the La Rivera neighborhood, in eastern Cali. The collection of debt is the suspicion for the motive of the crime. When he was in the front garden of his home, an unknown person attacked him with shots and then fled on a motorcycle. The authorities investigated the possibility that the shooting had to do with a recent lawsuit won by Piper against a businessman who had not paid him for presentations.

In the 1980s, his son, John Jairo, was murdered. On November 11, 1991, a fire destroyed his house, destroying his memories and his sheet music with all his musical history. Píper Pimienta lived his last years suffering from serious health problems. In 1992, a thrombosis paralyzed half his body, and he had to resort to the charity of his colleagues and the record label to cover his medical expenses. He acquired an unsteady gait with intensive therapy, accompanied by a cane, and continued singing wherever he was invited. The authorities have never been able to solve his murder.

—⚡—

Chamaco Ramírez, originally named Ramón Luis Ramírez Toro, was a renowned salsa singer and composer born on September 10, 1941, in Santurce, Puerto Rico. He gained fame for his singing talent after joining *Tommy Olivencia's Orchestra* at 16. Ramírez went on to record eight albums with the orchestra, which are now considered classics. In the 1960s, he also provided vocals for albums by the *Alegre All Stars* and *Kako and his Orchestra* while still being a Tommy Olivencia y Su Orquesta member.

Unfortunately, Ramírez faced frequent legal problems due to his use of illegal drugs during his later years. Tragically, he died at the youthful age of 41 after being shot in the borough of the Bronx in New York City in the early hours of March 27, 1983. He passed away in the ambulance while being transported to the hospital.

—⚡—

When Rogelio Martínez, the director of *La Sonora Matancera,* heard Celia Cruz's first single on 78 rpm, "Cao Cao Maní Picao" and "Mata Siguaraya," recorded in the studio of CMQ, he decided to record her. He told Sidney Siegel, the producer of Seeco Records in Cuba, about his plan, but he was unhappy. He asked Rogelio,

"But how is it possible? Have you gone crazy?" Rogelio replied that if Siegel didn't want to produce the album, he could look for another studio the next day because *"You can't tell me who I can or cannot record."* Rogelio then went to Havana to sign the contract with Celia Cruz, whom he called "La Guarachera de Cuba."

—⁂—

Chago Martínez, whom Willie Rosario considered the best baritone sax player he ever had, went on to become the mayor of his hometown of Juana Díaz, Puerto Rico.

—⁂—

His first wife, Angelina Bruschetta, inspired the song "Mujer" by Agustin Lara.

—⁂—

Trini López designed two guitars for Gibson, the Trini López Standard and López Deluxe.

—⁂—

In 1970, Gabriel Eladio "Yayo el Indio" Peguero became the lead singer of *La Sonora Matancera,* replacing Justo Bentancourt. He remained with the group for over two decades despite recording only forty-four songs.

—⁂—

In a significant turn of events in 1959, José Curbelo dissolved his orchestra and founded the Alpha Artists Music Agency. This agency swiftly rose to prominence as the leading Latin music broker on the East Coast.

Within a remarkably fleeting time, Curbelo had all the top bands under his contract. The exclusivity of the top spots in New York City was now under his control, as any band aspiring to perform there had to secure Curbelo's approval. This effectively established a monopoly, with promoters being mandated to hire his bands. The consequences of non-compliance were severe, as it meant they couldn't engage any bands at all.

La Sonora Matancera initially offered the position of trumpet player to a friend of Pedro Knight named Oswaldo Diaz. Unfortunately, he had to decline as he had prior obligations to his father's band. Instead, he recommended Pedro for the role. Pedro had been a childhood friend of the band members and lived just two blocks from where the band was formed. At the time, he worked as a typographer for *El Bodeguero* newspaper. When Pedro was called for a tryout, he agreed to accept the position, but only after finishing his job. On January 6, 1944, he visited the orchestra director, Valentin Cane, at his house in the city. Valentin's son, Humberto, then played some sheet music for Pedro, who started playing in the band at the Marte and Belona that night.

The 1968 album *Acid* by Ray Barretto, released on Fania Records, was a seminal work in Latin jazz. The title was suggested by Pete Bonet, who also wrote the liner notes on the back of the album. However, there was some controversy regarding the album's credits. While Barretto was credited with all eight songs on the LP, the truth was that the piano player Luis Cruz wrote "The Teacher of Love," and Gil López, the arranger, wrote

"Sola Te Dejaré." Four other tunes were the idea of Pete Bonet, who collaborated with Barretto on them. When confronted about the discrepancies, Barretto blamed Jerry Masucci for the mistake, but none of the musicians involved believed this excuse.

During the late 1920s, the son style of music was gaining respectability in Cuba, yet it was a source of controversy among the Cubans residing in Tampa. The Afro-Cuban Martí-Maceo Club's minutes revealed a deep-seated disagreement, with some members still considering the son music as provocative and vulgar. This controversy led to a brief ban on the son, a decision that further intensified the tension within the community.

In 1917, James Reese Europe's 369th Infantry "Hellfighters" Band needed musicians who could sight-read and play various military band instruments. To address this issue, Europe went to Puerto Rico, where he knew that every provincial city had musicians in their brass band who would suit the needs of the United States military. Puerto Rican musicians played a crucial role, with no less than 18 Puerto Ricans joining the band. Among them were trombonist Rafael Hernández, who would become Puerto Rico's most prolific and significant composer, and composer/conductor Rafael Duchesne, a veteran player of African American swing bands.

Sonny Bravo, an Afro-Cuban jazz and Latin jazz pianist, received a baseball scholarship to attend the University of Miami in 1954. He tried out for the Havana Sugar Kings of the International League AAA division, which was affiliated with the Major League Baseball's Cincinnati Reds. The team's home stadium was El Gran Estadio del Cerro in Havana. Unfortunately, during a game on a rainy day, he suffered a career-ending injury to his pitching arm before his second professional tryout.

Millie Donay

The dance team of Millie Donay, born Carmela Dante Di Stefano in 1934, an American of Italian ancestry, and Cuban Pete, born Pedro Aguilar in San Juan, Puerto Rico, in 1927, was historical, given that they were the first dance team of mix color to perform on stage in the United States. Millie was white, and Pete was dark, a significant contribution to race relations that has often been ignored.

Besides The Palladium, where Millie began as a soloist, they performed at Carnegie Hall, The Apollo Theatre, The Catskills, Waldorf Astoria, and Madison Square Garden for Israeli President David Ben-Gurion. They were also on the Jackie Gleason Show and trained the teachers of the Arthur Murray Dance Studios in Latin dances. After her divorce from Pete, Millie became the opening act for Jerry Lewis and opened for Pérez Prado in Las Vegas.

This author "re-discovered" her managing a beauty parlor in the late 1990s in New Jersey and brought her to a live interview together on N.J. Public Television. The interview can be seen on YouTube.

Simons Jou Llongueras was born in Spain on or about 1893. At an early age, he went to Cuba, where he was raised, and then to France, where he continued learning and improving his pastry skills. In 1923, at 219 West 116th Street, he established La Moderna Bakery. Besides delicious pastries, the business was famous for selling congas, bongós, maracas, claves, and other instruments. Marlon Brando bought his congas at this location. The place was known to be frequented by Mongo Santamaría, Willie Bobo, Machito, Cándido Camero, Bény Bonilla, and José Mangual, who would purchase their instruments or come to jam in the business's backyard. Jou imported most of the instruments he sold from Cuba, and it was the only place in town where musicians could purchase high-quality Cuban percussion instruments. It operated for four decades, during the 20s, 30s, 40s and 50s.

Joe Hernández

Luis Russell (1902-1963) was a talented jazz pianist, orchestra leader, composer, and arranger from Panama. When he was 17 years old, he was fortunate enough to win $3,000 in a lottery, which enabled him to move to the United States with his family. In today's economy, that amount is equivalent to almost $54,000.

The bass and tuba player Rafael Escudero (1891-1970) is recognized as one of the earliest Boricuas who significantly contributed to early jazz. Despite being Latino, he was a member of the highly regarded *Fletcher Henderson Orchestra*, a distinguished African American band of the Harlem Renaissance. Sadly, Escudero passed away at the age of 79 in a fire that occurred at the Roma Hotel in Old San Juan.

The Puerto Rican musician Ramón "Monchito" Muñoz Rodríguez played his first professional gig at 13, performing bongós with the renowned American jazz drummer, bandleader, and composer Gene Krupa. Monchito also recorded the song "Chiquita Banana."

Julio Iglesias is an investor in several prime properties in the Dominican Republic, including several hotel complexes and the Punta Cana International Airport, which he owns jointly with the fashion designer Oscar de la Renta.

Israel Vitenszteim Vurm, also known as Carlos Argentino, was a key figure in the history of Latin music. Born in Buenos Aires on June 23, 1929, he had Jewish roots. Israel was not just the first prominent Jewish recording artist to gain fame as a Latin and tropical-style singer in Latin America during the late 1940s and 1950s, but he also played a significant role in popularizing the Pachanga style. His career took off after joining *La Sonora Mantancera* in the 1950s, where he performed and recorded music. He earned the nickname "El Rey de la Pachanga." Israel's musical journey ended on June 20, 1991.

In 1988, Héctor Lavoe received a nomination for the Tropical Music Grammy Award for his album *Héctor Strikes Back*. Unfortunately, that same year, he was diagnosed with HIV. Héctor's heroin addiction had a devastating impact on his health.

He was scheduled to perform at a concert at the Rubén Rodríguez de Bayamón Coliseum in Puerto Rico alongside other notable musicians like Ray Barretto, Pete "El Conde" Rodríguez, Luis Perico Ortiz, and Johnny Pacheco. However, the event was ultimately canceled due to a lack of audience. Even though the Coliseum had a seating capacity of 8,000 people, only a few hundred tickets were sold.

The local promoters could not pay the performers or Ralph Mercado, and the event could have been better planned with promotion. Competing against a heavily promoted venue nearby, the concert was doomed. Héctor offered to perform for free for those who had attended, but the promoters cut the power and turned off the microphones to prevent him from doing so. It was a humiliating moment for Héctor Lavoe, who so desperately wanted to gain the love and support of his fans.

In the 1950s, Alberto Socarras, a Cuban flutist, appeared on Rod Sterling's TV show *The Twilight Zone*. However, by the mid-1970s, he had already been diagnosed with Alzheimer's disease. Due to his condition, he had trouble remembering where he lived, and the local police had to escort him home on multiple occasions.

Pedro Flores composed the bolero "Olga" in 1941, but it was not given a name at first. Julio Andino, the bass player, fell in love with a girl and promised her a gift. He asked Flores if he could name the song after her and offered him fifty dollars, which was a considerable amount of money at the time (equivalent to $1,025 in 2024). Flores agreed to the offer, and the song was named "Olga."

Willie Rosario, whose real name is Fernando Luis Rosario Marín, was born on May 6, 1924, in Coamo, Puerto Rico. He studied communications in college and received specialized training in the technical aspects of radio broadcasting. Apart from playing, he also worked as a disc jockey and news reporter for the New York-based Spanish-speaking station, Radio WADO.

Rosalía "Chalía" Herrera performed at Webster Hall in New York City in 1895 to raise funds for the Cuban War of Independence.

Isolina Carrillo was born in Havana on December 9, 1907. She started her music career at six, under the guidance of her father, who led a charanga típica. 1933 Isolina joined *Las Travadora del Cayo,* an all-female septet, as a trumpeter. Later, she founded the *Siboney* vocal group, which included renowned singers such as Celia Cruz and Olga Guillot. Isolina also organized and directed the *Giant Orchestra* of the *RHC Cadena Azul,* where she became one of the most significant figures of Cuban radio. In 1942, she formed the first orchestra of danzónes in Cuba. Isolina wrote many compositions, including "Dos Gardenias," "Miedo de Ti," "Increíble," "Canción Sin Amor," "Eres Parte de Mi Vida," "Cómo Yo Jamás," and "Has Cambiado Mucho." "Dos Gardenias" was composed in 1947 and premiered by Daniel Santos. He later recorded it with *La Sonora Matancera.*

Pedro Knight, who was married to Celia Cruz, lost his biological father when he was only a few months old. His mother, who was only 16 at the time, became a widow. Later, she met Angel Piedra, who became Pedro's stepfather. Pedro considered him to be his "real" father. Piedra was a skilled musician and played the clarinet, flute, and saxophone. He passed on his knowledge to Pedro, teaching him all he knew. Piedra owned a small printing shop and did his best to make time to teach young Pedro. However, as his business grew, he sought out a music professor who was the director of the Matanzas band and the composer of "Bemba Colora" to continue teaching Pedro music, José Claro Fumero.

Daniel Santos passed away on November 27, 1992, at 76, at his ranch in Ocala, Florida. He was laid to rest in the Santa María Magdalena de Pazzis Cemetery in Old San Juan, Puerto Rico. His tomb is close to the tombs of Pedro Flores, a renowned Puerto Rican composer, and Albizu Campos.

In 2022, Jaden from the group *Sophia,* at age 8, won the Latin Grammy for Best Latin Children's Album, making him the youngest winner ever.

It's worth noting that Celia Cruz was never officially a member of the *Sonora Matancera* band. Instead, she was invited to perform as a guest singer, along with another artist, usually Daniel Santos, during their tours. Celia contracted with *Radio Progreso* to perform their show *Cascabeles Candado*, and Sonora Matancera was part of it. This arrangement lasted for about fifteen years.

During the late 16th century, the first orchestra and composition with Cuban documentation was formed in Santiago de Cuba. This small ensemble comprised two fife players, a Sevillian violinist, Pascual de Ochoa, and two free black Dominican women, Teodora and Micaela

Gines, who hailed from Santiago de Los Caballeros. This orchestra played music for holidays and churches. Two of its members, Pascual de Ochoa and Micaela Gines, later moved to Havana. At the end of the century, they joined a quartet with Pedro Almanza, a violinist from Malaga, and Jacome Viceira, a clarinetist from Portugal. The group also included other musicians who played the guiro and castanets.

The Italian actor Rodolfo Pietro Filiberto Raffaello Guglielmi di Valentína d'Antonguella, famously known as Rudolph Valentino, arrived in New York when he was just 18 years old. Within a year, he was hired by Joe Pania, a restaurateur who owned *Castles-by-the-Sea, the Colón,* and the *Woodmansten Inn,* to dance the tango with vaudeville dancer Joan Sawyer for a weekly salary of $50. In today's currency, that would be equivalent to $900. Rudolph Valentino passed away due to sepsis at the youthful age of 31.

Agustin Lara studied at the Military College in Mexico and, by age 15, had joined the Personal Guard of Francisco Villa, a.k.a. Pancho Villa. However, due to his weak physical condition, he was discharged, putting an end to his military career.

Nilo Menéndez (1902-1987) was born in Matanzas, on September 26, 1902. He lived his adolescence in Havana, and in 1924, he left Cuba and went to New York. Nilo said that in 1929, he fell in love with a beautiful blonde with light green eyes. Her name was Conchita Utrera, and she was a Cuban from an upper-class and cultured family. The same night of the day he met her, he composed a melodic line. He asked the poet and talented tenor Adolfo Utrera, Conchita's brother, to put the lyrics to it, as he suggested the theme and some of the words, including "your eyes gave me the sweet theme for my song." The result was the birth of the beautiful and famous bolero "Aquellos Ojos Verdes" (Green Eyes).

Regrettably, Nilo Menéndez's relationship with Conchita was never meant to be. She penned him a farewell letter, expressing her fondness for the song but not for him, and they never crossed paths again. This poignant twist in their tale adds a bittersweet note to the story of the creation of "Aquellos Ojos Verdes" (Green Eyes).

Rafael Hernández

Rafael Hernández was a Puerto Rican composer who specialized in Romantic music. He was known for his love songs, which covered a range of themes, including erotic love, filial love, fraternal love, patriotic love, and love of God. One of his most famous songs, "Desvelo de Amor," was inspired by his close relationship with his sister, Victoria.

One day, Wito Kortright, Ray Barreto's lead singer, and the *Charanga Moderna Band* were on stage doing a gig with Tito Rodríguez and his orchestra. Wito was wearing a black suit with white socks. Barretto noticed and began to make fun of Wito's attire. This sarcasm by Barretto does not sit well with Wito, as he tells Barretto to go to hell, gets off the stage, and leaves, leaving Barretto without a singer and the guiro player. Barretto proceeded with no sweat and told Pete Bonet to do the singing.

During the Great Depression in the 1930s, Rafael and Victoria lived in an apartment in East Harlem and ran a music store together. Victoria was a significant help to Rafael, managing his Victoria Quartet and helping to keep him grounded. The composer relied on his sister's advice and guidance for all major decisions in his life.

In 1932, Rafael traveled to Mexico for a three-month contract but ended up staying for sixteen years. He greatly missed his sister and New York, and this nostalgia inspired him to write "Desvelo de Amor." However, to make the song more appealing to the public, Rafael changed the lyrics to focus on erotic love instead of his brotherly love for Victoria. In an interview with music historian Max Salazar, many years later, Victoria revealed that the song was written for her.

Joe Hernández

The great singer Celio González (1924-2004), born Celio González Adam Ascencio in Camajuani, Cuba, who at one time sang for *La Sonora Matancera*, was born with the inherited disease called phocomelia, which causes birth without two fingers and toes.

The success of the "El Manicero" song encouraged the Marks publishing house and other music publishers to include more Latin music in their repertoire. By September 1932, the Marks catalog had almost 600 Latin songs, mainly from Cuba.

"El Manicero" also became famous in the cinema and was used in the movie *Cuban Love Song,* filmed in 1931, and starred Jimmy Durante, Lawrence Tibbett, and Lupe Vélez. Carmen Burguette, the Cuban singer, dubbed Lupe Vélez's voice in "El Manicero," accompanied by the Palau Brothers Orchestra. The plot of the movie revolves around a marine (Lawrence Tibbett) who falls in love with a peanut vendor (Lupe Vélez) in Cuba, and after the war, he goes back with a friend (Jimmy Durante) to find her and their illegitimate child.

Metro-Goldwyn-Mayer released the film on December 5, 1931. Despite a favorable review, the film did poorly at the box office. However, two of the movie's songs, "The Cuban Love Song" and "El Manicero," became major hits.

Geoffrey Lamont Holder (1930-2014) was a Tony award-winning actor, singer, composer, choreographer, director, and dancer. He frequently performed at the Salsa dance shows at the Latin nightclub Corso on East 86th Street.

The day after Ismael Rivera's burial, La Toya Jackson visited his gravesite and placed flowers. She and her family, including Michael Jackson, were fans of Rivera's music.

In 2022, Angela Álvarez, a Cuban-born native, made history by becoming the oldest person to win a Latin Grammy at age 95. She tied with songwriter Silvana Estrada for the Best New Artist award. Additionally, Álvarez was the most senior person ever nominated for a Latin Grammy.

Unlike Celia Cruz, who voluntarily left Cuba because of Fidel Castro's revolution, La Lupe was asked to leave because the newly established government deemed her music and concerts anti-revolutionary.

The movie *Our Latin Thing* inaccurately documents the evolution of salsa music by misrepresenting its origins. It does not acknowledge the music's incubation and development in Cuba, leading viewers to believe that

Joe Hernández

it solely originated in Africa and continued to evolve in New York.

—∞—

In her autobiography, Celia Cruz claimed to have recorded 74 albums during her 15-year relationship with *La Sonora Matancera* and Seeco label, a discography that surpasses any uncovered until now.

—∞—

The Puerto Rico Theater, situated at 490 East 138th Street, at the intersection of Brook Avenue in the Mott Haven area of the Bronx, was constructed in 1917. It was previously known as the Forum Theater. After the massive migration of Puerto Ricans, the theater became a principal place to showcase musical performances by musicians from the island. Chucho Montalban, the theater manager, was the brother of the movie actor Ricardo Montalban.

—∞—

On June 24, 1935, Carlos Gardel, famously known as The King of the Tango, died in Medellin, Colombia, due to a tragic airline accident. The unfortunate incident occurred when two planes collided on the same runway, resulting in the loss of fifteen lives, with five more left with severe burns. The entire Hispanic world was devastated by the news of Gardel's sudden death, and tens of thousands mourned his passing. There were even reports that a famous singer retired to a convent due to the shock of his demise.

—∞—

Daniel Santos

One of the finest performers and interpreters of Pedro Flores's compositions was Daniel Santos, who delivered unforgettable renditions of songs like "Despedida," "Amor Prohibido," "Linda," "Obsession," and "Irresistible."

Julio Iglesias is fluent in seven languages, which allows him to enchant audiences worldwide with his suave voice and captivating stage presence.

One of Celia Cruz's most influential figures was Paulina Álvarez, a Cuban singer and bandleader whom she considered her disciple.

Joe Hernández

The *Grupo Folklórico y Experimental Nuevayorkino* was first the *Conjunto Anabacoa* formed by Andy and Jerry González.

Pete Bonet has been a lead singer or chorus member for more than fifty bands throughout his career.

Rubén Blades' father was a policeman in Panama who also played the bongós, and his mother was a Cuban singer and actress on radio soap operas.

Orquesta De La Luz, which was formed in 1984, is not just Japan's most famous salsa orchestra but a globally recognized musical entity. Despite being born, raised, and residing in Japan, its members have gained recognition worldwide for their exceptional music. However, they were not the first Japanese orchestra to play Latin music. This distinction belongs to Tadaaki Misago, a Japanese musician who organized the famous *Tokyo Cuban Boys Orchestra* in 1949. The Tokyo Cuban Boys Orchestra became Japan's longest-running Latin big band, paving the way for future Latin music enthusiasts in the country.

The Puerto Rican singer and guitarist José Feliciano was born José Montserrate Feliciano García on September 10, 1945. His first hit was his rendition of *The Doors* "Light My Fire," which sold over one million copies.

However, his best-seller has been "Feliz Navidad," a record that sells tens of thousands of copies every Christmas.

Manu Dibango was a tenor saxophonist from Cameroon Central Africa who was the songwriter of the worldwide 1972 hit "Soul Makosa." In 1973 he appeared with the Fania All Stars in Puerto Rico.

The Cuban trumpet player Rene Edreira, who played with Alberto Iznaga's *Siboney Orchestra*, was the first musician to play the Hawaiian guitar in Latin music.

In 1967, Cheo Feliciano had to leave the Joe Cuba Sextet to serve a prison sentence for drug use.

Bienvenido Granda, also known as "El Bigote Que Canta," holds the record for recording the highest number of songs *with La Sonora Matancera,* with over 200 tunes.

Tito Puente was a prolific musician; between 1950 and 1969, he produced 68 albums, which averaged an album every three and a half months.

Carlos Gardel remains the most successful tango singer ever, with record sales that no other tango singer has ever surpassed. He earned several nicknames throughout his career, including "La Voz" (The Voice), "El Zorzal Criollo" (The Creole Songbird), "El Mago" (The Magician), and "El Maestro" (The Master). He was also given accolades such as "El Que Cada Vez Canta Mejor" (The One Who Sings Better Every Day) and "Rey del Tango" (King of the Tango).

Jesús Navarro Moreno, popularly known as Chucho Navarro (1913-1993), was a Mexican guitarist and singer who initially wanted to pursue a career in medicine but later decided to become a musician. He moved to New York with a group named Los Capórales and subsequently became the leader of the famous El Trío Los Panchos. Chucho was a prolific composer of some of their greatest hits, including "Rayito de Luna," "Una Copa Más," and "Sin Remedio." He passed away in Mexico in December 1993.

There have been rumors for years that Libertad Lamarque had a brief romantic relationship with Juan Domingo Peron before he became the president of Argentina. At that time, he was an ambitious military officer. Lamarque had a problematic first marriage with Emilio Romero, who was an alcoholic, and her life was not going well. Her misery led her to attempt suicide in Santiago, Chile, by jumping from a hotel window. Fortunately, she survived the attempt as an awning broke her fall. After she recovered from her injuries, she ended her marriage in divorce, and that's when the short romantic interlude occurred with the man who would later become Argentina's authoritarian president.

—⚞—

Ruth Fernández

Ruth Fernández is the first Puerto Rican woman to record with a big band in the United States, the Vincent López Orchestra. She also achieved another milestone by becoming the first popular singer to be signed by the Metropolitan Opera House in New York.

—⚞—

In 1967, the famous musician José Feliciano was scheduled to perform in the United Kingdom along with his guide dog, Trudy. However, due to the strict quarantine regulations imposed by the government, Trudy had to be quarantined for six months, which left Feliciano devastated. These measures were designed to prevent the spread of rabies, but they caused immense frustration for Feliciano. He channeled his emotions into music and wrote the song 'No Dogs Allowed,' which became a top 10 hit in the Netherlands in 1969 and resonated with many people.

Yomo Toro

"Yomo" Toro, originally named Victor Guillermo Toro, was born on July 26, 1933, in Guanica, Puerto Rico. He was a skilled left-handed guitarist and cuatro player who recorded over 150 albums. Toro collaborated with musicians from genres such as Frankie Cutlass, Harry Belafonte, Paul Simon, Linda Ronstadt, and David Byrne. He also worked closely with Cuban legends Arsenio Rodríguez and Alfonso "El Panameño" Joséph, as well as salsa artists Willie Colón, Héctor Lavoe, Rubén Blades, and the Fania All-Stars. In addition, he recorded four albums with *Trío Los Panchos,* including one featuring Eydie Goemé. Despite his fame and virtuosity, Toro remained a modest man and only composed one song in his career titled "El Lechon de Cachete." He passed away on June 30, 2012, due to kidney failure.

La Lupe was married twice. First to Eulogio "Yoyo" Reyes and later to Willie García, a Cuban singer who recorded Ray Barretto, the Joe Cuba Sextet and Grupo Folklórico y Experimental Nuevayorkino. She had a son with Willie García.

Lucho Gatica, a prominent Chilean singer, was born on November 11, 1928, in Rancagua, Chile. He was married to the Puerto Rican actress María del Pilar Cordero, also known as Mapy Cortés, who appeared in several films during the Golden Age of Mexican cinema.

Jimmy Sabater played 23 years with the Joe Cuba Sextet, and Cheo Feliciano did nine. Jimmy sang the English lyrics while Cheo sang all the Spanish songs.

Willie Bobo used to perform regularly as a band member in Bill Cosby's variety show. They were good friends, and Willie occasionally appeared in comedy skits on Cosby's various TV comedy specials.

Joe Hernández

José Mojica, born Fray José de Guadalupe Mojica on September 14, 1895, was a former tenor and film actor. While in Buenos Aires, Argentina, he confided in Agustin Laras about his intention to become a monk and renounce his singing career before announcing it to the public. Laras tried to persuade Mojica not to take this step but was unsuccessful. As a result, Laras composed "Solamente Una Vez" and dedicated it to Mojica.

The Queen of Salsa, Celia Cruz, is buried at the Woodlawn Cemetery in the Bronx. This cemetery is the resting place of many other well-known people, such as Irving Berlin, Miles Davis, Louis Armstrong, Duke Ellington, George M. Cohan, Billie Holiday, JC Penney, Fiorello La Guardia, Bat Masterson, W.C. Handy, Herman Melville, F.W. Woolworth, Frank Grillo (Machito), Héctor Lavoe, Charlie Palmieri, Johnny Pacheco, La Lupe, and the gangster Bumpy Johnson.

The *Lecuona Cuban Boys* was founded in 1931 by the great Cuban composer Ernesto Lecuona. However, he appeared with the group sporadically, and the actual leader initially was Armando Orefiche, followed by the brothers Augustin and Gerardo Brugueras.

Casita María, a pivotal youth center located at 110th Street and Park Avenue in New York City, holds a rich historical significance. It served as a vibrant hub for numerous young Latin boys and girls, fostering a space for creation, learning, and skill development.

The center's profound influence is a testament to the collective effort of the community, evident in the many young individuals it nurtured, who later emerged as distinguished musicians, artists, and responsible community members. Today, it is in the Hunts Point section of the South Bronx.

The Victor label recognized the Trío Matamoros' potential and paid them $20.00 per side for their first recordings in New York City. These recordings, which include the immensely popular songs "Lagrimas Negras," "Mama Son de la Loma," and "El Que Siembra Su Maiz y Mientes," were not just successful but also became a part of the cultural fabric, resonating with people across generations.

Cuban pianist José Melis occasionally accompanied Frank Sinatra and Mel Torme, in addition to performing as a soloist with many symphony orchestras, including the Boston Pops.

Noro Morales was born Norosvaldo Morales, but he shortened it to Noro.

Tito Puente made his debut at the age of 13 as a drummer with the Noro Morales Orchestra.

Joe Hernández

The legendary conga drum player, Cándido, used to proudly display a reference letter given to him by the renowned bandleader Stan Kenton many years ago. The letter highlighted Cándido's exceptional talents, strong work ethic, admirable personal qualities, and unwavering loyalty. The letter also stated that Cándido was always "clean."

On March 16, 2011, the USPS issued five commemorative stamps honoring Latin Music Legends, including Selena, Carlos Gardel, Carmen Miranda, Celia Cruz, and Tito Puente, each with a denomination of 44 cents.

During the early years, Latin American musicians had to travel to New York or New Jersey to get their music recorded. RCA Victor, originally known as the Victor Talking Machine Company, had its recording facilities in Camden, New Jersey. As Latin music grew in popularity, RCA Victor established more recording facilities in other parts of Latin America, such as Mexico.

Panchito Riset, whose real name was Francisco Hilario Riser Rincón (1910-1988), became a singer in the *Antobal Orchestra* in New York in 1933. In one of the early records, he replaced Antonio Machín, who was misspelled as Riset. Thus, he adopted the name Panchito Riset for his musical career.

Antonio María Romeu Marrero (1876-1955) was not just a Cuban pianist, composer, and band leader. He was a musical powerhouse known as 'El Mago de las Teclas' (The Keyboard Magician), who left an indelible mark on Cuban music. His legacy includes over 500 danzónes, a testament to his prolific creativity and dedication to his craft. Among these, his most renowned piece is the arrangement of "Tres Lindas Cubanas," a *son* originally penned by guitarist Guillermo Castillo and later popularized by the Sexteto Habanero.

Joe Hernández & Marco Rizo

Marco Rizo was a talented pianist, composer, and conductor from Cuba. He gained recognition after performing with the *Don Azpiazú Orchestra*. However, he rose to fame as the music director of the famous American sitcom *I Love Lucy* featuring Desi Arnaz and Lucille Ball. Rizo even wrote the theme song for the show, but unfortunately, he never received credit due to "show-biz politics."

Before La Guaracha de Cuba, Celia Cruz was also crowned the *Queen of Salsa;* La Lupe had already been honored with the same title.

While in New York in 1935, Carlos Gardel appeared in the English-language musical revue *The Big Broadcast of 1935* with Spanish subtitles. Gardel shared the billing with many big names in the film, including Bing Crosby.

Roberto "Bobby" Valentín, also known as "El Rey del Bajo," meaning "King of the Bass," was born in Orocovis, Puerto Rico, on June 9, 1941. He started his musical journey by learning to play the guitar from his father. Later, he switched to the trumpet and eventually found his calling in playing the bass.

Alfredo Sadel, a famous Venezuelan singer and actor, changed his name as there were at least two professionals with similar names. To create his new name, he took the first two letters of his last name, SA, and the last three letters of his idol's previous name, Carlos Gardel, forming Sadel. He recorded more than 2,000 songs during his career and once performed a duet with Bény Moré.

Over the span of nearly four decades, from 1941 to 1979, the *Machito Orchestra* embarked on a prolific recording journey. They produced 52 albums and 17 LPs, many of which were collaborative projects with other artists. The orchestra's recordings spanned various formats, including 417 78-RPMs and 284 78-RPM recordings featuring Machito's voice. These recordings, made in collaboration with esteemed musicians such as Xavier Cugat, Noro Morales, Marcelino Guerra, Cané, La Siboney, Conjunto Batiri, Tito Puente, and the Gaucho All-Stars, stand as a testament to the orchestra's enduring legacy.

Sidney Siegel established the Seeco Records company in 1943. The company was originally a jewelry store named Casa Siegel, located on 115th Street and 5th Avenue. The label recorded several renowned artists, such as Bobby Capó, Celia Cruz, Vicentico Valdés, Joe Cuba, La Sonora Matancera, and many others.

Vicente Sigler, a Cuban musician and band leader, organized the first Latin orchestra in New York City in the early 1920s. Determining the exact date of the band's launch is challenging because Sigler had entered the country illegally. However, records indicate that as early as 1925, he performed at prominent hotels in midtown. The orchestra was primarily composed of Puerto Rican and Dominican musicians.

Joe Hernández

Gloria María Fajardo, a native of Havana, Cuba, found her second home in Miami, Florida, at the age of 16 months. Singing was not a career path she had considered during her teenage years. However, when she turned 18, her life took a significant turn. Emilio Estefan, the leader of a small group in Miami called The Miami Latin Boys, recognized her talent and invited her to join them. This pivotal moment marked the beginning of her singing career and the start of a lifelong partnership. Three years later, Gloria and Emilio's professional collaboration blossomed into a personal one as they got married.

Eduardo Sánchez de Fuentes

Eduardo Sánchez de Fuentes (1874-1944) was a Cuban pianist, composer, and author. He is best known for composing the habanera "Tu," which is considered a masterpiece among Latin American composers. The story behind the title of the piece is quite interesting. It is said that while playing the melody on the piano, a young lady approached Sánchez de Fuentes and asked him the name of the composition he was playing. In response, the maestro gallantly replied, "tu" (you), thus giving the habanera its famous name. Despite being the only habanera he ever wrote, "Tu" earned him a place in history and cemented his legacy as one of the greatest Latin American composers ever.

Arsenio Rodríguez

According to legend, Arsenio Rodríguez is credited with inventing the mambo, which he originally called "El Diablo" (The Devil). This name caused much controversy, particularly among the Catholic priests in his community, who were outraged by the music.

Arsenio changed the name to mambo, the Bantú Congo word for a song in praise of deities. In lengua bozal, the combination of Spanish and Bantú, the phrase *"Abre kuti guini mambo"* means, *"Open your ears and listen to the mambo I am singing to you."* However, in many live interviews, Arsenio is heard giving a more simplified explanation, stating he changed the name to "mambo," which in his Congolese ancestors' language meant *"Abre los Oídos y Oye Esto"* (open your ears and listen to this).

Joe Hernández

SMC (Spanish Music Center Records) is a record label established by Gabriel Oller in 1945. The label was named after the music store he owned in midtown on 6th Avenue, in the lobby of the Belvedere hotel called the Spanish Music Center. Tito Puente, his Picadilly Boys, Miguelito Valdés, and his Orchestra were among the first artists to record under this label.

Max Salazar was a journalist, collector, and Latin music historian who was born in New York City on April 17, 1932, and grew up in Spanish Harlem. In his youth, he was a boxer, and in 1953, he won a close decision over Clarence Brown, the then 118-pound national Golden Gloves champion. Max authored the book Mambo Kingdom: Latin Music in New York in 2002. He passed away on September 19, 2010.

Celia Cruz was terrified of flying, so she packed a Saint Christopher and listened to classical music to help her cope.

Despite all the compositions that Tito Puente wrote, he composed only one bolero, released as a 45 RPM titled "Sin Amor." The singer was a friend's girlfriend, who owned a dry-cleaning business in Manhattan. Her name was Hilda Nieves.

The Cuban pianist Alfredito Valdés Jr. was the son of the famous Cuban singer Alfredito Valdés. His mother, Ana María Punny, was a guitarist and vocalist of the all-female band Anacaona.

—⚊—

In 1927, Antonio María Romeu's orchestra made a memorable visit to New York to record a few danzónes. Among the members of the Philharmonic Orchestra of Havana, who were also part of Romeu's orchestra and accompanied him on this significant journey, was a remarkably talented young teenager named Mario Bauza, who was a mere 16 years old at the time.

—⚊—

Pacheco and his Charanga were the first Latin charanga to headline the Apollo Theater in New York City in 1962 and 1963. However, Machito and his Afro-Cubans headlined the Apollo as far back as the late 1940s, and Tito Puente did so in the 1950s.

—⚊—

The renowned Mexican tenor Pedro Vargas abandoned his medical studies to perform at the Teatro de la Esperanza Iris in Mexico City when he was 24 years old.

—⚊—

Bény Moré, born Bartolomé Maximiliano Moré in Camaguey in 1919, was the oldest of twenty siblings.

—⚊—

The inspiration for Mongo Santamaría's incredible composition "Afro Blue" came to him unexpectedly. He was at a television show in Los Angeles, waiting for Dinah Shore when he began joking around with the pianist. Suddenly, the idea for the song struck him. However, some musicologists believe that the idea for the song came from a piece that belonged to Ernesto Lecuona. Another explanation is that Mongo created the song by taking a melodic fragment from a familiar praise song for the Yoruba deity Obatala, the Lord of Creativity. However, Cuban violinist and flutist Felix "Pupi" Legaretta claims that he is the true author of the piece, and that Mongo stole the song from him when Pupi played in Mongo's charanga. Just reading this can give you the blues.

Rafael Hernández's composition of "Malditos Celos" resulted from rage and jealousy from a woman named Juanita, with whom Rafael had lived for 15 years in Puerto Rico. Rafael fell in love with a Mexican woman named María Pérez when they moved to Mexico. Juanita sensed she was losing him, became jealous, got drunk, made a spectacle of herself, and humiliated Rafael in public. Rafael then composed the song. He eventually left Juanita, married María, and had four children.

Cuban Pete earned his nickname after winning a dance competition at the Palladium Ballroom in New York City in 1950. The then-owner, Tommy Morton, declared him "Cuban Pete, King of the Latin Beat."

The first known Cuban manufacturer of string instruments was the dark-skinned Juan José Rebolla.

—∞—

In 1952, Tito Puente released thirty-seven swinging tunes.

—∞—

"El Manicero" (The Peanut Vendor) is the most listened-to Cuban song, followed by "Quiereme Mucho."

—∞—

At the age of eleven, María Teresa Vera made her debut at the Politeama Grande in a tribute to Arquimides Pous.

—∞—

Julio Iglesias has been married twice and is the father of eight children.

—∞—

Machito, a true titan of Latin music, left an indelible mark with over 75 LPs recorded over a remarkable four and a half decades.

—∞—

The famous line used by the Fania All-Stars, "Quitate Tu Para Ponerme Yo," debuted in Cuba in 1933 as part of a political slogan.

—∞—

The Cuban quartet that achieved the most success in the 1950s was an entirely female group organized by pianist Aida Diestro (1924-1973), known as the *D'Aida Quartet*. The group had three brilliant young singers, Elena Burke, Omara Portuondo, and her sister Haydee Portuondo. Two of these (Elena and Omara) would later achieve fame as soloists. When the group played at the Fontainebleau Hotel in Miami, Omara's sister, Haydee, decided to stay in the United States. Another brilliant singer replaced Haydee, Moraima Secada.

They performed on the most important radio and television programs and in nightclubs with Pedro Vargas, Nat King Cole, Édith Piaf, Rita Montaner, Bola de Nieve, and Bény Moré. Ironically, despite their popularity, the original group recorded only one LP. Throughout the years, other young singers would join the group as others left.

Antonio Machín was born in Sagua la Grande, Cuba, on January 17, 1903, to an impoverished family: a father who was Galician and a mother who was black with fifteen siblings. He was the first black singer to perform at Cuba's "El Casino Naciónal."

Pérez Prado's songs "Que Rico el Mambo" and "Patricia" are some of the best-selling Latin albums ever, having sold four and five million copies, respectively. As a result, the North American Critics Association chose Pérez Prado's orchestra as the most famous orchestra of the year 1955. RCA-Victor also awarded him with a gold record for "Cherry Pink and Apple Blossom White," which sold over a million copies that year, reaching a total of 1,800,000 copies sold.

The story is that Herbert Marks, son of the leading publisher E. B. Marks, was on his honeymoon in Cuba in 1929. Supposedly, he was staying at a hotel run by Moisés Simons's brother. This visit was his first visit to the island. There, Marks had an opportunity to listen to a lot of typical music, including "El Manicero." He brought the song back to New York and published it in 1930. The publisher hired Don Azpiazú's sister-in-law, Marion Sunshine, to write the lyrics in English with the help of Wolfe Gilbert. Wolfe was an American songwriter of Tin Pan Alley and best remembered as the lyricist for "Ramóna" (1928), the first movie theme song ever written.

As a teen, Tito Puente sang with a local barbershop quartet. He learned much about rumbas from a black Cuban drummer playing with the *Happy Boys Orchestra*. Cuban drummers Carlos Montesino and Antonino "Tony El Cojito" Escollies, the first drummer, timbalero with the *Machito Afro-Cubans*, taught him the basics of the timbales. He was also tutored by a pianist named Blue Mountain. He also studied the drum set with an African American show drummer named Mr. Williams. He mastered the alto saxophone and clarinet from a music teacher his parents rented a room to, Professor Millian.

Joe Hernández

William Correa, also known as Willie Bobo, began his career in the music industry in 1947 as a band boy for the Machito Orchestra.

Los Muñequitos de Matanzas is a Cuban musical group founded in the La Marina district on October 9, 1952. The group initially consisted of a few young street rumberos who used to hang out together after work. One day, while having drinks at a local tavern called El Gallo, they heard a song by Arsenio Rodríguez that impressed them. They started drumming on the counter, table, and other surfaces, and soon, the other customers and passers-by joined in with applause. One of the youngsters suggested forming a rumba group to play at local venues, and everyone agreed. With the help of a local singer and composer named Florencio Calle "Catalino," who became the group's director, *Grupo Guaguancó Matancero* was formed.

The group started performing all over the towns in the province of Matanzas, and in 1953, they were invited to perform in Havana. Their performances on radio and television earned them recognition, and they recorded their first 78 rpm record for Puchito Records. One side of the record featured a tune called "Los Muñequitos" (referring to The Newspaper Comic Strip Characters), which became incredibly popular among the listening public. As a result, the group changed its name *to Los Muñequitos de Matanzas,* becoming one of the most renowned Cuban music groups ever.

New York City television Meteorologist Audrey Puente is the daughter of the late Latin percussionist Tito Puente.

—⁂—

Celia Cruz and *La Sonora Matancera* left the island of Cuba soon after Fidel Castro toppled the government of the dictator Fulgencio Batista. The new dictator, Fidel Castro, would not allow Celia Cruz to enter the country even to see her parents at the end of their lives.

—⁂—

Gloria Estefan's father served in Vietnam and was exposed to Agent Orange. As a result of this exposure, he developed multiple sclerosis in 1968. Gloria herself began to fear that she might one day suffer from the same condition. These fears almost became a reality when, in 1990, she was involved in a severe accident that caused a fracture in her cervical vertebrae. The accident occurred when her tour bus crashed near Scranton, Pennsylvania.

—⁂—

In 1988, Gabriel Oller retired and relocated to Las Vegas to live with his brother Vicente Tatay. At the time, Mr. Oller had Alzheimer's disease. During the summer of the same year, Oller was struck and killed by an automobile while crossing the street. His brother's nephew, Andrew Tatay, inherited Oller's estate. Presumably, his brother must have passed away sometime between Oller's arrival and his death. Part of the estate was a six-story warehouse with thousands of 78 RPM recordings and tons of memorabilia. The nephew, clearly unaware of the value of the stored items, junked it all.

In Mexico and New York City, Cuban music, especially the mambo, took a life outside of Cuba. The mambo reached its zenith at the Palladium in New York City in the early 1950s. Here, the mambo got refined by the dancers, and like a "bug," it spread to the rest of the country and even the world. The orchestra of Machito, Puente, and Rodríguez played for all ethnic and Anglo audiences. "The Big Three" developed sophisticated arrangements and incorporated jazz instrumental solos. It was here where the stage was set for the *salsa* explosion as we know it today; Machito, Rodríguez, and Puente were the Father, the Son, and the Holy Ghost of the Latin music dance scene in New York City.

Julio Iglesias was born in Madrid, Spain, but his mother came from a Puerto Rican family.

Juan Tizol was one of many musicians who were recruited from Puerto Rico to play in the theater pit bands and jazz clubs that catered primarily to African American audiences in New York and Washington, D.C. Tizol, along with many other Puerto Rican instrumentalists in the early 1920s, played in the pit orchestra of the legendary Howard Theater in Washington.

In 2020, due to the pandemic, Record Mart, Manhattan's oldest record store in Times Square Subway station, closed after serving Latin music buyers and devoted fans for 62 years since 1958. Jesse Moskowitz and Bob Stack established it. The official address was 7 Times Square. IRT Subway Mezzanine. New York, NY 10036.

Ubaldo Rodríguez Santos, popularly known as Lalo Rodríguez (1958-2022), was a Puerto Rican salsero who kickstarted his music journey at 17. He made his debut on Eddie Palmieri's album "Sun of Latin Music," lending his voice to the hit song "Un Dia Bonito" (A Beautiful Day), along with "Nada de Ti" (Nothing of You), "Nunca Contigo" (Never with You), and the bolero masterpiece "Deseo Salvaje" (Wild Desire), which he wrote himself. This 1975 album was a game-changer in the salsa music scene, becoming the first "Salsa Album" to win a Grammy at the 18th Grammy Awards. The following year, in 1976, Lalo Rodríguez continued to make his mark with his performance on "Unfinished Masterpiece," which was nominated for a Grammy at the 19th Grammy Awards and won.

On March 20, 2011, Lalo was arrested on charges of domestic violence, accused of attempting to strangle his wife of twenty-five years. Shortly after that, he was arrested again for possession of cocaine and violating his wife's restraining order. Rodríguez died at the age of sixty-four on December 13, 2022. The cause of his death is unknown. Rodríguez was found dead outside a residential building in Carolina, in the north of Puerto Rico.

Joe Hernández

Jaime Sabater González, known to the world as Jimmy Sabater, was born on April 11, 1936, in El Barrio (Spanish Harlem), New York City. His musical journey was ignited by his teenage friend, Willie Bobo, with whom he shared a close bond as neighbors. Their mothers, who worked together for many years, further cemented their friendship. Their daily routine was a blend of sports, music, and making music. It was through Bobo that Jimmy was introduced to Tito Puente, a neighbor whose musical influence would leave an indelible mark on Jimmy's music.

Justo Betancourt, renowned for his rendition of "Pa' Bravo Yo," was born on December 6, 1940, in the La Marina neighborhood of Matanzas, Cuba. His early life was immersed in music, a legacy passed down from his family. His parents, both singers in amateur groups, and his paternal uncle, a skilled percussionist, were the pillars of his musical journey. At the early age of 11, Betancourt took his first steps into the world of music as a member of a group sponsored by a beer brand, *La Pandilla Cabeza de Perro*. This was just the beginning of his journey. At 16, he joined the *Guaguancó Matancero* group as a vocalist, where he honed his skills and learned the intricacies of rumba singing from the streets of Matanzas. His journey continued with the Genaro Salinas *Club Orchestra,* with whom he recorded his first single, "Para Gozar Cubita," for the Fama label, marking a significant milestone in his career.

He left Cuba in 1964 and embarked on a new chapter in New York, where he recorded with Orlando Marin for the Fiesta label on the album *Esta en Algo*. This album showcased his versatility as he sang some tunes, including "Aprende a Querer." From there, he collaborated with various singers and groups, such as *La Sonora Matancera,* Mongo Santamaría, Eddie Palmieri, Ray Barretto, and the Fania All-Stars. Additionally, he led a group called *Conjunto Borincuba,* further demonstrating his ability to lead and collaborate.

—⁂—

Celia Cruz's legacy includes several places named after her. Besides Celia Cruz Square in Los Angeles, three streets have been named in honor of La Reina de la Salsa. One of these streets is the iconic Calle Ocho in Miami, which has been renamed Celia Cruz Way.

—⁂—

Johnny Rodríguez, a Puerto Rican singer and older brother of Tito Rodríguez, was born on October 10, 1912, on a ship traveling from Cuba to Puerto Rico. His birth was registered in the Municipality of Camuy, Puerto Rico, and he grew up in the Membrillo neighborhood of the same town.

—⁂—

From an incredibly early age, their mother Doña Ercilia encouraged Tito Puente and his younger sister Anna to study music and dance. At twelve and seven, respectively, they became members of "Stars of the Future," an organization formed by the director of a local funeral parlor. The meetings were held at "La Milagrosa" Catholic Church on 115th Street and Lenox Avenue in New York City.

Joe Hernández

Joe Gaines of New York's WEVD radio station wrote the liner notes and suggested the title for Ray Barretto's album "Hard Hands."

Richie & Tito Puente

The famous musician Tito Puente had a son named Richard "Richie-Kiki" Puente, a percussionist and one of the founders of the disco group *Foxy*. Richie's mother, an Italian dancer named Ida Carlini, had a brief relationship with Tito Puente.

Richie was a talented musician who played multiple instruments. Ten years prior, he suffered a brain injury resulting from a mugging, which led to hospitalization due to viral encephalopathy. Despite this, he continued to pursue his musical career and played with famous artists such as Eddie Money, George and Gwen McRae, Peter Frampton, Blowfly (Clarence Reed), and ABBA.

In 1978, *Foxy* released their hit song "Get Off," which topped Billboard's R&B charts for two weeks and reached #9 on the Hot 100 pop charts. The group had two Grammy nominations and two gold records.

Richie also performed as a solo artist and played percussion for Edward Villela's Miami City Ballet production Mambo No.2 a.m. In February 2001, he appeared as a guest artist at Roseland Ballroom in New York City for the Linda McCartney Breast Awareness Garland Foundation in the Latin segment tribute to his father, Tito Puente.

Sadly, in 2004, Richie passed away in his sleep after waking up from a two-month coma induced by doctors to save him.

Singer and composer Pete Bonet began his singing career with *Alfredito Valdés y su Charanga Popular*.

Rafael Ithier, born in Moca, Puerto Rico, on October 3, 1926, is the creative force behind *El Gran Combo*. His musical journey began at an early age, and by 17, he was already showcasing his talent on the trumpet with a group called *Billo Frometa* in the Dominican Republic. After a period of musical exploration, he returned to Puerto Rico and founded his own group, *El Combo de Ayer*. This was a crucial step in his career, as it provided him with the platform and experience necessary to form the iconic *El Gran Combo* in 1962.

Tito Puente had a low opinion of Jerry Masucci, whom he referred to as a *"f**king sh**head."*

Don Azpiazú, credited with making the song "El Manicero" famous worldwide, came from a wealthy and influential family. His family had connections with people in political power and enjoyed certain privileges. His grandfather, José Azpiazú, arrived from Spain in 1840 and worked as a Colonel and an aide to General Máximo Gómez. Azpiazú's great-grandfather was a pianist who played for Queen Isabel II of Spain.

In 1956, Santos Colón met the King, Tito Puente, and that was the beginning of a successful sixteen-year relationship that took Santitos and the Tito Puente Orchestra on an extensive journey throughout the United States, Central and South America, Japan, the Philippines, and Hong Kong.

Pete Bonet was a successful Promoter who provided work for nine orchestras a week at the Corso for years. He was in the process of publishing his second book titled *Del Fanguito pa' Hollywood* before passing away due to cardiac arrest on March 30, 2022, in Rahway, New Jersey.

Despite always looking sharp and like a million dollars, Noro Morales had to work often and hard because he had to pay alimony to three wives.

José Melis had a successful career in the entertainment industry before joining the *Jack Paar Show*. For almost a decade, he performed at various venues across the United States, including the Hotel Sahara in Las Vegas, the Hotel Sherman in Chicago, Bassin Street, and the Park Sheraton Hotel in New York.

Andrés, the maternal uncle of the tremendous Cuban conguero Cándido Camero, who played for the *Septeto Segundo Naciónal*, taught Cándido how to play the bongós using condensed milk cans at age 4.

The Conjunto Kubavana was founded by Alberto Ruiz in 1936. In 1948, Carlos Barbería purchased the rights to the Kubavana name and formed his version of *Orquesta Kubavana*.

Although there are conflicting accounts of his date of birth, some sources state that Frank "Machito" Grillo, born Francisco Raúl Gutiérrez Grillo De Ayala, was born in Tampa on February 16, 1912. However, the evidence suggests otherwise. Like many other Cuban musicians,

Machito needed a more straightforward way to enter the United States. He solved his problem by taking advantage of a fire in the birth records in Tampa, Florida. Machito made a case to prove his birth between specific dates to register, taking advantage of the opportunity caused by the fire. However, others claim that he was born in the Havana neighborhood of Jesús María on December 3, 1908. The truth is that no one knows his actual date of birth, not even his immediate family.

For the next 30 years and until his death, Tito Puente maintained relations with Margaret Acencio. According to himself, these were the happiest years of his life. Prompted by his children, Tito Puente Jr. and Audrey Puente, Tito and Margaret married about 4 or 5 years before Tito's death.

In the mid to late 1920s, Rafael Hernández earned money by writing arrangements of danzas, danzónes, and boleros for pianola rolls.

In 1940, Victoria Hernández, a woman of remarkable resilience, ventured to Mexico to live with her brother, Rafael Hernández. She harbored a dream of establishing a business, but the harsh reality of Mexican law, which forbade foreigners from such endeavors, stood in her way. Undeterred, she returned to New York the following year and took the reins of a women's clothing store located at 786 Prospect Avenue from 1941 to 1969. Her journey was not without its twists and turns, but she ultimately returned the store to Casa de Música, later renamed Casa Hernández.

In 1969, Victoria Hernández passed the torch to Puerto Rican guitarist, vocalist, and composer Miguel Angel 'Mike' Amadeo, who transformed the store into 'Casa Amadeo, Antigua Casa Hernández.' This transition marked a significant chapter in the store's history, one that would be recognized years later. In 2001, the store was rightfully added to the National Register of Historic Places, a testament to its enduring legacy as the oldest continuously run Latin music store in New York.

Ray Barretto was known for being a dedicated and meticulous musician. Whenever he entered the studio, he was entirely focused on his work. One day, during a rehearsal, his wife Brandy came in with a tray of food and placed it in front of him. Ray and Brandy did not exchange words as Ray continued working and giving instructions to his band members. Ray's eyes were fixed on the studio window, wholly absorbed in his work. Ray began to pick at the food without looking down at the tray. After a while, he finally turned his attention to the tray and realized that he had eaten baby shrimp. Immediately, he got up from his chair and told Irv, the sound engineer, that he would return soon. He then instructed his wife to call the hospital.

Ray and Brandy rushed out of the studio, confusing Irv and the crew. After forty-five minutes, Ray returned to the studio as if nothing had happened. It turned out that Ray was asthmatic and allergic to shellfish, and Brandy had mistakenly given him shrimp. As a result, Ray had to rush to the hospital to get an antidote. It makes you wonder how Brandy could have made such a severe mistake.

Carlos Gardel recorded close to 518 tangos; among his best remembered are "A Media Luz," "Adios Muchachos," "Caminito," "Mi Buenos Aires Querido," "Por Una Cabeza," "El Dia Que Me Quieras," and "Mi Noche Triste."

In addition to appearing in 65 films across Argentina, Mexico, and Spain, and six telenovelas, Libertad Lamarque recorded 800 songs.

Tito Puente was declared the "King of the Mambo" by *La Prensa,* a Spanish newspaper in New York, on May 29, 1954. The coronation occurred at the Manhattan Center Ballroom on 34th Street, near 8th Avenue. However, Pérez Prado was already recognized as the Mambo King of the world by that time.

In 1927, the Cuban composer Ignacio Piñeiro wrote a tune titled "Echale Salsita." He wrote this tune while traveling from Havana to Matanzas and stopped at a roadside restaurant famous for its food. As reported by others, he did not write this song on his way to the Chicago World Fair.

The Latin Music Trivia Book

Pepe Sánchez was a troubadour who would serenade his sweethearts and was also a serenader for hire to sing to those sweethearts of other men who could not sing.

Olga Guillot has recorded over 60 LPs, with 30 reaching Gold Record status. Among her most successful songs are: "La Gloria Eres Tu" (The Glory Is You), "Cuando Estoy Contigo" (When I Am With You), "Soy Tuya" (I Am Yours), "No," "La Noche de Anoche" (The Night of Last Night), "Que Sabes Tu" (What do You Know), "Bravo," 'Voy,' "La Mentara," (The Lie), and "La Canción de Mis Canciónes" (The Song of My Songs)."

Latin jazz and boogaloo percussionist Joe Torre received his first set of timbales and lessons from his brother-in-law, Pete Terrace, who had married his sister.

On the evening of Tito Puente's passing away, June 1, 2000, Celia Cruz was in Buenos Aires. She claims in her autobiography that Tito left her a message on the same day on her answering machine in New Jersey, saying, *"See you later, Negra."* It couldn't be the same day since Tito underwent surgery early that morning; complications followed, and he went into a coma and then died.

Gilberto Monroig was born on July 2, 1930, in Santurce, Puerto Rico. His father gifted him a guitar when he was ten years old, and he began playing it while imitating his idol, Carlos Gardel. At 13, he became a professional singer with the *Conjunto Taone,* and later, he replaced the vocalist Santos Colón in 1945 in the *William Manzanos' Hatuey Orchestra.* He was known for singing with a cigarette and a glass of whiskey within reach despite abusing drugs, drinking, and smoking. Despite all this, he kept his beautiful voice intact until his last breath. He produced 40 single records and 30 LPs, winning two Gold Record Awards. Unfortunately, he died from throat cancer on May 3, 1996. He was laid to rest in the Santa María Magdalena de Pazzis Cemetery in Old San Juan, alongside fellow Boricuas and great singers and composers like Rafael Hernández, Pedro Flores, and Daniel Santo.

La Milagrosa Catholic Church, located on 115th Street and Lenox Avenue in El Barrio, used to organize an annual event to showcase the talents of its most gifted children. The event would culminate in the crowning of a King and Queen, chosen based on their artistic abilities and popularity. A young Tito Puente won the crown four times for his exceptional dancing skills.

Dancer Nilo Tandrón was the individual who sponsored Tito Puente's entry into Santería rituals.

Noro Morales was the first to record for Gabe Oller's Coda label in 1945; Noro recorded three numbers,

"Bangin the Bongó," "Linda Mujer," and "Rumba Rhapsody."

Marco Antonio Muñiz Vega, a Mexican singer from Jalisco, was a personal assistant for famous stars such as Libertad Lamarque and Bény Moré in the early 1950s. At that time, he was struggling to make a name for himself as a singer in Mexico City.

Machito & His Afro-Cubans Orchestra

Machito's Afro-Cubans is considered the greatest and most influential Latin band ever played.

On August 24, 1973, Jerry Masucci and the Fania Company organized the Fania All-Stars concert at Yankee Stadium. The concert included Típica 73, El

Joe Hernández

Grand Combo, and Mongo Santamaría as guest stars. Despite the media hype before and after the event claiming it was a success, the reality was far from it. Within a few songs, approximately 40,000 to 44,000 crowd rushed onto the stage, causing chaos and unrest. Johnny Pacheco, the musical director and one of the co-founders of the Fania label, repeatedly asked the crowd to back off, but they didn't listen. Some even climbed onto the stage, with one woman dancing on Larry Harlow's piano.

The situation became so dire that Masucci's brother had to intervene and declare the concert over. Desperate to seek safety, the performers ran for their lives. Some took refuge in trailers, while others hid in the clubhouse, afraid for their lives. Meanwhile, the fans ran rampant across the field, causing widespread destruction. They stole instruments, destroyed microphones and equipment, and caused much damage. It was an unmitigated disaster.

Masucci's foresight to film it was the only positive thing that came out of the event. However, to make up for the disaster, he organized another concert in Puerto Rico where Héctor Lavoe was filmed, as he could not perform at Yankee Stadium due to the chaos.

―⚉―

In the late 1960s, Pete Bonet, a Puerto Rican singer, organized dance events at the Brooklyn Roundtable, which had a capacity of 400 people and was owned by Maurice Levy. Tony Raimone, owner of the Corso at 205 East Eighty-six Street, would visit the Roundtable regularly and try to convince Pete to move to the Corso, but Pete refused, as he was doing well at his current

The Latin Music Trivia Book

location. One day, Mr. Levy demanded an extra 50 cents per person at the door, which Pete couldn't afford, so he decided to leave the Roundtable.

Pete then approached Mr. Raimone at the Corso, and they made a deal. Pete began promoting dances on Wednesdays, Fridays, Saturdays, and Sundays, forming a group that became the House Band. The Corso, which had a capacity for over a thousand people, became the hottest place in town and an enormous success after the Palladium Ballroom.

—⟁—

During his early youth, Tito Rodríguez aspired to be a jockey and tried out racing horses at *Hipódromo Las Casas* in Villa Palmera, Santurce, Puerto Rico.

—⟁—

Once, Oscar D'león was at the airport in Venezuela, ready to board a flight to New York, when the band members demanded more money, or they would not make the trip. Oscar then boarded by himself and got in touch with the Puerto Rican pianist Oscar Hernández, who was able to put a group together as he debuted at The Corso. That evening, he smashed it, sharing the billing with Willie Rosario and Tommy Olivencia with Frankie Ruiz.

—⟁—

Rafael Hernández participated in the first full-feature movie filmed in Cuba, Ahora Somos Felices, named after one of Rafael's compositions. The Puerto Rican actress/singer Mappy Cortés and the Mexican tenor Juan Arvizu were the stars of the movie.

Celia Cruz was a global performer who traveled worldwide but never really got to see the world. Her routine was always the same: she would arrive at the airport, go to the hotel, then to the venue, back to the hotel, and then back to the airport. Due to her tight and hectic schedule, she never had time to enjoy and explore the countries she visited.

Mario Bauza's masterpiece composition, "Tanga," emerged after several years of contemplating ways to blend Cuban rhythms with jazz. The piece ultimately came together during a rehearsal of the Machito band on May 29, 1943. As the composition was played, someone listening remarked that the music was exciting as "Tanga," the Bantú Congo word for energy and a word used as a synonym to describe the buzz given when smoking good Marijuana. And thus, the birth of Afro-Cuban jazz was christened with "Tanga."

The Xavier Cugat Orchestra was the first Latin music orchestra to record Latin tunes with English lyrics, with Dinah Shore and Buddy Clark as vocalists. However, the Hispanic community did not consider these recordings genuine Latin music.

It is believed that Rafael Hernández played the first Latin tune in New York City in 1919 when he sang and played his guitar at a house party on 99th Street.

Tito Puente & sister Anna

In 1925, Tito Puente's brother Alberto was born. Unfortunately, he passed away when he was only four years old due to a tragic fall from a fire escape while the family was visiting friends. Another version of the story suggests that Alberto fell from the fire escape of their tenement home while Tito was playing with him and witnessed the incident. In 1928, Tito's sister Anna was born. Sadly, she died of spinal meningitis when she was still a teenager.

Joe Hernández

In 2013, Cheo Feliciano was diagnosed with liver cancer during treatment for a dislocated shoulder. After undergoing chemotherapy, he was declared cancer-free by early 2014. Unfortunately, he was killed in a car accident on April 17, 2014.

On the evening of April 7, 1962, *La Sonora Matancera* with Celia Cruz debuted at the Teatro Puerto Rico in the Bronx with the Cuban performer Rolando Laserie, Mexican singer Armando Manzanero, Puerto Rican singer Lucecita Benítez, and Chilean singer Lucho Gatica. Earlier that morning, Celia learned that her mother had passed away the night before. *La Guarachera de Cuba* mustered all her strength, despite her extreme sadness and pain, and performed that night.

In January 1945, Gabe Oller established the Coda Recording Company at 1291 6th Avenue in midtown Manhattan. With Art Raymond, a radio talk host from WEVD, Oller formed the Spanish Music Center (SMC) recording company. Raymond, also known as "Poncho," hosted a one-hour program called *Poncho's Club Tico Tico,* during which he played recordings from the SMC and Coda labels.

Xavier Cugat was crucial in popularizing Latin music in the United States. Despite facing criticism, Cugat's approach to the American audience was brilliant. He initially presented a watered-down version of Latin music, accompanied by dancers and costumes, which helped the audience accept the genre. Gradually, he reduced the visual elements and provided a more authentic Latin sound, achieving what no one else could do for Latin music. He deserves enormous credit, not only for Latin music but also for exposing the talents of his orchestra. His version of Latin music became popular among the American audience, along with his taste for swing, and he was ranked alongside other great North American bands, such as Benny Goodman, Glenn Miller, and Artie Shaw. Many singers passed through his orchestra, becoming a launching pad for many famous soloists, including Miguelito Valdés, Dinah Shore, Frank Sinatra, Machito, Tito Rodríguez, Bobby Capó, Desi Arnaz, and many others.

The man who called all the shots and ran the Palladium was Tommy Morton; his name was on the lease, although he did his best to stay low-key and always had a "front man" representing the management of the place. It was Tommy Morton who contacted Machito and offered him a job. The Machito Orchestra was hired because of its ability to perform a variety of rhythms, such as Mambo, tango, ballads, and swing music. There wasn't any other orchestra that had those sets of skills.

The Mambo Kings Play Songs of Love, a novel by the Cuban American author Oscar Hijuelos, which won the Pulitzer Prize, did not feature the character of a black santera named Evangelina Montoya. It was the creative decision of the movie's producer, Arnold Glimcher, to include this role, which was brilliantly portrayed by Celia Cruz in the film.

Joe Hernández

Miguelito Valdés

In 1939, Miguelito Valdés recorded Margarita Lecuona's "Babalú," a few months later, he left Cuba for New York. The record company released the song in New York, and it was an instant hit. The demand for the song was so high that it became difficult to get a copy. Another young Cuban, Desi Arnaz, living in New York then, capitalized on the song's success by singing it everywhere he had an opportunity. This boosted his show business career immensely, making him the hottest star in New York City and giving him a ticket to Hollywood. The Babalú mania did not subside and continued to be popular in 1940.

The bolero, originally titled "Madrigal" or 'When I am With You," was first performed by the *Puerto Rican Sextet*. Later, Charlie Figueroa recorded it under the name "Estando Contigo." However, it was the creative genius of Felipe R. Goyco, affectionately known as Don Felo, that gave birth to this timeless piece of Puerto Rican music.

Roberto Ledesma at one time played timbales with flautist José Fajardo's charanga.

Most ballad singers from Cuba began their careers in their home country before gaining recognition abroad. However, Roberto Ledesma, born in Havana on June 24, 1924, started his singing career outside of Cuba when he was already approaching his 40s. In the early 1960s, he began singing in New York and Miami, but nothing extraordinary happened until fortune smiled.

The Gema label contracted him to record an LP, but he still needed one more song to complete the album. Ledesma requested the label's owner, Álvarez Guedes, to include the bolero "Con Mi Corazón Te Espera" by Humberto Suarez. Guedes was not thrilled with his choice, as Ledesma had already recorded that bolero twice on other labels without success. Nevertheless, he obliged. The third time was the charm, and suddenly, "Con Mi Corazón Te Espero" was all over the radio with tremendous success.

The Dominican composer Mario de Jesús spent six months composing the bolero lyrics "Y Que Hiciste del Amor Que Me Juraste" (And What Did You Do with the Love You Swore to Me).

Joe Hernández

Tito Rodríguez's oldest brother, Johnny Rodríguez, at the age of 20, had the burden of supporting his nine siblings after the death of their parents.

Marlon Brandon & Millie Donay

Cuban Pete, Millie Donay, and the *Machito Orchestra* were invited to perform at the first "Stars of Israel" show in Madison Square Garden. Prime Minister Ben Gurion graced the event and later sent a letter of appreciation to the performers with the official seal of the Government of Israel, thanking them for their remarkable performance and participation.

From the 1920s through the 1940s, Latin music bands were primarily employed as relief bands. The band would play during a mandatory fifteen-minute break for the featured American pop band. The pianist, Rafael Audinot from *El Conjunto Canéy*, created a signal, via a melody, that would alert the musicians that the break was over. This melody became "Rumba Rhapsody" for a 1940 recording under the Decca label.

Johnny Pacheco and Izzy Sanabria attended grammar school at P.S. 51 in the South Bronx.

Chano Pozo and Dizzy Gillespie

When Chano Pozo joined Dizzy Gillespie in 1946, little attention was paid by those in the music scene that Chano's introduction of the conga drum in American jazz was the first.

Despite being childhood friends, Tito Rodríguez and Tito Puente constantly riffed to satisfy their egos on who should get "Top Billing." This foolishness spilled over into other aspects of their professional careers. In 1954, Tito Rodríguez left Tico Records to sign with RCA. Then Tito Puente followed, went to Tico, and signed with RCA in 1956. Rodríguez then returned to Tico, only to have Puente, in 1959, return to Tico. Consequently, Rodríguez went and contracted with United Artists Latino.

The rivalry between Tito Puente and Tito Rodríguez began early in their careers and continued until Tito Rodríguez's last days.

Although downplayed by many, and both Titos would pretend otherwise, the rivalry did exist. However, the tension between the two brought out the best in them. It forced each to become the best he could be. They became better showmen, and their artistic and creative output, which was staggering, was no doubt fueled by this archrivalry. Yet, despite not speaking to each other much after being good friends in their early years, they both respected and admired each other's talent.

—ɯ—

Eddie Palmieri debuted as a timbalero at 13 in a conjunto called El Chino y Su Alma Tropical, formed by a fellow named Chino, who married Palmieri's aunt, whom his mother raised.

—ɯ—

Rosalía "Chalía" Herrera was the first singer of Latin origin to record and the first to record a habanera, the famous "Habanera Tu, " in New York City in 1901.

—ɯ—

Singer Tito Nieves's uncle, Miguel Amadeo, is the composer of "Que Me Lo Den en Vida," a big hit by El Gran Combo, and the proprietor of Casa Amadeo in the Bronx.

Machito's wife, Hilda Grillo, grew up and went to grammar school with Tito Puente.

Libertad Lamarque

The famous and talented Argentinian singer and actress Libertad Lamarque was known as "La Novia de America" (America's Sweetheart). She was born in Rosario, the largest city in the central province of Santa Fé, on November 24, 1908. Her father was a military anarchist who was in prison when Libertad was born. When the father was asked what his daughter's name should be, he said, "Libertad" (Liberty).

Joe Hernández

In 1932, Mario Bauza became a member of the *Orchestra of Noble Sissle*. The same year, he landed a job as the lead trumpeter for jazz drummer Chick Webb. Within a year, at twenty-one, he became the orchestra's musical director.

Tite Curet Alonso had over 1,000 recorded compositions and claimed to have had an additional 1,500 unpublished works.

In 1917, while Rafael Hernández was residing in San Juan, he composed his second waltz. He was encouraged by his bandmates to write a song, which he did and titled it "Mi Provisa." In coming up with the title, Rafael took the first letters of the names of his musician friends' girlfriends. They were Mi-caela, Pro-vidence, Vi-center, and the last, Ro-sa. We can assume that Rafael thought little of the song because he sold it to one of his friends for 25 cents, the equivalent of six dollars, in 2024.

Al Santiago, the owner of Casa Alegre, was inspired by the famous "Cuban Jam Sessions" and believed that the New York Puerto Ricans could also create a jam session. He put together a group of musicians but initially had yet to choose a leader. Santiago ultimately had to choose between Charlie Palmieri and Johnny Pacheco as the group's leader. He chose Charlie because of his philosophy of harmony.

Tito Puente also worked as a consultant, arranger, and musician for Roper Records during the 60s and 70s. This information was revealed for the first time by this author in an article he wrote paying tribute to Tito Puente for the magazine *Bochinchat* in 2000. Before this, it was discussed over the airwaves by the same author on the Vicki Sola Show *Que Viva La Musica* at WFDU 89.1 FM and on other radio shows with Chico Álvarez at WBAI 99.5 FM and Miguel Pérez on Spanish radio WADO 1280 AM, among others.

During his tenure with Roper Records, Tito Puente's name may not have been prominently featured on many albums, likely due to his other contractual obligations, particularly with Tico Records. However, his influence was undeniable, as he contributed around 40 to 50 tunes across approximately 12 albums and nine 45s. These recordings were released under various names, including Tito Puente, the *Latin All-Stars*, and the *Roper Dance Orchestra*. Notably, many of Puente's fellow musicians, such as Jimmy Friasura, Charlie Palmieri, and Al "Alfredito" Levy, also lent their talents to these projects.

On April 8, 1961, the Palladium ballroom was packed beyond capacity to nearly 800 swinging dancers when the music stopped in the middle of a tune, the lights went on, and over the loudspeaker, the police announced, *"This is a raid."* All you could hear was the noise of patrons throwing stuff on the floor. There were knives, guns, heroin, and marijuana, which the police confiscated, along with the arrest of approximately 25 patrons that resulted in 15 indictments. Among those arrested was the Cuban singer and percussionist Rolando Laserie.

The raid had been coordinated by detectives Sonny Grosso and his partner Eddie Egan, whose work on breaking up an organized crime ring in 1961 and seizing what was considered a record amount at the time of 112 lbs. of heroin led to the book (by Robert Moore) and subsequent Academy Award-winning film, The French Connection. The sting was in response to a woman who worked for the Manhattan DA's office, who, while attending the lady's room, was offered marijuana.

Max Hyman, the frontman, was handed three summonses alleging the establishment of permitting known criminals, prostitutes, and drug pushers to frequent the premises and conduct business. Max Hyman denied the allegations and insisted that he ran an honest business. Six months later, in September of the same year, the Palladium lost its liquor license.

The once-number-one stop in New York City for dancing and hearing the best in Latin entertainment continued to operate. Dancers still came to listen to great orchestras. Still, the business needed to be able to sell liquor and not be limited to selling sodas. On May 1, 1966, the headliners were *Orquesta Broadway,* Eddie Palmieri, and Richie Ray, and the last dance played was Broadway's "Pare Cochero." The Palladium was now closed forever.

Noel Epinanio Estrada Suarez was a Puerto Rican composer best known for his unforgettable song "En Mi Viejo San Juan." He has also written many other musical jewels, such as "El Amor del Jibarito" (The Poor Farmer's Love), "Rómance de Cafetal" (Romance of the Coffee Field), "Mi Amorcito Lindo" (My Cute Little Love), "Lo Nuestro Termino" (Our Love is Finished), and many others.

Don Ellis, also known as Donald Johnson Ellis (1934-1978), was a versatile American jazz musician who played trumpet and drums and composed and led his band. He was a member of Rudy Calzado's fourteen-piece orchestra, where he played trumpet. Ellis is best known for writing the soundtrack of the movie "The French Connection," for which he won a Grammy award for "Best Instrumental Arrangement." He also composed the music for the film's sequel, "French Connection II."

Tito Rodríguez's final concert took place on February 28, 1973, at Madison Square Garden in New York City, with the accompaniment of the *Machito Orchestra.*

In 1964, La Lupe's home burned down due to candles lit during her practice of Santería. Twenty years later, an electrical fire destroyed her apartment and left her homeless.

Cal Tjader, a renowned musician known for his jazz and Latin music, recorded his first Latin LP, *Mambo with Tjader,* in 1954.

According to some musical historians, Tito Rodríguez died in the same hospital room where Rudolph Valentino had died. However, this claim is not entirely accurate. Valentino passed away at the New York Polyclinic, located at 341-351 West 50th Street, whereas Tito Rodríguez breathed his last at the New York University Medical Center, situated at 550 First Avenue.

Tito Puente recorded almost 140 LPs throughout his lifetime, out of which 71 were recorded between 1950 and 1971. This period was marked by an astounding burst of creative energy, during which Tito produced one album every 14 and a half weeks. This count does not even include the numerous shorter plays on 78s and 45s.

In 1987, Celia Cruz and her husband, Pedro Knight, decided to renew their marriage vows. However, they faced a problem: several Catholic churches refused to perform the ceremony because they could not provide their baptism certificates, which were left back in Cuba, and obtaining them was almost impossible. Finally, after a long search, they found a Catholic priest willing to perform the ceremony. However, it is worth noting that Celia does not mention a church wedding in her autobiography.

Tito Puente used to tell a story about how almost nobody knew that he had written the song "Oye Cómo Va." Once, during a conversation with a music company executive, the executive mentioned Santana's song "Oye Cómo Va" without realizing that Tito was the actual composer of the song. Although Tito felt a bit uncomfortable, he didn't correct the executive. Later that day, he received a check in the mail worth $15,000.00 in royalties from the album recorded by Santana. From then on, Tito never got angry when someone didn't recognize him as the song's author. He had resigned himself to the fact that the public rarely remembered the composers of the songs. Some people believe this may be another one of Tito's exaggerated stories. Nonetheless, he proudly told the story's author that Santana's version of his song had paid his mortgage.

In a unique turn of events in 1955, Mongo Santamaría recorded the first-ever Afro-Cuban folkloric music album titled "Chango" in New York. What's intriguing is that there was no contract for the recording, and he was paid just $80 for his work, with each sideman receiving $40. Despite these unconventional circumstances, the album became the best in its genre. A notable detail is that the only non-Cuban musician on the recording was Willie Bobo, a Puerto Rican. This fact, often overlooked, adds an interesting layer to the album's history.

The word "Mambo" was first used in a New York recording in November 1946 on José Curbelo's "El Rey del Mambo" two years before Pérez Prado's first mambo release in the US.

Joe Hernández

Eddie Palmieri

Eddie Palmieri, a renowned musician, and the legendary record producer Harvey Averne were working on recording a new album. However, disagreements over musical and technical aspects arose when the session began, with Palmieri constantly demanding. The studio also needed to meet Palmieri's liking. Eventually, the producer, musicians, and Palmieri left the studio with the album unfinished.

However, Harvey was determined to finish the album with or without Palmieri. He believed that the album had the potential to receive a Grammy nomination. With the deadline fast approaching, Harvey worked tirelessly to complete the album. He and the recording engineer, Irv Greenbaum, worked long hours, sometimes working for 24 hours straight. They had much to do, including adding instrumental solos to some songs and doing creative reconstructive editing on others.

Against all odds, Harvey and Irv finished the album and submitted it in time for the Grammy nomination. However, Palmieri was not pleased with the album and publicly denounced it because it did not meet his high standards. Harvey decided to title the album Eddie Palmieri--*Unfinished Masterpiece*. In 1976, the album won a Grammy for "Best Latin Recording." Despite this achievement, Palmieri refused to accept the award, but Harvey did.

Irv Greenbaum, the sound engineer for Fania, once shared a story about a recording session he worked on with Rafael Cortijo. Greenbaum mentioned that during the recording session, he observed a peculiar ritual that Cortijo would perform after the orchestra finished recording a music track. Cortijo would go to a corner, and his musicians would line up behind him. One by one, Cortijo would place a small spoon filled with cocaine under their nostrils. This behavior continued until the recording session ended.

In 1939, the Mexican composer Alberto Domínguez composed the famous boleros "Frenesi" and "Perfidia." These two great songs soon became popular in Mexico and worldwide. The swing bands of Artie Shaw and Glenn Miller were among the first to record them in the United States.

The Palmieri brothers have a nine-year age difference between them.

Joe Hernández

Moisés Simons

In 1928, Moisés Simons Rodríguez, a renowned composer from Cuba, sat in a small coffee shop at the corner of San José and Amistad in Havana. Born in Havana in 1889, Simons came from a family of Jewish immigrants who hailed from the Basque region of Spain. The coffee shop was a small establishment with only six or eight tables. Perhaps Simons was sipping a cup of hot coffee when he suddenly heard the voice of a small man selling peanuts. The man's vendor cry was "pregonando mani." He had cans of peanuts heated with carbon to keep them warm, and he was crying out, *"Maniii... maniii...".* As Simons heard the vendor's cries, he was inspired and started writing on paper. He may have even used a napkin. This is one version of the story told by some musical historians about the creation of the song "El Manicero." Although there may be other versions, what is important is the impact this song had on the history of Latin music in the United States and worldwide.

It's worth noting that the Cuban singer Rita Montaner recorded the song first for the Columbia label in the late 1920s, even before Don Azpiazú's recording for RCA Victor in May 1930, which also featured Antonio Machín, trumpeter Julio Cueva, and composer-saxophonist Mario Bauza.

During the 1950s, Jose Fajardo was a highly sought-after musician in Cuba. He was so popular that he led three different bands and performed concerts across the island, from one end to another. His fame was such that he often had multiple performances in a single night and traveled between cities by helicopter.

Due to the ongoing feud between Tito Rodríguez and Tito Puente, Rodríguez decided to sign with United Artists. He ensured his contract stipulated that he would be the only Latin bandleader allowed to record under the U.A. label. Unfortunately, this move hurt Charlie Palmieri, whose Charanga L.P. was also recorded under the U.A. label. Palmieri was allowed to leave his contract, which he did, and he signed a few months later with Al Santiago's new label, Alegre.

At some point in the 1950s, Arsenio Rodríguez met Pérez Prado in New York, and the well-known Puerto Rican promoter Federico Pagani asked both, "Who was the inventor of the mambo?" Pérez Prado promptly replied that Arsenio was the inventor of the mambo;

however, Pérez was the only one who made money playing it.

Cal Tjader's "Soul Sauce" sold over 150,000 copies in 1964 and contributed to using the word "Salsa" before the Fania label used it. On the recording, you can hear Willie Bobo exclaiming the word "Salsa" in the background.

Rudy Calzado (1929-2002), a Cuban percussionist, vocalist, arranger, and composer, was requested by Tito Rodríguez to take over and sing for his orchestra at the Palladium in 1964. This was because Tito needed a much-needed rest. Rudy fulfilled this role for fifteen days.

The compositions "Yo Soy La Voz," "En El Cafetal," "No Hay Manteca," and "Tumba La Cana" were all recorded by Celia Cruz and written by Rudy Calzado.

The 1972 album "La Voz Sensual de Cheo" by Cheo Feliciano was recorded in Argentina. It features arrangements by the six-time Grammy winner, Argentinian composer, arranger, and conductor Jorge Calandrelli. This album is notable for being the first to combine a harp and violins in a salsa recording.

La Lupe's smash-hit and best-selling recording with Tito Puente, "Que Te Pedí," composed by Fernando Mulens, was a variation of "Jugué y Perdí," recorded by Héctor Fernando and composed by the Cuban pianist-flutist band leader Lou Pérez.

—ഡ—

Marc Anthony, whose birth name is Marco Antonio Muñiz, was named after the famous Mexican singer by his father, Felipe Muñiz, who played jibaro music.

—ഡ—

In Venezuela, Bény Moré was arrested and jailed for injuring the head of an emboldened businessman, a certain Maz Pérez, who tried to get away with not paying his orchestra.

—ഡ—

At one point, Jerry Masucci began an extensive campaign promoting the Fania label products, producing over 75 hours a week of salsa programming in the top Latin Markets through five Spanish-language radio stations.

—ഡ—

Cuban Pete and Millie Donay got their first professional break with the *Xavier Cugat Orchestra*. Cugat hired them and took them on the road with the band. They performed at the best hotels and theaters and were also part of a show called "Havana Nights," which traveled to the same venues. Another great dancer on the show was

Joe Hernández

Cacha Pozo, the wife of the legendary Chano Pozo. Pete and Millie learned a lot by watching her dance.

—⚎—

1966 was a big year for the Boogaloo, which had three hits: "I Like It Like That" by Pete Rodríguez, "Boogaloo Blues" by Johnny Colón, and "Bang Bang" by Joe Cuba.

—⚎—

Arsenio had another brother, other than Israel, who lived in the Bronx in the 1950s, Raúl Rodríguez. Raúl owned the El Dorado restaurant on East 163rd Street and Intervale Avenue between 1956 and 1958.

—⚎—

Esy Morales, the younger brother of Noro Morales, was a talented flutist in American Jazz. Tito Puente held him in high esteem. Sadly, Esy passed away in 1950 at the age of 33 due to drug abuse.

—⚎—

Catalino "Tite" Curet Alonso, a name that echoes with "sauce, rhythm, and flavor," Is widely regarded as the most influential composer of the Salsa musical movement during the 70s and 80s. His work has left an indelible mark on the genre, inspiring countless musicians and captivating audiences worldwide. Born on February 12, 1926, in Guayama, a region in the southeast part of the island of Puerto Rico, known for its carnivals and Afro-Borinquen musical and religious traditions, he graduated from the University of Puerto Rico with a degree in journalism. He worked for Tico Records in Puerto Rico and was a postal worker for 37 years. Curet Alonso had been interested in and practicing journalism since the 1940s and began his career as a sports journalist for *Diario La Prensa* in New York.

—ᴍ—

During her performance in Santa Cruz de Tenerife, Canary Islands, Spain, on March 3, 1987, Celia Cruz made history by setting a new Guinness Book of World Records record for the largest number of people attending a single concert, with 244,000 attendees.

—ᴍ—

After Rafael and Victoria Hernández opened the first Spanish music store in Harlem, Gabriel Oller's Tatay's Spanish Music Center was established in 1934 at 1315 5th Avenue, a few blocks from Casa Hernández.

—ᴍ—

Nat King Cole, a crooner and jazz pianist, embarked on a series of visits to Cuba between 1956 and 1958. During these visits, he graced the stage at the Tropicana, commanding a fee of $5,000 per show (equivalent to over $55K in purchasing power in 2024). However, he was barred from the prestigious hotel due to his skin color, a policy that affected him despite his international fame. With over 97% of the hotel's occupants being North Americans, he had to seek more modest accommodations. Yet, he found comfort in the respect shown to him by the Cubans, a respect that was often denied to him in the United States. In a beautiful exchange of cultures, Cole recorded instrumental tracks at a Havana studio for his 1958 LP "Cole Español." The album, a testament to

Joe Hernández

his appreciation of Cuban music, is mainly composed of Cuban songs, including his popular rendition of "Quizás, Quizás, Quizás."

During the early days of Gabriel Oller's record label Dynasonic, which lasted from 1934 to 1941, he recorded several local tríos and quartets, including Noro Morales and Cáney. However, due to limited resources, the label was only able to press two hundred copies at once. Moreover, the shellac used in manufacturing was in short supply due to the war, which made these recordings fragile and allowed for at most fifteen plays.

A few months before undergoing the six-hour surgery to remove a malignant brain tumor that was growing in her brain, Celia Cruz had to have her left breast removed due to cancer. This was the same illness that had claimed the life of her mother. Despite being in the middle of her recovery, the strong-willed Queen of Salsa continued to work tirelessly to promote her album "La Negra Tiene Tumbao."

During World War II, Tito Puente, on a brief respite, married his girlfriend, Mirta Sánchez. Their love story continued to unfold in 1947 with the birth of their son, Ronald. In the 1950s, Tito's life took another turn when he found companionship with a captivating young woman, Ida Carlini. Their union brought forth a son, Richard Anthony Puente, in 1953.

Noro Morales got his first gig in New York, playing in the pit band of Teatro Hispano on 116th Street and Fifth Avenue.

In February 1947, Tito Rodríguez gathered a remarkable group of musicians to support Chano Pozo during his initial recordings in New York. The session included tracks such as "Rumba en Swing," "Porque tu Sufres," and "Cómetelo to," on which Pozo not only played the conga but also sang. Among the notable musicians that Tito brought to the recording were Arsenio Rodríguez, Rene Hernández (Machito's talented arranger and pianist), Mario Bauza and various trumpeters, Eugene Johnson (an African American alto player), and Machito's rhythm section.

Mario Bauza and Fernando Arbello, a Puerto Rican jazz trombonist, played together in the Chick Webb band. Arbello attended the Puerto Rico Conservatory of Music in Ponce.

Alfredo "Chocolate" Armenteros played on an album called "Rhumba a la King" that Nat "King" Cole recorded in Cuba.

Joe Hernández

8th Calvary Mexican Band

Sig. Encarnación Payen

When the 8th Calvary Mexican Band performed at the New Orleans World's Industrial and Cotton Centennial Exposition in 1884, under the direction of Sig. Encarnacion Payen they were a big hit performing all forms of Latin and Caribbean-based music, mainly Cuban. Many of the musicians fell in love with this cosmopolitan city's culture. They, in turn, would influence New Orleans musicians. This opened the gates for other musicians from Mexico to follow. One fellow who visited and stayed in 1884 was a saxophone, clarinet, and flutist player named Florenzo Ramos (1861-1931), who was one of the founders of the New Orleans Musicians' Union and considered by many to be New Orleans's first resident saxophonist.

—⚋—

Joseíto Fernández, the Cuban composer of the famous song "Guantanamera," unfortunately never received royalties for his work. Despite the song's popularity and success, he didn't receive a single penny.

The Happy Hill Orchestra was founded in 1929 in San Germán, Puerto Rico, also known as the "City of the Hills." In January 1930, the orchestra was named after the city's characteristic hills. It is also known as the "Dean of the Orchestras."

At its founding, the orchestra was under the musical direction of Luis A. Lamboy Toro and had seven founders. Ramón Collado, a trumpeter, pianist, organist, composer, and arranger and the author and arranger of the Puerto Rican anthem "La Borinqueña," was one of the first arrangers of the Happy Hill Orchestra.

This ensemble is also notable for being the first Puerto Rican orchestra directed by a woman, the pianist Pepita Nazario Alsina.

Despite the fluctuations in popular taste, the changes in musical genres, and the difficulties and setbacks it has faced, the Happy Hill Orchestra has managed to stay together, distinguishing itself as a legendary orchestra that has outlived many other recognized orchestras.

Salsa dancing is an excellent way to exercise and get your body moving. Depending on the style you dance (such as mambo, cha-cha-chá, or bolero), a dancer's heart rate can range from 150 BPM to close to 220 BPM. Dancing Salsa can burn between 300-400 calories per hour, a fantastic way to stay fit and healthy. While a

Mambo can accelerate your heart rate and burn more calories than a cha-cha-chá, both styles will work your muscles, flexibility, and nervous system differently. On the other hand, Bolero may burn fewer calories but can do wonders for stimulating your hormone system. Salsa dancing can also help you improve your flexibility and strength and benefit your brain.

Author and Joe Cuba

In 1954, Jimmy Sabater began his music career with a quintet led by Joe Panama, a pianist. When Joe left the group, Jimmy asked his friend from the neighborhood, Sonny Calderón, also known as Joe Cuba, to join the band and take Joe Panama's place. Together, they restarted the band.

Arsenio Rodríguez resided in Puerto Rico for a brief period. He first lived in Santurce and then moved to Cataño.

The Frank H. Campbell Funeral Home, where the services for Celia Cruz were held, has also hosted many funerals of famous personalities, including Jacqueline Kennedy Onassis, John Lennon, Judy Garland, Tommy Dorsey, Arturo Toscanini, Rudolph Valentino, Herman Badillo, Joan Crawford, Lauren Bacall, Irving Berlin, James Cagney, Jack Dempsey, Mario Cuomo, Greta Garbo, George Gershwin, Rita Hayworth, Robert F. Kennedy, Ed Koch, Héctor Lavoe, Billy Martin, Mary Tyler Moore, Joan Rivers, Ed Sullivan, Tennessee Williams, and Mae West, among many others. The funeral home was previously located on Sixty-sixth Street and Broadway.

Benny More was known for his extraordinary ability to improvise. Once, while playing for a TV show in Venezuela, his band had 10 minutes to fill before they went on stage. The band started improvising, and Benny began to create lyrics on the spot. The result was the popular hit "Que Bueno Baila Usted" (How Well You Dance), one of his signature songs. However, this story contradicts the original narrative of the song's creation in 1958 on the Puerto Rican TV show *La Taberna India*.

The first recorded merengue was an instrumental composition titled "Rubén" by Juan Bautista Espínola in 1922, performed by the International Novelty Orchestra, a band under RCA Victor. This lively and upbeat tune began a musical genre that has captivated audiences worldwide.

Héctor Ulloa R., known as the "chinche" of Colombian television, wrote the bolero "Cinco Tavitos," which Julio Jaramillo popularized.

Vernon and Irene Castle

On February 3, 1913, the Knickerbocker Theatre on Broadway premiered a new musical comedy called The Sunshine Girl. It starred Julia Sanderson, a new singing sensation, and the young dancing couple Vernon and Irene Castle. The production featured the popular Cuban habanera's one-measure clave pattern, significantly boosting its popularity.

Within a few months, the Argentinian tango, became a national obsession. The Castles were in high demand

and were paid a thousand dollars for a single appearance, equivalent to around $31,000 in 2024. The Castles also owned a dance school, and their orchestra was conducted by two of New York's most famous African American composers, W. H. Tyers and James Reese Europe. James was not only the Castles' musical director but also recruited, at a later date, the Puerto Rican composer Rafael Hernández, along with seventeen other Puerto Ricans for the U.S. Army 359th Regimental Band during WWI.

In 1936, 13-year-old Tito Rodríguez joined *Conjunto de Industrias Nativas,* led by Ladisalo, as a singer. At 16, he recorded with the renowned *Cuarteto Mayarí.*

In a television interview, Cheo Feliciano recalls living at 35 East 110th Street in Harlem in the mid-1950s, and Arsenio Rodríguez lived at 23 East 110th Street. Cheo claims to have witnessed the fire at 23 East 110th Street, where Arsenio lived, and escaped with his life. The problem with Cheo's story is that Arsenio never lived at 23 East 110th Street, and that building has never had a fire. The fire was at 23 West 65th Street, where in 1955 Arsenio lived. The second version of the song "Hay Fuego en la 23," played by *La Sonora Ponceña,* changed the lyrics to 110th Street.

Arsenio's life was a journey across different neighborhoods. In the 1950s, he resided in the heart of Puerto Rican culture, 'El Barrio,' with his wife, Emma Lucía Martínez, at 152 East 116th Street, between Third and Lexington Avenue. However, he also found solace with his brother Israel 'Kíke' Rodríguez and his family in the Bronx, at 811 Tinton Avenue, between East 160th Street and 161st Street. This diverse living arrangement reflects the rich tapestry of his life and music.

The Roper Dance Orchestra was the music sold to all dancing schools at the time, including the Arthur Murray dance studios. The Anglos learned how to mambo and cha cha chá to these arrangements, courtesy of Tito Puente. Only an earnest student of Puente's style could have detected the "Maestro" in these recordings.

Based on these facts, it is evident that the number of albums Tito Puente recorded is much greater. The album marketed and promoted as his 100th album, *The Mambo King: His 100th Album,* in 1991 is inaccurate since all the Roper Records he recorded were done before, mainly in the 1970s. It is most likely that his 1981 recording *C'est Magnifique (with Azuquita)* was his 100th album.

Oscar Hernández is an American pianist, producer, band leader, and arranger of Puerto Rican descent and the youngest of eleven siblings. He was the producer, arranger, musical director, and conductor for the Broadway musical *The Capeman* and the musical director and arranger for the off-Broadway show *Quién Mató a Héctor Lavoe* (Who murdered Héctor Lavoe). Oscar is also the musical director of the multi-Grammy winning *Spanish Harlem Orchestra.*

Izzy Sanabria designed the 1970 album cover for *Wanted By FBI/The Big Break-La Gran Fuga*. It featured a black-and-white photo of Willie Colón taken in a photo booth for 25 cents.

Tite Curet Alonso, Cortijo, and Ismael Rivera were close friends, almost like brothers—however, their friendship changes when Ismael and Cortijo are sent to jail. Despite Rafael Ithier creating El Gran Combo, Tite never wrote a composition for the band out of loyalty to his friendship with Cortijo and Ismael. Eventually, when Andy Montañez decided to leave El Gran Combo to pursue a career with the Venezuelan group La Dimensión Latina, Tite immediately gave him one of his compositions.

The habanera is a stimulating and versatile rhythm that has powerfully impacted music. It is considered the precursor to many music genres that were born in the Caribbean, including the Cuban Danzón, the Puerto Rican Danza, the Tango, and American ragtime.

Charlie Palmieri was the first to sign with José Curbelo's Alpha Artists Music Agency in 1959.

Cheo Feliciano interpreted 45 of Tite "Curet" Alonso's compositions from the moment they met in the 1970s. Because of Curet's music and other composers like Nick Jiménez, Cheo was able to revive his singing career with tunes like "Anacaona," "Salomé," "Canta," "El Ratón," "El Día Que Me Quieras," "Naborí," and "Así Soy," among many others.

As a teenager in Cuba, Mario Bauza played alongside the father of José Curbelo.

Justo Bentancourt and Ismael Miranda became friends early in Miranda's career. The mega-hit song "Pa' Bravo Yo" was composed by Miranda, and he had every intention of recording it. Bentancourt told Miranda that he could not record the song because it belonged to him. Miranda laughed and reminded Betancourt that he wrote the song and could do what he pleased. Bentancourt insisted that he could not. Miranda, jokingly, asked why he couldn't. Bentancourt told Miranda because *"...you are not mulato oscuro"* (dark skin), given that Miranda was very "white", and the theme of the song was of a singer that was "black." Miranda laughed, agreed with Bentancourt, and allowed him to record the song, which became Bentancourt's signature piece.

The *Carmelo Díaz Soler Orchestra*, one of the first in Puerto Rico to incorporate vocalists and perform on the radio, was a testament to the unwavering dedication of its founder, military bandmaster Díaz Soler. Established in the early 1920s in the town of Ciales, the orchestra's journey took a significant turn in 1927 when it traveled to Camden, New Jersey, under contract by Columbia Records to record 52 songs.

A young Desi Arnaz auditioned for the *Xavier Cugat Orchestra* at the Brook Club. At that time, the orchestra was a five-piece quintet that included Al Capone's son. Desi and Al Capone's son, Albert Francis "Sonny," had already become friends in Miami while attending Saint Patrick's High School.

Celia Cruz was matron of honor at Willie Colón's wedding.

From 1967 to 1975, Willie Colón and Héctor Lavoe collaborated to produce twelve albums.

The Cuban government had the distinguished historian and musicologist Helio Orovio delete from his first edition of "Diccionario Enciclopédico de la Música Cubana" (1981) any mention of Cuban musicians who left the island after 1959. The Cuban government continues to censor the play or mention of Cuban musicians who abandoned the revolution in all Cuban media. Fidel Castro went as far as to destroy all recordings from Cuban musicians who fled. However, Mr. Orovio, to his credit, made corrections and reinstated those previously deleted in his 1992 second edition.

Joe Hernández

In 1945, Uncle Sam called on Joe Loco; he had been called on before but was rejected because of poor eyesight. However, with the war intensifying, restrictions were lifted, and Joe could no longer escape the draft. Pianist Rene Hernández replaced him in the *Machito Orchestra*.

Tito Puente and musical historians claim that Tito was the first to move the timbales to the front of the orchestra, which he did with *Machito's Orchestra* when he performed a "solo." Technically, this is not accurate. Tito can claim that he was the first in a dance setting, but the first to have done so, many years before, in 1936, in a movie titled *Go West Young Man,* percussionist Mano López, then playing for *Xavier Cugat's Orchestra,* did so in the film. However, Tito Puente was the first to play the timbales while standing up. Before him it was the norm to play sitting down. He continued this practice when he began his own band. He was also the first to move the entire battery of Afro-Cuban percussion - timbales, congas, bongó - to the front of the band, whereas as in the past they were relegated to the back of the orchestra.

Pedro Albizu Campos was the nephew of the Puerto Rican composer Juan Morel Campos. He was an attorney, a politician, a president, and a spokesperson for the Nationalist Party of Puerto Rico. He was a strong advocate for Puerto Rico's independence and led the nationalist revolts of October 1950 against the United States government in Puerto Rico. For his fight for independence, he spent twenty-six years in prison at various times.

—⚝—

Margo was a member of the dance team Augie and Margo, who also happened to be Tito Puente's cousin.

—⚝—

Johnny Rodríguez (Upper Right)

In the mid-1940s, Johnny Rodríguez became the first Puerto Rican to be featured on NBC and CBS television.

—⚝—

Despite touring extensively throughout the United States and playing at some of the best-known upscale venues, Pérez Prado may have performed at the Palladium Ballroom only once and rarely at any other New York City nightclub dominated by the Afro-Cuban sound.

—⚝—

In January 1948, the Cuban drummer Chano Pozo purportedly embarked on a tour to Europe with the Dizzy Gillespie Orchestra. As the tour progressed, his drums were mysteriously stolen. Chano decided to return to New York to procure a replacement set. However, fate had a different plan. He never made it back to Europe. Instead, he found himself lingering in the bustling streets of New York City. This enigmatic figure met his untimely end on the tragic evening of December 2, 1948, when an infamous character that was a local bookie and marijuana dealer, Eusebio Muñoz, known as "Cabito" (Little Corporal), extinguished his young life over a drug deal gone awry.

Another narrative emerges, painting a different picture of Chano's final days. In this version, Chano is said to be in Georgia when he returns to New York to replace his stolen drums. Chano goes to La Moderna, the bakery run by fellow Cuban Simón Jou, who, besides selling baked goods, also sells conga drums. There, Chano bumped into his colleague Mario Bauzá; he recounted to him the extreme racism he had encountered down in Georgia and told him he would not return to rejoin the Gillespie tour. However, a thorough examination of the records from late 1948 reveals no trace of Chano with Dizzy Gillespie in Georgia. Moreover, the logic of returning to New York for new drums, only to head back to Georgia, seems questionable at best. Later in the year, as described above, Chano is killed by a local drug dealer over some "weak" marijuana.

An interesting side note: supposedly, the birth of the background chorus/coro, "I'll never go back to Georgia," stemmed from this experience.

After Pérez Prados's astounding ten weeks at number one in the pop charts with the extraordinarily successful "Cherry Pink and Apple Blossom White," Tito Puente arranged his "softer" version on a 78 RPM recording with him playing the alto saxophone giving a solo performance.

The dress code to enter the Palladium, like in many other dancing night spots in New York City at the time, required men to wear a jacket and a tie. However, if a patron needed the proper attire, the club provided the means to rent a coat or tie for a fee.

The bolero began to be danced as bolero-son in 1927-29 when a montuno (vamp) was added at the end for improvisation.

Johnny Albino (1919-2011) and his *Trío San Juan,* a quality group similar to *Trío Los Panchos,* recorded only for the Verne label, a record company in New York with little international circulation. This situation limited them enormously as they could not achieve the popularity of Los Panchos, who recorded on CBS, or that of Trío Los Tres Diamantes, who recorded for RCA VICTOR. Thankfully, the Fuentes label represented the Verne house in Columbia, and Johnny Albino's boleros are now as popular, if not more than Los Panchos. It is worth mentioning that they only visited some countries once. For example, they visited Colombia without any publicity, and if they had received any, they would have known the love and enthusiasm they caused with their boleros. "Cosas Cómo Tú" was a musical sensation in Colombia and continues to be played today. No bolero from Los Panchos achieved this level of popularity.

Due to its frequent use, the Savoy's floor had to be replaced every three years. The house band during the 1930s was led by Chick Webb and directed by Mario Bauza, making it the most popular band at the time. At the Savoy, Ella Fitzgerald, a teenage vocalist fresh from a talent victory at the Apollo Theater in 1934, became a part of their band.

Izzy Sanabria would tape his 1970s show "Salsa" from the Cheetah Dance Club.

Morris Levy, a prominent figure in the music industry, was long suspected of having ties to organized crime, specifically with the Genovese family. Besides owning his record labels, including Roulette Records, he owned several nightclubs in New York City, including the legendary jazz club Birdland. He was known for being good friends with Tito Puente, so much so that many musicians called him Tito's Godfather. However, Levy was constantly under scrutiny from the law, and in 1986, he was finally tried and convicted of extortion. Unfortunately, he never served time for his crimes, as he passed away in Ghent, New York before he could be put behind bars. Levy always said that he would never go to jail.

Rafael Lay and Richard Egues contributed the greatest number of works to the Aragón orchestra repertoire.

In 1996, Johnny Pacheco became the first Latino music producer to receive the NARAS (National Academy of Recordings Arts & Sciences) Governor's Award in New York City.

It's difficult to imagine another orchestra like the one Tito Puente brought together, with the exceptional percussionists Willie Bobo, Cándido Camero, Carlos "Patato" Valdés, Mongo Santamaría, and Tito himself.

Ironically, *Machito and his Afro-Cubans* were often a large orchestra composed mainly of Puerto Ricans, Anglos, and Jewish musicians in the early 1940s, with only a few Cubans.

Panart Record company, which was founded by Ramón Sabat, an engineer in 1944, was one of the first and most successful independent record labels in Cuba. In the 1950s, the label invited an all-star cast of some of the best musicians from Cuba and the United States to record an album. The finished product was released six months later as *Cuban Jam Session, Volume I,* and it enjoyed worldwide sales of over one million dollars over two years. However, the musicians who played in the album were paid only $20.00. Unfortunately, the Castro communist regime's seizure and nationalization of the company, renaming it "Panart Nacionalizada," marked a significant turning point in the history of Cuban music. It was eventually absorbed by EGREM shortly after.

Tito Puente never felt at ease with using the term "salsa" to define the music he played. Instead, he preferred to refer to his music as "New York Afro-Cuban music." He believed that his term more accurately described the "New York Latino" sound that originated from the Afro-Cuban roots.

The famous Cuban Flutist and bandleader José Fajardo was the cousin of José Manuel Fajardo, the father of singer Gloria Estefan.

The intersection of Saint Ann Avenue and 140th Street in the Bronx was named after La Lupe on June 13, 2002.

Celia Cruz went to the National Teachers College in Cuba to fulfill her father's desire to become a teacher. However, she did not pursue teaching as a career, as singing was her true passion. So, she enrolled at the Havana National Conservatory of Music to pursue her dream of becoming a singer.

Alfredo "Chocolate" Armenteros & Author

The Cuban trumpeter Alfredo "Chocolate" Armenteros (1928-2016) earned his nickname "Chocolate" after being mistaken for the International Boxing Hall of Fame boxer Kid Chocolate.

Before she defected from Cuba in the 1950s, Celia Cruz toured Mexico, South America, and the United States. Her debut was at the Teatro Puerto Rico in New York, with additional performances at the Club Caborrojeño and the Palladium Ballroom.

In the late 1960s and early 1970s, the Hotel St. George in Brooklyn Heights hosted big dances featuring multiple Salsa bands. Interestingly, in the past, this hotel was where the Brooklyn Dodgers of the National League stayed whenever they played their home games at Ebbets Field.

Paulina Álvarez

Paulina Álvarez, also known as Raimunda Paula Pena Álvarez (1912-1965), was a renowned Cuban-born singer who had a significant impact on the music industry. She was highly regarded by many prominent singers, including Celia Cruz and Omara Portuondo. Paulina was a trailblazer and made history as the first woman to lead her own orchestra. José Fajardo, a skilled flutist, was a part of her orchestra.

Agent and Record Producer Ralph Mercado was infamous for bouncing checks and not paying.

Tito Puente had great admiration for Celia Cruz and considered her to be a wonderful lady. Still, at times, he felt that she was overly particular and thought she had a "...bug up her a**" because she would never stay in the same hotel with any native Cuban performing in the same venue.

'Guantanamera' resulted from a series on Radio CMCD that began in 1935. Joséito Fernández was hired to write songs for a soap opera to accompany the sketches depicting feuds and love dramas in a family. There were hundreds of 'Guantanameras,' each telling a different storyline. It was this versatility in the song that made it an enormous success.

Compay Segundo, also known as Máximo Francisco Repilado Muñoz Telles, was born on November 18, 1907, in Siboney, Cuba. He earned his nickname by singing the second voice in his musical partnerships. 1947, Segundo formed the successful and popular duo *Los Compadres* with Lorenzo Hierrezuelo. He composed more than 100 songs, including the famous "Chan Chan," also the opening track of the *Buena Vista Social Club*. Other notable songs he composed include "Sarandonga," "Macusa," "Mayari," "La Calabaza," "Saludo Compay," and "Hey Caramba." He invented the "armonico," combining seven strings between the Spanish guitar and the tres. He even performed for President Fidel Castro and Pope John Paul II at Vatican City. Compay Segundo passed away on July 13, 2003, due to kidney failure, just two days before the death of Celia Cruz. He was 95 years old.

Joe Hernández

Another tale from Daniel Santos in his autobiography was that on one occasion, he was playing dominoes in a gambling den, and among those present was a Dominican named Carrasquillo, from whom Santos won fifty-six dollars in a game that night. Carasquillo thought he was cheated and waited for Santos to leave the joint. Santos went out, and in the middle of the block, Carasquillo took advantage of the darkness of the night and stabbed Santos in the chest, close to the heart.

To prevent so much blood from coming out, Santos put his right index finger into the wound and walked towards the nearest hospital. He claims he was fighting death every step of the way.

Things stayed that way until he joined the army, and one day, while he was on guard duty, one of the soldiers informed him that he had seen Carasquillo in a gambling house. Since he had friends in the battalion, he asked one of them to take over his guard. So, he went home, put on civilian clothes, grabbed a baseball bat, and headed to where Carasquillo was playing with his hand of dominoes. When Santos entered, Carasquillo immediately ran towards the bathrooms, and Santos followed him. Santos grabbed him and gave him fifty-one hits for every dollar he accused him of having earned from him illegally.

Orquesta Aragón evolved from the Charanga Francesa, a brass orchestra famous in 19th-century Cuba.

Pedro Knight had been married twice and had seven children before he met Celia Cruz. In 1950, a year after Celia had joined *La Sonora Matancera,* Pedro got a divorce. They kept their relationship a secret and low-key between themselves. Pedro asked Celia several times to marry him, but Celia refused because she had heard rumors that Pedro was a womanizer. Pedro denied these rumors and called them gossip. Despite a ten-year courtship, Pedro never gives up and finally convinces Celia to agree to marry him.

They got married on July 14, 1962, before a Connecticut judge. The ceremony was simple, with singer Rolando Laserie as the best man and his wife, Tita Borggiano, as the matron of honor. Dance promoter and Laserie's manager Catalino Rolón served as the witness. There was no party or honeymoon since Celia was still mourning the death of her mother. Celia and Pedro were in their late thirties at the time of their wedding.

—∞—

In the mid-1940s, Xavier Cugat opened and operated the Casa Cugat Mexican restaurant in West Hollywood. The elite Hollywood celebrities visited the restaurant. A feature of the service provided was two singing guitarists who would stop by each table and play diners' favorite songs upon request. The restaurant closed its operations in 1986.

—∞—

In 1900, the Gramophone Company had a catalog for sale with 5,000 different recordings.

—∞—

Joe Hernández

María Teresa Vera

María Teresa Vera composed 26 songs, the most important being the bolero-son "Veinte Anos" (1935), which she also lists as habanera. But undoubtedly, her work as an interpreter of the bolero that had recently begun to be known was extraordinary. Her discography is quite extensive. The songs that had the most success in her voice were: "Santa Cecilia," "Doble Inconciencia" (or "Falsaria") "Longina' by Manuel Corona, and "Perjura" by Campanioni.

—⚜—

Pérez Prado received criticism from Cuban and New York musicians, particularly the Big Three - Machito, Tito Puente, and Tito Rodríguez. However, he developed a unique formula that fused Cuban and jazz flavors to create an unprecedented sound. Prado initially worked as a pianist and arranger in Cuba, earning a meager $50 weekly. However, within a few years, he had become so successful that he was making over $5,000 each week (equivalent to around $60,000 today). Pérez Prado was incredibly popular in Mexico and was so well-regarded that police officers would accompany him to his performances. Pérez Prado is credited with popularizing the mambo and has significantly contributed to the music industry.

—⟶—

Before forming the Trío Matamoros, Miguel Matamoros worked as a driver and private mechanic, Siro Rodríguez was a blacksmith, and Rafael Cueto was an apprentice tailor. In the mid-twenties, they met and abandoned carts, hammers, anvils, scissors, and everything that linked them to their respective jobs to form the group that would quickly begin to achieve success in the traditional carnivals of Santiago.

On December 11, 1516, a ship arrived in San Juan, Puerto Rico, with a silversmith named Pury Diaz, who introduced the first Spanish guitar to the Island, then known as San Juan Bautista (St John the Baptist). The name was soon changed to Puerto Rico, or "rich port," when the Spaniards realized the impressive gold in its rivers. Once the port city was established as the capital city, it took the name of San Juan.

—⟶—

The first Tango song to be published was "Toma Mate Che."

—⟶—

Joe Hernández

Celia Cruz at the Int'l Latin Music Hall of Fame

Celia Cruz, the renowned Cuban singer, was born on October 21, 1925, in the Cerro district of Havana. She was the only daughter of Simón Cruz, a railroad worker. Her mother, Catalina Alfonso, had a daughter named Dolores from a previous relationship with a man named Aquilino Ramos. After Celia was born, Catalina had two more children, Bárbaro and Gladys, with Alejandro Jiménez. In 1999, Celia Cruz was honored and inducted into the International Latin Music Hall of Fame.

In the 1950 filme *Ritmo del Caribe*, *La Sonora Matancera* musical accompaniment Rita Montaner.

In 1992, Willie Colon performed at President Bill Clinton's Inauguration Ball.

Johnny Pacheco and Pete "El Conde" Rodríguez collaborated on recording seven albums between 1964 and 1973.

On March 13, 1988, 119,986 people gathered at Miami's Calle Ocho and danced the conga, breaking the Guinness World Record.

Ismael Rivera had an older brother named Carlito who died when Ismael was eight months old due to an intestinal infection.

María Teresa Vera, also known as "Mother Trova," became the first Cuban feminist heroine on 78 RPM (Rosalía "Chalía" Herrera was the first to record on cylinders). She had a fondness for smoking cigars and drinking cognac. While touring as a guitar duo with her longtime partner Lorenzo Hierrezuelo, she made her debut recording with Sexteto Habanero in New York in 1918.

The Cuban singer Omara Portuondo won a Latin Grammy award in 2009, becoming the oldest award recipient at 79.

By the mid-1940s, Walt Disney wanted to take Bény Moré and the Trío Matamoros to Hollywood to stage them in his cartoons. Matamoros, who was an immensely proud man, refused.

Davilita, or Pedro Ortiz Dávila, was the first singer to record tangos in bolero time. One of his notable recordings was "Niebla del Riachuelo" with the Noro Morales Orchestra in New York.

The Cuban flutist Alberto Socarras hired a young Dizzy Gillespie to add authentic American flavor to his small Cuban and jazz mix group.

In the autumn of 1953, Edyie Gormé became a permanent member of Steve Allen's Tonight Show cast. She sang, wrote, and performed in sketches with Steve Lawrence for the following four years. They had much in common, and their friendship gradually turned into romance. However, they had met casually before at the Brill Building, the historic landmark on Broadway in midtown Manhattan, which was the center of the American music industry. Edyie was three years older, and they got married in 1957 in Las Vegas.

The verses of the bolero "Boda Negra" (Black Wedding) that the Cuban Alberto Villalon set to music, although attributed to the Colombian poet Julio Flórez, belong to the dark Venezuelan priest Carlos Borges, who claimed to have written them in the year 1885.

Marlon Brando Playing the Conga

Marlon Brando, the renowned actor, was not just a fan of Afro-Cuban music; he was a devotee. His love for this genre was so profound that he journeyed to Cuba to master the art of playing the bongó. On one memorable evening, Marlo invited the legendary Celia Cruz and her husband, Pedro Knight, to his Hollywood home for dinner. He eagerly promised to showcase his bongó-playing skills after the meal. However, amidst the delightful food and sparkling champagne, Celia succumbed to a peaceful slumber, missing Marlon's musical performance.

In the early days of the Fania enterprise, the founders, Jerry Masucci and Johnny Pacheco, would work tirelessly around the clock delivering records in Johnny's

Joe Hernández

Mercedes. They literally would not sleep; Masucci would listen to Symphony Sid on the radio every night to listen to his music. If by 2 a.m. Sid had not played one of Fania's songs, Masucci would creep out of bed, buy a pastrami sandwich to take to Sid, and wait until he played one of Fania's numbers.

The *Tito Puente Orchestra's* historic 1949 album *Mamborama* featured "Abaniquito," the first American mambo and Puente's first hit. It's a hard-driving mambo featuring Mario Bauzá on trumpet, with Graciela helping out on coro and Vicentico Valdés on lead vocals.

The first recordings of Cuban music were made in Havana in 1904 with the Cuban pianist and bandleader Antonio María Romeu Marrero (1876-1955) and a small orchestra specializing in danzones, of which his brother Armando was a member. Antonio wrote and arranged over 500 danzones, many adapted for other Cuban rhythms. His most famous composition was "Tres Lindas Cubanas."

Rafael Muñoz Medina (1900-1961), a well-known Puerto Rican band leader, mentored many young musicians who later became accomplished artists in New York. Some of his notable students include Noro Morales, a pianist, and César Concepción, a trumpeter. Muñoz's son, Ramón Monguito, followed in his father's footsteps and played with the Tito Rodríguez Orchestra at the Palladium as his timbalero.

Miguelito Valdés

When Miguelito Valdés replaced Desi Arnaz in 1940 in the *Xavier Cugat Orchestra,* billed as *Mister Babalú,* he earned $150 a week, about $3,300 in today's market.

During his presidential campaign 1959, *Fajardo y sus Estrellas* performed for the young Massachusetts Senator John F. Kennedy.

Rafael Ithier, founder of the *Gran Combo*, is a veteran of the Korean War.

The Dominican percussionist, guitarist, singer, and songwriter Cuco "Pupo" Valoy worked as a gardener until he formed a guitar duo, *Los Ahijados,* with his brother Martín.

Joe Hernández

Marty Sheller takes the trumpet solo on Mongo Santamaria's 1963 guajira/cha-cha-chá version of Herbie Hancock's tune "Watermelon Man." It reached number 10 on the Billboard pop charts and was inducted into the Grammy Hall of Fame. Mongo's version would become the forerunner to the coming Latin Boogaloo craze in N.Y.C.

In the mid-1980s, Dizzy Gillespie sent a book to Celia Cruz. However, he only printed her name and "New York, New York" on the package, but it still reached her successfully.

Libertad Lamarque was a talented singer with a beautiful voice that quickly gained recognition and admiration from many. As a result, the directors of the Argentine RCA label signed her as their exclusive artist. On September 8, 1926, she began recording her first album, which featured popular songs like "Gaucho Sol" and "Chilenito." In the following five years, she recorded a hundred more songs. Throughout her long and distinguished musical career, she recorded 800 songs.

María Teresa Vera continued to create music until 1961. However, in 1962, she suffered a concussion that permanently removed her from the world of music. She passed away on December 17, 1965, after suffering from cerebral thrombosis.

Ernesto Lecuona's older sister, Ernestina Lecuona y Casado (1882-1951), taught him to play the piano and performed for President Hoover.

In 1928, Pedro Flores met Rafael Hernández and they became great friends. Pedro often accompanied Rafael to his *Trío Borinquen* performances. At the age of 34, Pedro, despite his limited musical knowledge, took the initiative to create a new musical group. His vision was to play more upbeat music that people could dance to, a departure from the romantic songs performed by Rafael's group. Pedro formed this new group and named it the *Trío Galón*. They performed at many of the same venues as Trío Borinquen, marking the beginning of Pedro's musical journey.

Ernesto Hoffmann Liévano, the author of the lyrics of the bolero "Cosas Cómo Tu," was Colombian. He was working as an announcer for a station in New York when Santiago Alvarado, the music author, met him.

Fernando López, who appears as the author of the music of many boleros with lyrics by the Argentine Roberto Lambertucci, is actually the Cuban Fernando Mulen López.

Joe Hernández

Salsa Queen Celia Cruz sang jingles in Cuba during the early 1950s to promote various products and brands such as Coca-Cola, Bacardi rum, Pilon coffee, Candado soap, Colonia 1800, Guraina cheese, Jupina pineapple soft drink, H. Upmann, and Partagas cigars. Surprisingly, all these brands still exist today. For each recording, Celia was paid between eighteen and fifty pesos. Although it's challenging to find them, some CD recordings in the United States contain these jingles by Celia.

Ismael Rivera, born on October 5, 1931, in Santurce, Puerto Rico, was a man destined for a musical journey. His talent as a singer and songwriter was nurtured by his childhood friend Rafael Cortijo, who introduced him to the vibrant world of Afro-Caribbean music. In 1955, *Cortijo y Su Combo* made their debut in Puerto Rico, with Ismael as their lead singer, and they quickly became a sensation, riding the wave of television's growing popularity in the country.

Ismael's influence extended beyond his collaborations with Cortijo. He revolutionized the montuno by incorporating new variations in the melody and expanding his improvisations beyond the traditional four lines. Together, they recorded more than twenty-five albums. Although the band disbanded in 1962, Ismael's musical journey continued. He started his group, *Los Cachimbos,* and recorded nine albums. Unfortunately, Ismael passed away due to a heart attack on May 13, 1987.

Despite his premature death, Ismael Rivera's legacy lives on as one of Puerto Rico's greatest singers. His fans still cherish his famous cry, "¡Ecua Jei!" which resonates in their hearts today.

—◊—

Tito Puente was fond of La Lupe's voice, but he found her personality and behavior irritating and exhausting. She had a knack for getting on Tito's nerves. Tito's close friend, trumpeter and band manager, Jimmy Frisaura, said, *"Tito was very close to throwing her out of the window."*

—◊—

Rosalía "Chalía" Herrera

The Cuban singer Rosalía "Chalía" Herrera made her professional debut in New York City in 1894, two and half years after Carnegie Hall opened. It would be another twenty-one years (1915) before she would debut at Carnegie Hall.

—◊—

Joe Hernández

Chico O'Farrill, Author & Matt Dillon

Arturo "Chico" O'Farrill (1921-2001) was a highly skilled musician who excelled in composing, arranging, conducting, and leading bands. He received his training under the guidance of renowned figures such as Stokowski and Eugene Tedesco. O'Farrill began his career as a ghostwriter for the famous jazz arranger Gil Fuller. Throughout his career, he wrote music for and played with a wide range of artists such as Benny Goodman, Count Basie, Dizzy Gillespie, Gato Barbieri, David Bowie, Machito, Frank Sinatra, Wynton Marsalis, Stan Kenton, Glenn Miller, "Cachao," Mario Bauza, and many other notable figures in the music industry. He was among the first to be inducted into the International Latin Music Hall of Fame in 1999.

El Gran Combo debuted on Puerto Rican radio on May 21, 1962.

Tito Puente

During World War II, the US Navy assigned many enlisted musicians to bigger ships such as battleships, aircraft carriers, and destroyers to boost morale, especially on long voyages. Tito Puente was transferred to the Santee, where he played the alto saxophone and clarinet in the ship's big band and the drums and piano during mealtimes. He was also responsible for playing the bugle. But it was during the battles that Tito's true bravery shone. He was assigned the role of a machine gunner, a task that required immense courage and skill, earning him the respect of his fellow soldiers. In addition to his musical duties, he also rotated guard duties, cleaned restrooms, and performed other tasks as needed, demonstrating his dedication to his service.

Ismael Rivera was able to secure a job in the newly formed *Orquesta Panamericana* with the assistance of his friend Cortijo after being discharged from the military. The orchestra was created by the Puerto Rican saxophonist and composer Lito Peña. Ismael's first recording with the orchestra was "Cha-cha in Blue." His performance of the plena "El Charlatan" with the Orquesta Panamericana was an enormous success, marking the beginning of the legend of El Sonero Mayor de Puerto Rico.

Francisco "Chino" Pozo was a renowned percussionist from Cuba, known for his exceptional skills on the bongó. He arrived in the United States in 1937 and joined Machito's Afro-Cubans as their bongócero. At the suggestion of Mario Bauzá, he developed modern syncopated cencerro patterns still used today in Afro-Cuban big band mambo music during the montuno section, where instrumental soloists are featured. These patterns became so popular that other musicians called them "Golpes de Chino" or "Golpe Chino." Candido Camero, a fellow percussionist, said, *"Chino was the most sought-after percussionist of his time, having recorded with numerous artists across various genres, including jazz, Latin, TV, and movies."* Chino's final significant performance was with vocalist Paul Anka in Las Vegas. Sadly, he passed away on April 28, 1980, due to complications related to AIDS.

Louis Moreau Gottschalk, a talented pianist and composer born in New Orleans, was deeply moved by his visit to Puerto Rico, which inspired him to compose Souvenir de Porto Rico (Recuerdo de Puerto Rico) with the subtitle Marche des Gibaros (La Marcha de Los Jibaros). During his trip, he was enchanted by a native melody in the "Aguinaldo" style played by local folk musicians, which he incorporated into the composition. The name Jibaros refers to peasant farmers on the island. Gottschalk's journey continued to Cuba, where he was further inspired to create La Nuit des Tropiques (A Night in the Tropics).

Joe Ginsburg, also known as Joe Gaines, was born on December 13, 1937, in Brooklyn, New York. He attended the New York School of Announcing and Speech. He interned with some of the greatest disc jockeys in Latin music, including Dick "Ricardo" Sugar and the incomparable "Symphony Sid" Torin. In 1971, Joe Gaines launched one of the most successful and popular Latin radio shows in New York, called The Joe Gaines Express Show, which was broadcast on WEVD. Joe had an illustrious career in Latin music that spanned over four decades. He passed away on August 2, 2016, at the age of 78.

In 1934, Davilita embarked on a new chapter in his career, joining *Alberto Socarras' Orchestra* as a singer. His talent and dedication led him to a momentous opportunity-performing "Lamento Borincano" for the legendary Argentinian Tango singer Carlos Gardel at the grand inauguration of the Campoamor Theater on August 10, 1934. However, the magnitude of the occasion overwhelmed him, and he forgot part of the song's lyrics.

Joe Hernández

The musical group *La Sonora Matancera* was named after Matanzas, Cuba. It was active for 79 years until 2003, making it one of the longest-lasting groups in the history of Latin music. On January 12, 1924, in the Ojo de Agua neighborhood of Matanzas, at 41 Salamanca Street, a musical group was founded by Valentín Cané and Pablo "Bubu' Vazquez Gobin. Initially called *Tuna Liberal,* the group was named after Governor Juan Gronlier, in whose honor they performed their debut. In 1926, when Carlos Manuel Díaz joined, the group changed its name to *Septeto Soprano,* and with the inclusion of Rogelio Martínez in the early 1930s, they became *Estudiantina Sonora Matancera.*

Over the years, the group's name changed to *Sonora Matancera, Conjunto Sonora,* and *Matancera,* reflecting a change in instrumentation and style. *The Sonora Matancera* entered the Guinness Record in 1996, after seventy-two years of existence, as the oldest orchestra in the world. It also has the most radio programs, the largest number of recordings issued (including reissues), and the most singers of different nationalities.

Johnny Pacheco and Jerry Masucci came up with the idea of creating the Fania label during a party at Jerry Masucci's home on March 23, 1963.

In Bobby Capó's famous bolero, "Piel Canéla", the word "tú" is repeated 40 times.

Machito recorded over 75 LPs in four and a half decades.

Ismael Rivera

Ismael Rivera started his journey from a humble beginning - he began by shining shoes at an incredibly early age. His mother, Doña Margarita, remembers fondly how he earned his first wage, a modest sum of 27 cents. Demonstrating his entrepreneurial spirit, he gave all the money to his mother, who returned 7 cents and kept the rest. Ismael spent 5 cents to watch a movie at the Savoy theatre and used the remaining 2 cents to buy himself a sweet treat. As he improved his shoe-shining skills, his earnings also improved, reaching an impressive amount of 3 to 4 dollars per day, a significant amount for a young boy.

Before the invention of the disk system, recordings were made individually on cylinders or discs, making it impossible for artists to achieve commercial success as they had to record every disc one at a time. Can you imagine an artist like Teresa María Vera singing one of her songs 50,000 times? However, with the introduction of the disk system, a master recording could be created and duplicated, allowing for recordings to be sold on a large scale for the first time.

In addition to appearing in 65 films in Argentina, Mexico, and Spain and six telenovelas, Libert Lamarque also recorded 800 songs.

Marlon Brandon and Sammy Davis Jr. would often sit in with the orchestras of Machito, Puente, and Tito Rodríguez at the Palladium Ballroom on bongó or conga.

The Palace Theatre is a famous landmark located at 1564 Broadway, in the heart of Times Square. This area is known for its lively entertainment scene and is in the Midtown Manhattan district of New York City. The theatre was built by Martin Beck, a renowned vaudeville impresario and booking agent responsible for constructing all the Martin Beck Theatres in New York City's Broadway District. He was also the founder of the Orpheum Circuit. The Palace Theatre is known for hosting the debut performance of Don Azpiazú with Antonio Machín and "The Peanut Vendor," an event that has since gone down in history. Martin Beck was a visionary booking agent and was responsible for launching the legendary Escape Artists Harry Houdini's career.

—⁂—

The Cheetah nightclub was initially situated at 1686 Broadway, near 53rd Street in New York City. It opened on April 27, 1966, and moved to 310 West 52nd Street, near Eight Avenue. Previously, in October 1968, the Cheetah was known as the Palm Gardens. In the 1970s, the club became a famous Latin-American dance club that Ralph Mercado managed. At this new location, the Fania All-Stars performed their second concert. The Cheetah was part of a series of clubs with the same name in Los Angeles, Chicago, and Montreal.

—⁂—

Before the mid-1920s, danzón was primarily instrumental. But by then, bands began to add singers to their performances.

—⁂—

Lou Pérez was born in New York and is a Cuban Descendant. In 1955, Pérez recorded with his orchestra of 15 musicians for Columbia under the name of Orchestra Belmonte.

—⁂—

Cheo Feliciano was the owner of a recording company called "Coche Records."

—⁂—

Joe Hernández

When Tito Puente was just 16 years old in 1939, he participated in his first recording session with Johnny Rodríguez at the Stork Club. During the session, he played timbale and also used a bass drum while performing a solo on the song "Los Hijos De Budda."

The word "Tango" originated from slaves. Additionally, the dance salons where Tango is performed are commonly called "milongas."

In 1958, the Cha Cha Chá championship was held in Hong Kong, and 17-year-old Bruce Lee emerged as the champion. This was the same year he won the Hong Kong School Boxing Tournament, defeating the previous champion, Gary Elms, in the final. What made his victory even more remarkable was his dance partner, his ten-year-old brother, Robert Lee. Bruce's journey in dance began at the age of 13, and even in his leisure time in the States, he taught Cha Cha Chá in Chinatown to earn some extra money. Bruce was fond of saying: "Think of a fly, think of a flea, when you do the cha-cha, you'll think of me."

Although the Dominican Republic has been at the forefront of promoting and popularizing this infectious rhythm, the dance originated in the Dominican Republic and Haiti and was strongly influenced by Venezuelan and Afro-Cuban musical practices and dances throughout Latin America.

Tito Puente introduced the vibraphone in the late 1940s to cater to the listening and dancing pleasures of both Anglos and Latinos.

Mr. & Mrs. Sanabria

Israel "Izzy" Sanabria, a graphic designer who transformed the visual style of Salsa music, was born in Mayaguez, Puerto Rico, in 1939. His family later moved to the Bronx, New York City, where he grew up. After attending the School of Visual Arts, Izzy began his career at Alegre Records in 1961. Here, he refined his skills, designing album covers for renowned artists such as Kako y su Combo and Johnny Pacheco. His talent caught the attention of Pacheco, who recruited him for his first major project - the iconic retro logo for FANIA.

Izzy Sanabria's influence on the design of Latin and Salsa album covers was profound, leaving an indelible mark on the industry. His designs, inspired by the vibrant sounds of Salsa, used bold colors and shapes to create visuals that mirrored the excitement of the music. His impact was not limited to Fania and Alegre; he also designed album covers for numerous other labels, including Cotique, Cesta, Inca, and many more. This extensive body of work solidified his status as a true pioneer in the field of album cover art.

Andy Montañez had never performed salsa before joining El Gran Combo de Puerto Rico. He had been part of a trio before.

Louis Moreau Gottschalk's final public appearance was a global affair in Río de Janeiro, a testament to the universal appeal of his music on November 24, 1869. The program, a rich tapestry of sounds, required a massive ensemble of 650 musicians. It featured a diverse array of performers, including four national guard bands, a band each from the Brazilian navy and army, two German orchestras, a professional orchestra of seventy 'professors,' and even the pit orchestra from the infamous Alcazar, Río's most notorious theatre. This cultural amalgamation attracted the entire elite of Río de Janeiro, resulting in a sold-out show that celebrated the diversity of music and culture.

Chano Pozo

Chano Pozo (Luciano Panzo Gonzales), the composer of the famous songs "Tin Tin Deo" and "Manteca," was shot and killed at the age of 33 in a Harlem bar called the Río Café on December 2, 1948. Chano lived at 127 West 111th St. During the previous 18 months, he had been appearing with the *Dizzy Gillespie Orchestra.*

The incident occurred after Chano got into a physical altercation with a fellow Cuban named Eusebio "Cabito" Muñoz. The reason for the fight was that Cabito sold Chano some marijuana that was not strong enough and then refused to refund his money. Muñoz was quickly apprehended.

The police reconstruction of the shooting stated that Pozo was standing at the bar around 10:15 PM in conversation with two women identified as Bernice Best and Florence Martin when Muñoz appeared at the doorway. Muñoz, in his statement to the DA, said that Pozo had taken $15 from him earlier in the evening, threatening him with bodily harm at the time. Whether or not Muñoz, who was identified by the police as Puerto Rican, was coming to take his money back isn't known;

however, he did pull out a .38 automatic and fired five shots directly at the Cuban musician. Following the shooting, Muñoz fled the scene.

Pozo was hit in the chest, heart, left forearm, shoulder, and right forearm. He was pronounced dead at New York City Sydenham Hospital.

Muñoz was arraigned in Felony court and held without bail for action by the Grand Jury. Muñoz, the perpetrator of the crime, was convicted of manslaughter and served only five years in prison for his actions.

The incident was covered in *The New York Age* on Saturday, December 11, 1948, on page 18.

Juan Arvizu, the famous Mexican tenor, was lucky to discover the two great composers: Agustín Lara in Mexico and Mario Clavell in Argentina.

It is believed that Tango sprung from poor and underprivileged areas of the docklands of Buenos Aires, with the genesis of its dance in the middle of the 19th century in the south of Buenos Aires, where African and European immigrants would dance in the streets and the brothels. Tango is a fusion of European, African, and gaucho styles. For instance, the European influence can be seen in the formal structure of the dance, while the African influence is evident in the rhythmic patterns. The gaucho style, on the other hand, is reflected in the passionate and improvisational nature of the dance. Although it is widely accepted that Argentine Tango has its roots in Argentina, this musical style's exact emergence and development remain a mystery. The earliest known musical scores of Argentine Tango only date back to the 20th century, adding to its origins' enigma.

Delve into the linguistic history of Tango and discover its fascinating journey. The term 'tango' was not new during that time. It was already used to describe a type of music introduced to Europe from Cuba in the second half of the 19th century, often alongside the more popular habanera. The terms' tango' and 'habanera' were sometimes used interchangeably, a linguistic dance mirroring the fluidity of the music itself. The name 'American tango' was synonymous with 'habanera,' further blurring the lines between these musical styles. Tangos were even composed for Spanish zarzuelas, light opera's known as 'Andalusian tangos' (Tango Andaluz), showcasing the versatility and adaptability of Tango.

―⚏―

Jerry González (1949-2018) was an American bandleader, trumpeter, and percussionist of Puerto Rican descent. He graduated from the New York College of Music and paid his tuition by playing gigs with the Beach Boys.

―⚏―

Trini Lopez left behind a significant musical legacy, having produced a remarkable discography that included over 60 albums.

―⚏―

Joe Hernández

Johnny Pacheco Oil Painting Commissioned by Author

Johnny Pacheco was born on March 25, 1935, in Santiago De Los Caballeros, Dominican Republic. He attended the Julliard School of Music and later formed his first orchestra, Pacheco y Su Charanga, which became famous. Their first record, Pacheco Y Su Charanga Vol 1, was released under the Alegre Records label owned by Al Santiago and sold over 100,000 copies in only two months!

About The Author

Joe Hernández was born and raised in New York City. Growing up in the 1960s and '70s, he experienced the "Salsa Explosion." He lived through the excitement of dancing to the live music of Johnny Pacheco, Ray Barretto, Tito Puente, Tito Rodríguez, Larry Harlow, Willie Colón, Eddie Palmieri, Joe Bataan, Richie Ray, La Lupe, Celia Cruz, Ismael Miranda, Orchestra Broadway, Charanga America, Típica Novel, Típica 73, Charanga 56, Luis Perico Ortiz, Machito, Joe Cuba, etc.

Joe frequented many of the dancing clubs, such as The Corso, Casa Blanca, La Epoca, Hipocampo, The Chez Sensual, Ochentas, Cork-n-Bottle, Copacabana, The Marion Manor, Ipanema, Boombamakao, The Cheetah, Casino Fourteen, Ochentas, Casa Borinquen, Side Street, Sweetwaters, La Maganette, etc.

Joe is the founder and past president of the International Latin Music Hall of Fame (ILMHF) and a frequent guest on radio and television. He has authored articles for magazines on the history of Latin music. Joe also served as a talent judge for several years on the National Hispanic Youth Showcase in association with NJ public Television and the New Jersey Performance Arts Center.

He was also friends and spent much time talking to many who were part of the salsa scene and with those who preceded it. Joe was friends with Cachao, Marco Rizo, Chico O'Farrill, Graciela, Lou Pérez, Joe Cuba, Johnny Albino, Raúl Azpiazú, Patato, Yomo Toro, Ernie Ensley, Millie Donay, Joe Gaines, Chico Álvarez, Miguel Pérez, Vicki Sola, Franc Peri, Ida Carlini, Roberto Torres, Richie Puente, Dr. Cristobal Díaz Ayala, and Max Salazar.

Joe knew and had in-depth conversations with Johnny Pacheco, Tito Puente, Jimmy Friasura, Ray Barretto, José Fajardo, Larry Harlow, Margie and Augo, Cándido, Chocolate Armenteros, Irv Greenbaum, Izzy Sanabria, Héctor Casanova, Jimmy Sabater, Cheo Feliciano, Cuban Pete, Johnny Ventura, Johnny Colón, Richie Bonilla, Trini López, etc.

Joe holds an MBA in Strategic Leadership and an M.S. in Human Relations and Business from Amberton University. He has been a lifetime entrepreneur, owning over a dozen businesses, and was an Adjunct Instructor at the State University of New York (SUNY). Currently, Joe is the Executive Director of the Joseph David Hernández Foundation, a 501(c) (3) non-profit organization dedicated to improving the lives of children through sports. He is a member of the Society of American Magicians and the International Brotherhood of Magicians and a monthly columnist for M-U-M and The Linking Ring magazines. He has published numerous books on the history, practice, and philosophy of the art of conjuring. Joe lives in New Jersey with his wife, Isabel, and has two children, Natalie and Joseph.

Index

A

Aguilar, Pedro, see Cuban Pete
Albino, Johnny, 84, 410-411
Alcaraz, Luis, 272
Alonso, Curet Tite, 80, 129, 277, 287, 291-292, 382, 405
Álvarez, Paulina, 280, 333, 416
Amadeo, Miguel, 381
Amalia, Paoli Doña, 117
Anabacoa, conjunto, 334
Anacaona Septet, 135, 173, 276, Pres. FDR, 276, Graciela 284, 298, Anna María Punny, 349
Andino, Julian, 195, 324
Anthony, Marc, 178, 225, named after, 393
Apollo Theatre, 89, 104,139, 308, J. Pacheco, 349, E. Fitzgerald, 412
Aquellos Olos Verde, the song, 171
Aragón, 133, 184, 418
Armenteros, Chocolate, 39 113, 397, 415
Armstrong, Louie, 26, 189

Arnaz, Desi, 33-34, father prohibit drums, 54, 120, Cuban Pete film, 126, popularized the Conga dance 203-204, singer for Xavier Cugat, 226; Babalú, 376, Al Capone's son, 407, 427
Augie and Margo, 260, Margo, Tito Puente's cousin, 409
Averne, Harvey, dispute with Eddie Palmieri, 388-389
Avilés, Vitin, 79
Azpiazu, Don, 56-57, 82, 94, 102-103, sister-in-law, M. Sunshine, 133, 135-136
Azpiazu, Raul, 80-81

B

Baker, Josephine, 71
Barretto, Ray, 28, 76, 93 103, 108, 114, 138, 187, 226, 287, Greyhound bus, 293, 318, food poisoning, 365-366
Bataan, Joe, 136
Batista, Fulgencio, 264, 355

[449]

Bauza, Mario, 67, 89, 112, 123, 201, 218, 238, 382
Bentancourt, Justo, 317, "Pa Bravo Yo," 406
Birdland, 87
Blades, Rubén, *Siembra,* the álbum, 24, 26, 144, 154, 158, 190, presidency, 303, 334
Bobo, Willy, 151, 277, Bill Cosby Show, 339
Bolero, 15
Bonet, Pete, 53, 108, 271-272
Boogaloo (bugalú), 292, 394
Brachfield, Andrea 189
Brandon, Marlon, 378, playing for Celia Cruz, 425
Bravo, Sonny, 320

C

Cachao, 88, 105, 228
Calle Ocho, Guinness World Record, 423
Calloway, Cab, 189
Calzado, Rudy, 392
Camero, Cándido, 342, uncle Ándres, 363
Campo, Pupi Orchestra, 183, 257
Capó, Bobby, 241
Capo, Bobby, 55, 265
Carlini, Ida, Tito Puente's girlfriend, 37-38
Carlos Argentino, 323
Carr, Vicki, 214

Carrillo, Isolina, 325
Caruso, Enrico, 172
Casals, Pablo, 174
Casino de la Playa, 87
Castellanos, Daniel, 168
Castro, Fidel, 355
Cepeda, Rafael, Don, 123
Chano, Pozo, 109, 119, 133, 189, 379, 397 410, 443
Chappottín, Felix, 188
Charanga, 174
Cheetah, nightclub 65, 439
Claves, 95
Clooney, George, 252
Cohen, Augusto, 59, 210, 243
Cole, King, Nat, 157, 352, 395-396
Collazo, Fernando, suicide, 283
Colombia, country 306-307
Colón, Johnny, 178, 188, 394
Colón, Willie, 45, 51, 95, 190, *Los Dandies,* 272, "Asalto Navideño" album, 279, politics, 287, President Bill Clinton, 420
Columbia Records, 38, 154
Companioni, Gómez, Rafael, Miguel, 98
Contigo en la Distancia, the song, 309
Copacabana, 70
Corso, The, 116

The Latin Music Trivia Book

Cortés, Mappy, 372
Cortijo, Rafael, 86
Cruz, Celia, 33, 41, 53, 61, 67, 74, 77, 81, 100, 102, 104, 162, Radio Progreso, Cuba, 241, hospital, 253, 325, Guinness record, 395, breast removal, 396, Int'l Latin Music Hall of Fame, 422, Cuban jingles, 430
Cuba, Joe, 42, 111, 144, 198, 222, 261, 267, 275, 291, 292, 297, 302, 314, 400
Cuban Jam Sessions, 209
Cuban Pete, 31
Cubanacan, El Club, 301
Cucaracha, La, 140, 143
Cugat, Xavier, 161, 170, 205, 228, 233, 239
Curbelo, Celido Faustino, 225, 317-318
Curbelo, José, 210, 317

D

D'León, Oscar, 36, 246
Davidson, Eduardo, 121, 163
Davilita, 435
Davis, Sammy Jr., 438
De La Luz, orquesta, 334
De Nieve, Bola, 211, 221
Delfin y Figueroa, Eusebio, 141
Delirio de Grande, the song, 309
Díaz, Soler, 406

Diestro, Aida, 352
Donay, Millie, 31, 145, 320, 378, 393
Drum Prohibition, 64

E

Echale Salsita, 321
Edmundo, Ros, 200
Edreira, Rene, 335
El Canario, 63
El Indio, Yayo, 317
Ellington, Duke, 189
Escalona, Dalona, Fidias, 17
Escollies, Antonio, 194, 353
Escudero, Rafael, 322
Estefan, Gloria, 122, 242, father, 255, 280, 346
Estrada, Noel Epifiano, "En Mi Viejo San Juan, song, 247-249
Europe, Reese, James, 176, infantry Hellfighters, 319

F

Faílde, Miguel, 43, 172
Fajardo, José, 233, 391, John F. Kennedy, 427
Fania All-Stars, 58
Farrés, Osvaldo, 217
Feliciano, Cheo, 49, 67, 222, 265, 302, 334, 339, cancer. 373, 392, 403, 405, "Coche Records, owner" 439

[451]

Index

Feliciano, José, 334-335
Fernández, Joséito, 137, 397-398
Fernández, Ruth, 87, 185 337,
Figueroa, Charlie, 286
Fitzgerald, Ella, 196, 412
Flor Pálida, the song, 310
Flores, Pancho, 289
Flores, Pedro, 111-112, 128, 158, 168, 178, 180, 201, 284, 289, 324, 429

G

Gains, Joe, WEVD, 435
Galón, Trío, 429
Garay, Sindo, 256
Gardel, Carlos, 97-98 128, 133, death, 332, 335, 344, 366, 435
Gatica, Lucho, 339
Gershwin, George, 221
Gilbert, Dick, 103
Giovanni, Hidalgo, 298
Gonnzalez, Celio, 330
Gonzalez, Jerry, Beach Boys, 445
Gormé, Eydie, 38, 77, 80, 86, 90, 102, 424
Gottschalk, Moreau, Louis, 153, 163, 245, 296, 434-435
Gramaphone, 261-262
Grand Combo, El, radio debut, 432
Granda, Bienvenido, 279, 335

Greenbaum, Irv, Cortijo behavior, 389
Grenet, Eliseo, 203
Guantanamera, 129-130, 137, 398-339, 417
Guillot, Olga, 32, 85, 130, 222

H

Habanera, 405
Happy Hills orchestra, 399
Harlow, Larry, 107, 216, in Cuba, 299
Harlow, Rita, 69
Hayworth, Rita, 205
Hernández, Joe, 139, 150,
Hernández, Oscar, 404
Hernández, Rafael, "El Cumbanchero," the song, 27, 47, 85, "Lamento Borincano," the song, 91-92, 152, 192, 201, travel too Mexico, 328
Hernández, Victoria, 93, 169, 195, 364-365, 395
Herrera, Rosalía, Chalía, 111, 431
Holder, Geoffrey Lamont, 331
Hotel, St. George, 415
Hyman, Max. 47

I

Iglesias, Julio, 81, 191, 253, 282, 321, 332, 333, 351, 456

Infantry, Hellfighters, 319
Inolvidable, the song, 312
Int'l Latin Music Hall of
   Fame, 150
Ithier, Rafael, 146, 271,
   361, 405, 427

J

Jaramillo, Julio, 108
Jay and the Americans, 30
Jiménez, Manuel
   "Canario," 211, 230
Joe Cuba Sextet, name
   origin, 275
Jorrín, Enrique, 58, 64, 83,
   187
Junco, Pedro, 230-231

K

Kalaff, Luis, 273
Kennedy, F. John, 27 250,
   261, 427
Knight, Pedro, 33, 200,
   255, 303, 318 previous
   marriage, 419
Kortright, Wito, 45, 138,
   156, 222, 329
Kubavana, conjunto, 363

L

La Negra, Toña, 40
Lágrimas, Negras, the
   song, 311-312
Lamarque, Libertad, 163,
   336-337, 366, 381,
   428
Lara, Agustín, 130, 177,
   193, 315, 317, 327,

"Solamente Una Vez,"
   the song, 340
Lasalle, Erasmo, 122
Lavoe, Hector, 36, 154,
   158, 178, 205, 225,
   death of mother-in-
   law, 235, 245, 323-324
Lecompte, María Luisa,
   207
Ledesma, Roberto, 377
Lee, Bruce, ch-cha-chá
   champion, 440
Lecuona, Margarita,
   "Babalú," song
   written, 297
Lecuona, Ernesto, 35, 72,
   74, 106, 159, 160,
   172, 210, 340, 350,
   President Hoover, 429
Liévano, Ernesto Hoffman,
   "Cosas Cómo Tu," 429
Linda, the song, 147-148
Llongueras, Simon Jou,
   321
Loco, Joe, 184, 194
López, Mano, first to play
   timbales standing, 408
Lopez, Trini, 250, 253,
   guitars, 317
Lupe, La, 38, 48, 60, 126,
   151, 153, 166, 175,
   209, 331, 385

M

Machín, Antonio, 34
Machito, 16, 90, 107,
   120, debut, 121, 138,
   arrived in NY, 139,
   179, Hilda, wife, 208

Index

302, 345, 349, 351,
  date of birth, 363
Mambo # 5 the song, 310
Mambo Kings, 73, 94
Manicero, El, 75, 102, the
  song, 330
Manu, Dibango, 335
Manzanero, Armando,
  213, 242
Marco, Rizo 343
María, Casita, 340-341
Mariachi, 99
Marin, Muñoz, 27, 232
Marks, E.B (music
  publisher), 184, 330
Marks, Herbert, 353
Martin, Ricky, 238
Martínez, Chago, 317
Martinez, Ignacio Piñieiro,
  198
Martínez, Juan Tizol, 236
Martínez, Rogelio, 264,
  282, 316-317
Masucci, Jerry, 19, 62, 81,
  death, 308
Matamoros, Miguel, 54,
  114, auto mechanic,
  421
Matamoros, Trío, 54, 341
Matancera, Sonora, 40,
  125,177, 180, 181,
  181, 182, 208, 234,
  239, 264, 267, 276-
  277, 291, 304, 436
Mateo, Joséito, 307
Medina, Rafael Muñoz,
  426
Melís, José, 120, 363
Menéndez, Nilo, 327-328

Mercado, Ralph, bounce
  checks, 416
Merengue, 99, 189, 196,
  308, first recorded,
  401
Mexican Band, 8th
  Calvary, New Orleans,
  398
Miranda, Carmen, 206,
  295, 308
Misago, Tadaaki, 334
Mojica, José, 340
Monroig, Gilberto, 244,
  367-368
Monroig, Glenn, sued
  RMM, 304
Montaner, Rita, 139, 154
Montañez, Andy, 68, trío,
  442
Montuno, Son, 15
Morales, Noro, 106, 213,
Moré, Bény, 38, 48, 101,
  103, 119, 157, 168,
  marriage, 258
Moreno, Rita, 212
Morris, Levy, 214, 303,
  412
Muñequitos de Matanzas,
  Los, 354
Muñoz, Monchito, 242
Musicians, Puerto Rican
  147, 171, 306, see
  Juan Tizol, 356

N

Nater, Pete, 295
Nixon, Richard, 261

O

O'Farrill, Chico, 197, 271, 278, Matt Dillon, 432, Int'l Latin Music Hall of Fame, 432
Oller, Gabriel, 355, Dynasonic, 396
Orovio, Helio, 407
Our Latin Thing, the movie, 265, 331
Oye Come Va, 64, 66

P

Pacheco, Johnny, 19, 57, NARAS, 413
Pagani, Federico, 58, 217
Palladium Ballroom, 78, 83, raid. 383-384
Palmieri, Charlie, 50, 259, *Conjunto Pin Pin,* 280, debut, 288
Palmieri, Eddie, 79, 80, 146, 198, La Perfecta, 1st band, 254,
Paloma, La, 118
Panamericana, Orquesta, with Ismael Rivera, 432-433
Panart Records, 52, 413-414
Panchito, Riset, 128, 190, 342
Pedro Navaja, 24
Peraza, Armando, 61, 224
Pérez, Graciela, 179, 201, 284
Pérez, Lou, 229
Peri, Franc, 51

Pete, Cubban (Pedro Aguilar) 31, 138, 145, 320, 350, 378, 393
Piñieiro, Ignacio 198, "Echale Salsita," the song, 366
Piper Pimienta, 315-316
Pirela, Felipe, 237
Paoli, Antonio, 127
Ponceña, Sonora, 45, 177, 403
Population, Puerto Rico, 29
Pozo, Chano, 68, 95, 98, 109, 119, 133, 188, Conjunto Azul, 189, 379, Cacha Pozo, wife, 394, 397, stolen drums, 410, death, 443-444
Pozo, Chino, 68, Paul Anka, Las Vegas, 434
Prado, Pérez, 91, 215, 280, blacklisted, 285
Puente, Tito, 36, Ida Carlini, girlfriend, 37, 49, 51, 62, "Oye Come Va," the song, 64, 66, war hero, 66, Roper Records, 72, 73, 90, 100, Antonio Puente, grandfather,101, honored, post office, 114, 115, 124, 139 156 Picadilly Boys, 183, student of Victoria Hernández, 195, White House, 199, 249, dancer,

[455]

Index

251, "riff" with Tito Rodríguez, 260, 266, 274, 305, *Abaniquito*, album, 307, debut, 341, Richie Puente, son 360-361, wife, Margaret, 364, crowned King, 366, death of brother and sister, 373, opinion on La Lupe, 431, Navy, 432

Q

Queen Elizabeth, 261
Quiéreme Mucho, the song, 313-314
Quijano, Joe, 137, 170, 196
Quimbara, 30
Quizás, Quizás, Quizás, the song, 309-310

R

Radio Cuba, 198, 253
Radio Difusura, 18 La Hora del Sabor, La Salsa y él Bembe, 17
Radio, Puerto Rico, 172
Raimundo, Corona, Manuel, 101
Ramírez, Chamaco, 316
Rebolla, Juan José, 351
Record Mart, oldest store, 357
Rexach, Sylvia, 162
Riset, Panchito, 128, 342

Rivera, Ismael, 54, 207, 218, jail, 257, "Maquinolandera," the song, 271, La Toya Jackson, 331, 430-431, shinning shoes, 437
Rivera, Mon, jail, 264, played baseball, 270, *trabalengua*, 294
Rivera, Niño, 226
Rodríguez, Arsenio, "Fuego en la 23," 44, 87, 109, 166, 347-348, with Pérez Prado, 391, Puerto Rico, 400
Rodríguez, Felipe, 31, 136
Rodríguez, Johnny, 151, 171, 1st Puerto Rican on NBC & CBS, 409
Rodríguez, Lalo, debut, 305, death, 357
Rodríguez, Pete "El Conde," 279
Rodríguez, Tito, 53, 70, 168, 197, wife Tobi, 240 jockey, 371, final concert, 385, 397
Roena, Roberto, 158
Rogers, Barry, 73
Roman, Joséito, 189
Romeu, Antonio María, 219, 343, 349, 1st Cuban recordings, 426
Roosevelt, Franklin D., 276
Roper Records, 72
Roque, Julio, 209
Rosario, Willie, 324

[456]

Ruiz, Frankie, 31
Ruiz, Hilton, 269-270
Russell, Luis, 322

S

Sabater, Jimmy, "El Pito," the song, 297, 339 358,
Salazar, Max, 348
Saldel, Alfredo, 344
Salsa, 15-24, as exercise, 399-400
San Juan, Olga, 265
Sanabria, Izzy, 17, 35, 171, 230, 405, 412
Sánchez de Fuentes, Eduardo, 346-347
Sanchez, José, Pepe, 15, 367
Sandoval, Arturo, 278
Santamaría, Mongo, 63, 91, 216, 350, "Chango," 387
Santiago, Al, 35, 181, 202, 205, 224, 254, 382, 391, 446,
Santos, Daniel, 45, 103, 110, 132, 191, FBI, 205, 223, 268, 286, 288, death, 326, stabbed, 417
Saquito, Nico, 192
Sarandonga, the song, 314
Segundo, Compay, 417
Selena, 61, 147
Serranno Gladys, 54
Severison, Doc, 49
Sheller, Marty, 428

Siegel, Sidney, 345
Sigler, Vicente, 345
Silva, Myrta, 125, 182, 227, 283, 289, 291
Simons, Moisés, 202, 390
Sinatra, Frank, 253
Socarras, Alberto, 59, 170, 177, 203, 288, *Twilight Zone*, 324, 424, 435
Solis, Javier, 121-122
Sonero Mayor, El, story behind, 262-264
Sophia, youngest, 326
Sugar, Dick "Ricardo," WEVD, 307
Sunshine, Marion, 56, 133
Symphony Sid, 237, 426

T

Tanga, the song, 372
Tango, Tango foot, 27, *Tango,* the movie, 156, 168, Tango myth, 177, 304, 405, 421, Brett & Jennifer Griswold, longest danced Tango, 140, first tango, 421, origins, 444-445
Theater, Puerto Rico, 332
Tico Records, 267
Tizol, Juan, 356
Tjader, Cal, 16, 62, 87, 121
Toña, La Negra, 252
Toro, Yomo, 338-339
Torres, Willie, 16, 278, bus driver, 287
Torresola, Antonio, José, 31

Index

Touzet, René, 141
Tristeza, 15

U

Una Palabra, the song, 311
Utrera, Adolfo, "Those Green Eyes," the song, 259

V

Valdés, Bebo, 302
Valdés, Carlos "Patato," 207, 227, 261, 271
Valdés, Gilberto S., 254
Valdés, Miguelito, 88, 113, 124, 143
Valentín, Bobby, 344
Valentino, Rudolf, 161, 327, 386
Valoy, Cuco, 427
Vargas, Pedro, 349
Varona, Carlos Luis, 205
Ventura, Johnny, 219
Vera, María Teresa, 40, 46-47, 78-79, 280, 419, 427

Vereda Tropical, the song, 269
Vernon & Castle, 402-403
Victor Records, 52
Victor Talking Machine, 134
Vilato, Orestes, 76

W

Watusi, El, 138
Webb, Chick, 194
White House, 27, 164, 199, 261

Y

Yankee Stadium, 75, 369-370

Z

Zequiera, Rafael, 281
Zervigon, Eddy, 285

Made in the USA
Middletown, DE
31 May 2024